Entrepreneur®
MAGAZINE'S

startup

Start Your Own

WEDDING CONSULTANT BUSINESS

Your Step-by-Step Guide to Success

Eileen Figure Sandlin

EP
Entrepreneur
Press

Editorial Director: Jere L. Calmes
Managing Editor: Marla Markman
Cover Design: Beth Hansen-Winter
Production: Eliot House Productions
Composition: Ed Stevens

This publication is designed to provide accurate and authoritative information in regard to
the subject matter covered. It is sold with the understanding that the publisher is not
engaged in rendering legal, accounting or other professional services. If legal advice or other
expert assistance is required, the services of a competent professional person should be
sought.

Library of Congress Cataloging-in-Publication Data
Sandlin, Eileen Figure.
    Start your own wedding consultant business/by Eileen Figure Sandlin.
        p.   cm.   —(Entrepreneur magazine's start ups) (Entrepreneur magazines's
business start-up series; #1330)
    Includes index.
    ISBN 1-891984-74-8
        1. Wedding supplies and services industry—Management. 2. Consulting firms—
Management. 3. New business enterprises—Management. I. Title: Wedding consult-
ing service. II. Entrepreneur (Santa Monica, Calif.) III. Title. IV. Series. V.
Entrepreneur business start-up guide; no. 1330.

HD9999.W372S26 2003
392.5'068—dc21   2002192841

Printed in Canada

Contents

Preface ix

Chapter 1

What Dreams Are Made Of 1
    Know Thyself 3
    The Joys of Consulting 4

Chapter 2

The Wonderful World of Wedding Consulting 7
    Something New 9
    Bridal Business Basics 9
        A Day in the Life 9
        The Consultation 10
        Wedding Day Duties. 11
        Consulting Services and Fees 12

Chapter 3

To Market, To Market. 13
    Defining Your Audience 14
        Targeting Professional Women 15
    Economic Environment 16
    Conducting Market Research 17
        Primary Research 17
        Surveying the Market 20
        Cash as Bait 21

Pick Up the Phone 21
A Job for the Pros 21
Secondary Research 22
Mission Possible 22

Chapter 4

Business Underpinnings 25

The Name Game 26
Registering Your Company Name 28
Your Corporate Structure 28
Sole Proprietors 30
General Partnership 30
Limited Liability Company 30
Corporations 30
The Home Zone 31
Other Licenses and Permits 32
Getting Down to Brass Tacks 32

Chapter 5

Getting Professional Help 37

The Legal Eagle 38
Money Managers 40
Covering Your Assets 42
Insurance Riders 42
Business Owner's Insurance 43

Chapter 6

The Wedding Bell Bills 45

Tools of the Trade 46
Office Equipment 47
Personal Computers 47
Software 49
Fax Machines 50
Telephones, Answering Machines, and Pagers 50
Copy Machines 52
Postage Meters and Internet Postage 52
Office Supplies 53
Adding It All Up 53

Chapter 7

Establishing a Supplier Network 57

General Rules of Engagement 58

Major Suppliers 59

The Host with the Most 59

Fanciful Feasts 60

Floral Fantasies 60

A Joyful Noise 62

Say Cheese 62

Lights, Camera, Action! 63

A Little Slice of Heaven 63

Wedding Wheels 64

Chapter 8

Certification and Professional Development. 65

Making It Official 66

Industry Publications 69

Trade Publications 69

Consumer Publications 70

Event Planning Publications 70

Chapter 9

Spreading the Word. 71

Your Marketing Plan 72

SWOT Analysis 72

Read All About It 74

Let Your Fingers Do the Walking 75

Magazine Display Ads 77

Brochures 78

Business Cards 80

Word-of-Mouth Advertisting 80

Chapter 10

The World Wide Wonder 83

A Phenomenal Resource 85

Your Cyber Salesperson 88

Back to Basics 88

Building a Better Web Site 89

▲

Home Sweet Home Page 90
Name that Domain 90
Your Web Host 91

Chapter 11

Generating Positive Press **93**
News Releases 94
Writing the Release 97
Producing the Release 97
Promoting Your Cause 98
Feature Articles 98
Submitting Your Manuscript 99
Newsletters 99
Bridal Shows 100
Networking 102

Chapter 12

Here Come the Finances **103**
Income and Operating Expenses 104
Telephone Calls 104
Office Supplies 105
Postage 105
Wages 105
Insurance 108
Transportation 109
Online Service Fees 109
Other Miscellaneous Expenses 109
Receivables 110
Paying the Piper 110
High-Tech Bookkeeping 111
Where the Money Is 112
Uncle Sam to the Rescue 113
Do-It-Yourself Financing 114

Chapter 13

Happily Ever After **115**
Why Businesses Fail 116
Hindsight Is 20/20 117

Wedding Stories to Learn From 118
   Saving the Day 118
   The Case of the Disappearing Guests 119
   Butterflies Aren't Free 119
   Head Over Heels 120
   Ants for the Memory 120
Your Formula for Success 121

Appendix
   Wedding Consultant Resources 123

Glossary. **131**

Index **135**

Preface

Imagine having a job where the clients are usually deliriously happy, the job site is beautifully decorated, the food is delectable, and the financial rewards are excellent. That's what it's like being a wedding consultant.

Today's wedding consultants are more in demand than ever. Women now make up nearly 47 percent of the work-force, according to the Bureau of Labor Statistics. Brides-to-be are turning to wedding consultants in ever increasing numbers to handle the multitude of details they don't have time to handle personally. And these potential clients aren't necessarily wealthy, as clients tended to be in the past. Rather, they're often ordinary working women who want to have a fairy tale wedding, but who realize they need the services of an organized, detail-oriented wedding planner to make it happen.

This is where you come in. But there's more to being a wedding consultant than just selecting flowers for the head table and auditioning bands. You also have to be a savvy businessperson who can adroitly do things like manage your clients' finances while paying your own bills on time, juggle schedules and resources to accommodate multiple weddings, and handle the paperwork and personalities that go along with employees or contract help.

The book you're holding can help. It's a comprehensive guide to establishing your own wedding consultant business and making it run smoothly. It contains crucial information on setting up your business structure, determining your market area, hiring professionals to keep your business on track, advertising and marketing your services, using the Internet to generate new business, and finding financing. It has worksheets to help you calculate your costs and keep your budget in line. It also has words of wisdom and tips from successful wedding consultants around the country. Now just add your own determination to be a successful business owner and a genuine love for people, and you'll have all the tools you'll need to help both your brides' and your own dreams come true.

Good luck, and best wishes for a long and happy union!

1

What Dreams
Are Made Of

Once upon a time on a perfect summer day, guests in colorful wedding finery filled an old cathedral. The fragrance of dew-kissed blossoms wafted through the air as soft organ music played. A radiant bride walked up the aisle on the arm of her father to meet the handsome groom waiting at the altar....

Fairy tales like this do come true. Now more than ever, wedding consultants are making them happen. In the last decade, the need for professional wedding consultants has grown exponentially. Today, women are often simply too busy juggling the demands of their professional and personal lives to oversee the details necessary to create the wedding of their dreams. This has created an enormous opportunity for anyone considering becoming a wedding consultant.

Although it is difficult to pinpoint an exact figure for how many wedding consultant businesses there are nationwide, the best guess is approximately 10,000, according to Gerard Monaghan, president of the Association of Bridal Consultants (ABC). Monaghan says that although no one formally tracks these figures, his estimate is based on the number of people who pay for memberships to the various professional associations, as well as the number of people on mailing lists available from list brokers.

According to Monaghan, one out of every eight retail dollars is spent on wedding-related products and services. That makes the wedding industry a $42 billion business, although some estimates put that figure as high as $70 billion. Part of the reason for the propensity to spend big bucks on a dream wedding is that there are often six wage earners funding the event: the bridal couple themselves, and the bride and groom's parents. This has driven the cost of the average wedding up over the years. Robbi G.W. Ernst III, president of June Wedding Inc., An Association For Event Professionals, says the average cost of a wedding in the United States is now around

$17,500 for 125 to 150 guests. However, the average cost of a wedding can be $35,000 or more in larger metropolitan areas, where incomes are higher and services more expensive.

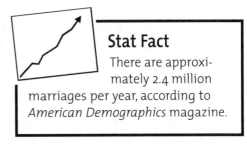

Stat Fact

There are approximately 2.4 million marriages per year, according to *American Demographics* magazine.

This industry outlook sets the stage for success for both new and established wedding consultants. According to Ernst, a novice consultant who coordinates ten weddings a year and charges the industry's standard fee of 10 to 15 percent per event can expect to gross $17,500 to $26,250 in sales. A more experienced consultant who handles 40 weddings a year can earn $70,000 and up.

"The earnings potential for wedding consultants is awesome," says Richard Martel of the Association for Wedding Professionals International. "Those who are better connected and better educated will do the best in this business, as will those who network as a way to build their reputations."

Know Thyself

So what does it take to be a successful wedding consultant? Loreen C., who owns a wedding consultant business in Ypsilanti, Michigan, says emphatically, "A sense of humor." And she's not kidding.

In a business where you're depending on the professionalism and reliability of up to a dozen or more people to create a bride's dream wedding, there's always the possibility that something will go askew or bomb out completely. That's why having a sense of humor and the ability to think on your feet are key to keeping things on track or fixing the problems that will inevitably crop up.

"I do laugh a lot, but that doesn't mean I'm taking anything lightly," Loreen says. "I'll put my foot down when necessary. But being warm and friendly puts clients who are tired and frustrated at ease, which makes my job easier."

In fact, being a people person is pretty much a requirement for this job. You'll be dealing constantly with weepy brides, demanding mothers, cranky suppliers, and others who will vie for your attention. You'll be bargaining with vendors, overseeing the activities of hordes of hired helpers, and mingling with the guests at wedding receptions. So it helps if you really love working with people and have an upbeat, positive outlook that will help you weather the inevitable problems that can arise when you're coordinating countless details.

On the more practical side, it also helps to have a strong business background. While it's not impossible to make a go of a wedding consultant business if you've never balanced a checkbook, previous experience with handling finances (even household budgets) as well as managing day-to-day office details is certainly valuable. After all, you will be coordinating budgets and overseeing finances for your clients. Plus you'll be taking care of the details of running your own business, which will include taxes, billing, and other financial matters. You may even have to deal with personnel administration at some point in your career. So business experience—or barring that, at least a good head for numbers and details—is very important.

"An entrepreneurial spirit is also very important," says Julia K., who runs a successful wedding consultant business in a suburb of Dallas. "You have to be able to identify what's good for the business and what isn't, then make the appropriate moves."

The Joys of Consulting

There are many challenges in this business, to be sure, but along with these challenges come great rewards. Assuming there's no shotgun involved, you are always working with happy (though understandably nervous) people. You are the catalyst that makes the biggest moment of their lives special and memorable. And you can have the satisfaction of seeing all the details you have so painstakingly planned come together seamlessly and effectively.

"The end result is definitely the best part," says Loreen, the wedding consultant in Ypsilanti, Michigan. "All I do is eat, sleep, and dream weddings, but it's worth it because it's so much fun."

In addition to the satisfaction of being able to make dream weddings come true for your clients, there's another really appealing reason for embarking on a career in wedding consulting: You become the proud chief executive officer of your own small business. As such, you answer to no one, except maybe the IRS. You can do things your own way. You can set up shop in a spare bedroom or opt for a commercial space. You can set your own hours and make your own schedule. You can take on as much or as little work as you wish. Not that you'll have lots of free time for lazy days on the beach in Maui or strolls down the Champs Elysées. Wedding consulting is hard work. You'll have a mind-boggling number of details to coordinate, oodles of suppliers to baby-sit, long days shifting from one achy foot to the other, and legions of anxious brides (not to mention their mothers) to reassure and soothe.

Does this sound like fun to you, too? Great! Then you have come to the right place. The guide you're holding in your hands will show you how to start a wedding consulting business. We'll cover day-to-day responsibilities and the various tasks integral to running this type of business. We'll also touch on the myriad issues a new business owner will face, such as taxes, insurance, and financing issues. But perhaps best of all, you'll find that this guide is punctuated with advice and words of wisdom from successful wedding consultants who have turned their personal dreams of working in an industry they love into reality. You can do it, too! So turn the page, and let's get started.

Do You Have the Right Stuff?

Take this short quiz to see if you have what it takes to become a successful wedding consultant:

1. Can you juggle a variety of tasks at various stages of development all at the same time?
   ❑Yes ❑No

2. Are you detail oriented?
   ❑Yes ❑No

3. Are you motivated and able to work without direct supervision?
   ❑Yes ❑No

4. Are your calendar and other important papers within reach rather than hopelessly buried under piles of office detritus?
   ❑Yes ❑No

5. Are you disciplined enough to work even when the birds are singing, it's sunny and warm outside, and the house needs painting?
   ❑Yes ❑No

6. Are you comfortable working alone without the benefit of chattering co-workers, coffee klatches, and holiday parties?
   ❑Yes ❑No

7. Can you handle emotionally fragile brides, demanding mothers, and irritable suppliers without succumbing to the urge to deck them?
   ❑Yes ❑No

8. Can you say "no" and mean it?
   ❑Yes ❑No

9. Can you laugh genteelly when things go wrong, then think fast on your feet to fix them?
   ❑Yes ❑No

10. Can you lead a conga line and do the Macarena when called upon?
    ❑Yes ❑No

Add up your "yes" answers. Scoring:

8 to 10 = Congratulations! You have the makings of an excellent wedding consultant.

4 to 7 = With some hard work, you can go a long way in this field.

1 to 3 = Thank goodness you bought this book.

0 = Maybe you should try a career in trucking or construction!

2

The Wonderful World of
Wedding Consulting

For pomp, circumstance, and sheer drama, there are few events in life that can equal that of a carefully planned wedding. From the solemn ceremony to an elegant country club reception, dresses with yards and yards of pristine white peau de soie and tulle, debonair tuxedoes, and sleek stretch limousines, weddings are as much a staged production as the most elaborate Broadway show. Even if the nuptials are more intimate and the budget more modest, weddings still require a great deal of advanced planning and follow-up to make sure every element of this momentous day comes together as planned—on time and within budget.

In the past, wedding planning activities were often relegated to the mother of the bride or another female family member who had an eye for fashion and a flair for floral design. There was a strict code of appropriate behavior and proper etiquette that dictated exactly how the bridal party should dress and interact.

All has changed with the influx of women into the workplace over the past 30 years. Today's mother of the bride is probably a working woman herself who does not have any more time to attend to details such as limousine rentals or reception hall contracts than the bride herself does. This has opened up a world of opportunity for well-organized, enthusiastic consultants. Professional wedding consultants treat their vocation as a business, not as a pleasant hobby or sideline.

"Today's consultants are men and women trained in the administrative and legal affairs of their industry," says Robbi Ernst, founder and president of June Wedding Inc. "They are the team leaders who orchestrate the entire wedding, including the wedding day itself."

Words from the Wise

Robbi Ernst of June Wedding Inc. offers these sage words of advice to anyone contemplating a career as a wedding consultant:

○ Seek out the best and most competent professional training in the wedding industry. "Go to the experts and let them teach you not to make the mistakes they made. This can save you a small fortune," Ernst says.

○ Take business and computer courses, including classes on marketing, at your local community college.

○ If possible, work for a well-known consultant for a while as an apprentice.

○ Have enough funds to carry you through three years, since it will take that long before you see a profit.

○ Decide whether you are going to do this as a hobby or as a career. "If you don't make this decision early on, you're going to be frustrated and unhappy," Ernst says.

Something New

Toward that end, many wedding consultants routinely serve as event planners, budget watchdogs, etiquette experts, troubleshooters, and on-site supervisors. They accompany brides-to-be to appointments for fittings, floral consultations, and other services. They provide a shoulder to cry on and a sympathetic ear for stressed-out clients. They also act as creative problem-solvers who can quickly assess a situation and devise a viable solution—often without anyone in the bridal party ever knowing a potential disaster has been averted.

Some wedding consultants prefer to offer consulting services only, and may provide a comprehensive "wedding blueprint" package that consists of realistic budgets, detailed schedules, and lists of reliable vendors. Still others provide insight and assistance with the social etiquette part of the wedding experience.

The scope of your own involvement is entirely up to you. The trend in the industry, however, has been toward offering total coordination of the entire blessed event because, as noted earlier, brides and their mothers just don't have time to attend to the mountain of details necessary to pull off the wedding they dream of. That means you must have an in-depth knowledge of every aspect of wedding planning and know how to make all the details mesh smoothly and effectively.

Bridal Business Basics

Let's start with some administrative basics. No matter where you decide to conduct the majority of your business, or what your personal management style may be, there are certain tasks that are common to all wedding consultants. Among them are day-to-day business administration, bridal consultations, and vendor and service coordination. Here's a look at each of these activities.

A Day in the Life

Even though no two days tend to be alike for wedding consultants because the tastes and needs of their clients vary so widely, there are certain tasks you can expect to do on a regular basis. To begin with, you'll spend lots of time on the telephone every day, fielding inquiries from interested brides, following up on vendor leads, and checking on the status of wedding preparations. If you employ contract or temporary help during weddings, you'll have to meet with them on a regular basis to provide instructions and go over details. You will also spend a significant amount of time with the brides themselves, either conducting consultations or accompanying them to appointments with suppliers.

Then there is the paperwork. You'll have contracts to review, tax forms to file, and other business-related papers to shuffle. You will also have to keep meticulous records on the choices that your brides make, the status of wedding day plans, and other details. A word of advice: No matter how good your memory is, you should always jot down every appointment and activity. The number of details you will have to attend to as a wedding consultant will be truly mind-boggling, and when you're busy and short of time, it will be too easy for something to fall through the cracks—possibly with disastrous results.

The Consultation

The first step in determining what a bride wants and how much she wants to turn over to you is to schedule a consultation. Although some planners offer a free consultation of no more than one hour, it makes sense to charge at least a nominal fee—say, $50 per hour—for your time. In his book, *Great Wedding Tips From the Experts* (Lowell House), Robbi Ernst of June Wedding Inc. says, "A genuinely professional wedding consultant isn't going to talk with [anyone] for free, unless it is simply an introductory meeting...to determine if you are a good match for each other."

According to Ernst, the fee for a single consultation meeting typically ranges from $175 in smaller communities to as much as $500 in metropolitan areas. Charging a fee will help to cut down on the number of women who are just "shopping around" for services without making a commitment.

On the other hand, Dolores E., a wedding consultant in Larkspur, California, offers a two-hour complimentary consultation for brides who wish to execute their own plans. She earns her fee by preparing a "blueprint" package for these brides, which provides a preferred vendor list, a detailed schedule, and ready-to-use budget spreadsheets. It takes her about two hours to prepare the package, and she charges a flat rate for the service.

During a consultation, it is important to determine exactly how much the bride wants you to do. Sometimes, she will prefer to do much of the groundwork herself (such as selecting a reception hall, ordering the cake and flowers, and auditioning the band or DJ), then will ask you to coordinate all the services and be on site during the reception. Other times, a busy bride will want to turn over all or many of these tasks to you, limiting her involvement to approving the choices presented to her and signing checks for the deposits.

For this reason, it's advisable to offer a variety of packages with varying levels of service. The idea is to provide choices that will allow the bride to customize her wedding to her exact specifications.

Stat Fact

You probably can guess that Las Vegas is the wedding capital of the nation, with 100,000 weddings a year. But you may be surprised to know that Gatlinburg, Tennessee, is number two, with 42,000 nuptials, according to Richard Martel of the Association for Wedding Professionals International. How's that for southern hospitality?

Suggested wedding packages might include:

- *Full-service package:* wedding planning and event supervision from beginning to end
- *Rehearsal and wedding day package:* on-site coordination and execution
- *Wedding-day-only package:* full or day supervision of wedding party festivities and vendors
- *Planning package:* budgets, spreadsheets, vendor recommendations, and other details
- *Party package:* planning and coordination of the engagement party, rehearsal dinner, and bachelor and bachelorette parties

Wedding Day Duties

All the wedding consultants we spoke to said they act as the bride's advocate on the happy day—running interference with suppliers, making sure the wedding party is dressed and where they're supposed to be on time, and so on. Some consultants, like Julia K. in Oak Point, Texas, and Packy B. in Broadview Heights, Ohio, prepare snacks and drinks for the wedding party to nibble on before the wedding so they don't go up the aisle with rumbling stomachs. To make sure all these tasks run like clockwork, most wedding planners create a detailed wedding day schedule that's provided to each member of the wedding party, the parents, and other relatives, as well as to the vendors who are responsible for providing various services.

Consultants often hire extra help on a contract basis to assist with wedding day activities. Their duties may range from greeting guests to taking care of the wedding party and families (refilling drinks, assisting the bride in the powder room, and so on). These contractors are hired on an as-needed basis and are paid either by the hour (around $10 to $15 per hour) or by the function ($100 to $150 per day).

Consulting Services and Fees

Stat Fact
Coordinating ten weddings a year is a good goal to shoot for during the first year of operation, says Gerard J. Monaghan of the Association of Bridal Consultants. An experienced consultant who doesn't have employees can handle about 30 to 40 nuptials per year.

Charges for consulting services vary widely. Typically, consultants charge by the hour or by the package. Some consultants will charge up to 15 percent of the total wedding cost, but this is a more common practice in larger cities where disposable income is higher and there are more top-level female executives footing the bill.

According to Ernst, preparation-planning fees, which include everything except wedding day coordination, usually range between $2,000 and $4,500, depending whether your business is in a rural or metropolitan area. Full production coordination, which includes everything from early planning and budgeting to wedding day activity coordination, will cost an additional $1,500 to 3,000 on average. A wedding that's very large or complex may cost much more.

According to the wedding consultants interviewed for this book, full production package rates ranged from $1,000 to $5,000. The higher prices were found in the largest metropolitan areas, where one consultant even offers a $10,000 "concierge" package for the bride who wants to do nothing more than verbally approve the consultant's selections and write checks to pay the suppliers.

To arrive at a price for your wedding packages, Gerard J. Monaghan of the Association of Bridal Consultants suggests using this formula to come up with an hourly rate:

(amount you want to net annually) ÷ 50 weeks
÷ 5 days per week x 2.5 (factor for
expenses) = per diem ÷ 8 hours =
hourly rate

The Small Business Administration says the average for service industry pay rates is $25 to $125 per hour. Where you price your services in this range depends on what your local market will bear. In the next chapter, we'll discuss how to go about researching your market.

To Market,
To Market

The place to start when establishing your wedding consulting business is with market research. Market research will help you lay the groundwork for creating a viable and successful business. It will help you to identify exactly who might be interested in using your services, and whether the area where you want to set up shop can actually sustain your bridal business. Market research will also provide you with useful information and data that can help you avoid problems down the road.

Now, you might be thinking, "Whoa, there! I'm an aspiring wedding planner, not a statistician. Besides, people get married everywhere. There's bound to be enough business in my area to keep me busy."

Maybe, maybe not. The wedding industry may generate annual retail sales of $42 billion, but not every part of the country has the same need for consultants. Take, for instance, those parts of Florida that are heavily populated by senior citizens. It's a safe bet that the chances of making a go at running a successful wedding consultant business in those areas are probably slim to none. Likewise, in rough-and-tumble states like Alaska or Montana, where new jeans are considered formal wear, there is probably a maximum number of consultants the economy can support.

You have to think this way if you want to be successful, and the only way you're going to find out about these kinds of shortcomings—as well as the potential opportunities—is by researching your target market. Fortunately, this is something you can undertake yourself even if you don't have a background in statistics or research, says David L. Williams, Ph.D., an associate professor of marketing research at Wayne State University in Detroit.

"With the exception of questionnaire development, which can be difficult for a beginner to do well, you can pretty much handle all of the research by yourself on a reasonably small budget," Williams says. "The problem is, many small business owners view market research as an optional expense. But it's the only accurate way you have to find out what's important to your customer."

This chapter will show you how to find out who will use your services, learn where they live and work, and determine the kinds of services they'll want you to provide. Armed with this information, you'll be able to make informed decisions that can help your business grow and prosper.

Defining Your Audience

As the song says, "Love makes the world go 'round," which means there should be plenty of people who will need your services, right? In theory, yes. But you'll be much more successful if you study the demographics of the area you wish to do business in, then tailor your services to a specific group within that market.

Demographics are defined as the characteristics of the people in your target audience that make them more likely to use your services or products. These characteristics may include age, education and income level, gender, type of residence, and geographic location.

Stat Fact

Eighty-three per-
cent of brides and
89 percent of grooms are
employed full-time, according to
Synchronicity Licensing, an
online statistician.

Probably the most significant demographic for wedding consultants to consider is age. According to The Knot, an online source of wedding information, the average age of today's bride is 26, while the average age of the groom is 28. So while you certainly can serve people of any age group, you'll probably have the best success and garner the most business if you target brides in their mid-20s. This also means that if the population base in the area where you wish to do business doesn't have brides in this age group, you must either reconsider your market or adjust your marketing strategy.

Case in point: Brides may be the ultimate consumer for your services, but who often foots the bills for those dream weddings? Mom and Dad, of course. So a viable way to adjust your strategy if you aren't based where 20-something consumers live is to target their parents instead. That's what Julia K. of suburban Dallas did when her market research showed that the communities around her were populated by couples that were long-time residents and were likely to have children of marriageable age. As a result, she concentrates her advertising efforts in those communities and now coordinates an average of 30 weddings per year.

This is not to say there's no market for your services among older brides. According to the Stepfamily Association of America, 43 percent of all marriages are remarriages for at least one of the adults. These brides are usually older (early 30s and up) and also are prime candidates for your services given the demands of their careers—and their children.

Yet another factor to consider is where your prospective clients live versus where they work. Julia says that brides may look for information, use bridal registries, or purchase their invitations in the area where they work, but they'll go home to get married. That means the wedding consultant may have to travel if he or she wishes to serve the brides who work in the local business community.

Targeting Professional Women

One demographic segment, which many wedding consultants serve successfully, is that of professional women. These corporate executives or business owners often hold advanced college degrees and have high incomes. Because they don't have time to plan their own weddings, they're more likely to favor full-service packages that make it possible for them to turn all the details over to an experienced planner. Since full-service packages are usually a consultant's highest priced offering, this can translate into significant profits.

Marsha F. and Jenny C., wedding consultants based in Dallas, found their niche by targeting professional women. Originally, they intended to coordinate high profile and celebrity weddings, but found the market was very difficult to break into. By refocusing their efforts on serving professional women instead, the weddings they book now average $30,000.

Packy B., the wedding consultant in Broadview Heights, Ohio, has also successfully captured the professional woman's market. She often communicates with her executive-level brides solely by e-mail, and has coordinated every detail of some of her most elaborate and lavish weddings this way.

Economic Environment

Before we move on, there's one more very important factor to consider in your market research efforts. That's the economic base in your prospective market area.

Obviously, a wedding consultant is not an absolute necessity when it comes to coordinating a wedding. People get married all the time without ever using consultants' services. What you offer is experience, convenience, and the ability to step in when the details become too time-consuming or overwhelming for a busy bride to

Destination Unknown

Richard Martel, president of the Association for Wedding Professionals International, estimates that by 2005, 12 percent of weddings will be destination weddings. The reason? "The Internet," he says. "It's given us the capability to find anything anywhere. People are now forming tour companies all around the country just to handle destination events like weddings."

The Internet has opened legions of new opportunities for wedding consultants who live and work in highly desirable locations such as Orlando (with Disney World), Hawaii (with its slice of paradise), and New York City (with its cosmopolitan flair). Wedding consultants who are willing to handle the extra challenges involved in coordinating destination weddings may find they're not as restricted by the vagaries of the local economy.

manage. So your task not only becomes making your services irresistible to brides, but making sure the people who will pay the bills are financially able to afford your services.

If you've done your market research right, you already have some idea of the average income levels in your neighborhood. Now you need to look at data like the percentage of people who are employed full-time and the types of jobs they hold. If the local market is driven by blue-collar, heavy, industry jobs, a downturn in the economy could make cash tight and affect your ability to book weddings. So could a plant shutdown or a scaling back of services. A call to your city's economic development office is an easy way to get a handle on the health of local industry in your area.

Beware
Mailing lists are purchased for one time use. Lists are "seeded" with control names so the seller will know if you use the list more than one time. If you wish to use the list more than once, you'll have to ante up again.

While you're at it, ask about the area's white-collar jobs and the types of companies that support them. One industry to be wary of is the high-tech industry. Jobs in the computer and dotcom sectors are red hot right now, and the people who hold them are earning tons of money. But you only have to glance at the Dow Jones industrial averages to know that tech stocks experience huge swings in both directions. So again, an economy that's based on high tech-jobs has the potential to go south, taking your prospective customers with it. You need to make sure you have a back-up survival plan if you aspire to serve an area that's heavily dependent on a single industry.

Conducting Market Research

Now that you have a general idea about the types of people who might be responsive to your marketing efforts, you can proceed to the next step, which is to conduct an organized market research study. Your goal is to touch base with potential customers to find out whether they'd be interested in using the services of a wedding consultant, as well as exactly what types of services they may require.

There are two kinds of research: primary, which is information gathered firsthand; and secondary, which is information culled from external sources. Each has its own merits as well as costs.

Primary Research

The most common forms of primary research used by wedding consultants are direct mail surveys, telemarketing campaigns, and personal interviews. Assuming that you'll

Market Research Questionnaire

(For use with a mailing list purchased from a bridal show.)

Special Occasions Bridal Consulting

1010 Park Avenue
Lincoln Park, Michigan 10101

July 5, 2002

Ms. Susan Pfeiffer
10 Spring Lake Road
Bloomfield Hills, Michigan 10101

Dear Ms. Pfeiffer:

Congratulations on your recent engagement! This is an exciting time in your life and I wish you much happiness.

I am about to start a wedding consulting business in the metro Detroit area that will assist happy brides-to-be like you with the many details necessary to organize a picture-perfect wedding. Would you please take a few minutes to answer the following questions so I can assist brides like you better?

What is your age?

❑ 18–24   ❑ 35–39

❑ 25–29   ❑ 40–44

❑ 30–34   ❑ 45 and up

Which of the following services might interest you as you plan your wedding? (Check all that apply.)

❑ Assistance with setting up and staying within budget

❑ Information about reliable vendors (i.e., florists, caterers, bakers, etc.)

❑ Assistance with selecting and meeting with vendors

❑ Assistance with planning your entire wedding

Market Research Questionnaire, continued

❏ Services of a wedding consultant on the wedding day

❏ Services of a wedding consultant to handle the entire event

❏ Coordination of the rehearsal dinner

❏ Handling of honeymoon arrangements

Have you ever considered using a wedding consultant?

❏ Yes   ❏ No

Would you prefer to pay a flat fee or a percentage of your wedding costs for wedding consultant services?

❏ Flat fee   ❏ Percentage

If you hired a consultant who charged a flat fee, how much would you be willing to pay?

❏ $1,000–$1,500

❏ $1,501–$2,000

❏ $2,001–$2,500

❏ more than $2,500, depending on the complexity of the wedding

What is your household income?

❏ $25,000–$50,000   ❏ $50,001–$75,000   ❏ $75,000 and up

What is your educational level?

❏ High school diploma   ❏ College degree

❏ Graduate school degree   ❏ Doctorate degree

What is your profession?

_____

_____

If you would like to be contacted by a wedding consultant, provide your phone number here:

(   ) _____

Stat Fact

According to Richard Martel of the Association for Wedding Professionals International, at any given time, just 1 percent of the population is planning a wedding. The trick is to find that part of the 1 percent in your geographic area and target your marketing efforts toward them.

want to save your start-up capital for equipment and advertising, you should probably try a survey first since it's the most cost-effective way to gather information. By the same token, you might try doing the survey yourself rather than hiring a marketing research firm because that can be quite expensive.

Your survey should be no more than a page long, since it's difficult to get busy people to fill out anything lengthier. The questions should be well-phrased so they're direct, clear, and unambiguous. They should also be constructed so the information they gather is conducive to analysis. For example, a question like "Would you be interested in hiring a wedding consultant?" isn't very useful because it's closed-ended, meaning it's possible for the respondent to give a "yes" or "no" answer without elaborating. That's not going to give you much insight, which is the whole point of this exercise.

Although you can certainly draft the questions yourself, you should consider asking someone experienced in market research for help. Since a marketing research firm tends to be pricey, Williams, associate professor at Wayne State University, suggests contacting the business school at your local university instead. A marketing professor on staff might be willing to draft your questionnaire for $500 to $1,000, or may even assign your questionnaire as a class project, as Williams himself has done. In the meantime, you'll find a sample market research questionnaire on pages 18–19 that you can use as a guideline.

Surveying the Market

This part is easier than you might think. Start by purchasing a mailing list that's targeted to the market you wish to reach. Local trade associations, list brokers, and even daily newspapers in major metropolitan areas can sell you a list of heads of households that can be sorted in many ways, including by ZIP code, so you can target a specific geographic area. You can find a huge listing of publications that sell their lists in the *Standard Rate and Data Service* (VNU) directory, which can be found in many libraries. Some other criteria you are bound to be interested in will include occupation (if you are looking for professional women), gender (since women are the primary consumers of bridal consulting services), and age (as in 20-ish or the parental age brackets). Need another list source? Try the *Directory of Associations* (Gale Research), which can be found at most large libraries.

Once you have your list in hand (which is usually priced as a flat rate per 1,000 names), you're ready to produce your questionnaire. To keep the cost down, format it yourself on a home computer, then bop over to a quick print shop like Kinko's and have copies run off on your company letterhead.

Another good source of lists is bridal shows. These trade shows can attract thousands of prospective brides, and the companies that run them often compile the names and addresses of attendees for their exhibitors. You may be able to purchase a copy of the list directly from the trade show organizer. Look for information about some of the largest bridal shows in Chapter 11.

Cash as Bait

How would you like an easy way to improve your response rates? Try enclosing a crisp, new dollar bill with your survey. The dollar is sent as a thank you to the recipient for taking the time to fill out and return the questionnaire. Although it does not guarantee a response, the buck certainly is an attention-getter, and direct marketing studies have shown that sending even a small cash honorarium does tend to improve the rate of return.

Of course, this trick could cost you a pretty penny, so to speak, since Williams says that surveys should be sent to a sample of at least 300 people to get useful data. However, even as few as 100 surveys would be useful, and would only require a $100 investment if you choose to include a monetary incentive.

Pick Up the Phone

Since you probably love people and already have strong people skills if you're planning to get into a service industry like wedding consulting, telemarketing is a natural, if time-consuming, way to gather information. As with surveys, you'll need a strong telemarketing script with questions similar to those on your market research questionnaire and a good prospect list. But when you call, don't just fill out the form. Listen carefully to the person on the other end of the line. She's bound to make comments and have concerns about things you've never even considered. That helps you add to the storehouse of knowledge you'll tap into when you're ready to go after your first client.

A Job for the Pros

If you're really nervous about doing your own market research and have a sufficiently large start-up budget, you could engage a market research firm to help you. These firms are located in most large cities and will be listed in the Yellow Pages. They will not only collect information for you; they'll also handle all incoming data, then analyze the results, and prepare a report for your review.

Williams says a smaller firm might charge you $2,000 to $3,000 to handle a survey project and prepare a simple report. The cost for 200 to 300 interviews and a report would be about $4,000 to $8,000.

Secondary Research

If you're looking for real cost savings when doing market research, try using secondary research. Someone, somewhere has probably researched something that relates to what you want to know, and you can often put your hands on that information free of charge.

The mother lode of statistical information can be found at state and federal agencies, since they collect data on everything from income levels to buying habits. Although this data may be a year or two old, it can still be very useful, particularly for the fledgling wedding consultant who does not have much money to spend on research. Some great sources of information are the U.S. Census Bureau (www.census.gov), the Small Business Development Administration (www.sbda.gov), local economic development organizations, and even utility companies, which often have demographic data they will provide free of charge or for a very nominal fee.

Other sources of useful secondary research include your local library and chamber of commerce, your state's economic development department, trade associations, and trade publications. You can find the names of thousands of trade publications in *Standard Rate and Data Service* (VNU). And of course, the Internet is an invaluable source of just about any information you require. Just be sure to gather information only from reputable sites, such as those posted by organizations with good business reputations or those that appear to have rock solid data sources themselves.

Smart Tip

Tip...

Compiled lists are lists of names that have been culled from published sources such as telephone directories and organization rosters. *Hot lists* consist of the names of known buyers, and are usually taken from magazine subscription lists, mail-order buyer lists, and so on. Hot lists cost more to rent, but are worth the cost because the information is usually fresher and more accurate.

Mission Possible

Understanding your market and the people you'll serve is critical to the success of your business. But understanding yourself and defining exactly what you plan to do as a wedding consultant is equally important. So follow the lead of America's most successful corporations and write a simple mission statement that includes your company's goals and outlines how you will fulfill them.

What might a typical mission statement for a wedding consulting business say? Here are a couple of examples:

Bride's Choice will serve the needs of busy professional women by providing a full range of wedding consultation services. Thanks to my prior hands-on experience with wedding planning for several friends and family members, I am confident that I will be able to coordinate ten weddings in my first year of operation.

Here's another possible approach to a mission statement:

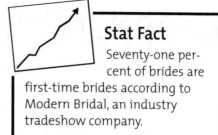

Hearts and Flowers Inc. is poised to become the premier wedding consultant service in greater Ashtabula. With our network of reliable suppliers, our personal background in business management, and our extensive network of social and business contacts, we bring an extra measure of experience to the business that will inspire confidence in our clients. Our goal is to achieve sales of $50,000 in calendar year 2002.

Your mission statement is your compass as well as the foundation on which your business' future is built. It can be one sentence long, as in the case of Pepsi's mission statement—whose succinct version is "Beat Coke"—or it can be several paragraphs. The length doesn't matter; the direction it provides is what's important. We've provided a work sheet on page 24 to get you thinking about what you want to include in the mission statement for your business.

Mission Statement Worksheet

Here's your opportunity to try your hand at writing your own mission statement. Start out by answering the following questions:

1. What are your reasons for becoming a wedding consultant?

_____

_____

2. What are your personal objectives? How do you intend to achieve them?

_____

_____

3. What skills do you bring to the business that will be of benefit?

_____

_____

4. What is your vision for this business? Where do you think you can take it in one, two, and five years?

_____

_____

_____

Using this information, write your mission statement here:

Mission Statement for

_____
(your company name)

_____

_____

_____

_____

_____

_____

4

Business
Underpinnings

Just as a bridal gown has a couture "superstruc-
ture" made of satin overlays, lace insets, and rustling tulle, a
wedding consulting business needs a formal framework to
ensure compliance with commonly accepted business prac-
tices. This chapter delves into standard operating procedures

Photo© PhotoDisc Inc.

for everything from legal matters to business insurance and shows you how to get your business machine oiled, cranked up, and ready to run.

The Name Game

Choosing a name for your company should be high on your list of priorities in the early stages of business development. Many wedding consultants opt to use their own names combined with a business description, like "Eileen Figure Bridal Consulting." But this can present a problem when it comes to cashing checks. If a client makes out a check to the business name rather than you, your bank probably isn't going to cash it. Then you'll have to ask the client to issue another check, which can make you seem unprofessional. In addition, using this type of name can lead to confusion with the IRS because it may be harder for those busy bureaucrats to distinguish between your personal income and your business income.

Even so, it is possible to incorporate your own name in the business name if that's what you really want. One wedding consultant in Austin, Texas, did this successfully when she named her homebased business "Elegant Weddings by Donna." But generally speaking, you should select a catchy, creative name that identifies who you are without being too cute. That means staying away from names that are over-the-top,

Dollar Stretcher

You can do your own name search for free if you have access to the Internet. Check for trademarks registered nationally on the U.S. Patent and Trademark Office Web site at www.uspto.gov. You can also search for the name using popular portals like America Online, Yahoo, Google, and Lycos. Network Solutions (www.networksolutions.com) can tell you if there's a Web site that already uses the name you've chosen.

like "Smart Broads Wedding Service," "Hugs and Kisses Weddings," or "Your First Wedding." Not only are they not professional; they won't inspire confidence in your clientele.

Simple, business-like names are always a better choice. Another of the wedding consultants interviewed for this book chose her romantic-sounding name, "Ever After Weddings," specifically because she didn't want her own name in the title.

"It seems to me that these are not ever my weddings and by using a name like 'Weddings by Lisa,' it implies control," she says. "That's a myth [about wedding consulting] that I wanted to discredit, not encourage."

There can be other compelling reasons for a name choice. Dolores E., the wedding consultant in Larkspur, California, started her business in 1991 under one name.

In Search of the Perfect Moniker

Wedding consultants frequently put a great deal of time and thought into selecting a name for their business—and with good reason. It's a big responsibility selecting a name that's clever and evocative, yet accurately describes what you do.

One wedding consultant we interviewed says, "I labored extensively over this decision. I once started a gourmet baking and chocolate candy company that I named Cocoa Bear Cuisine, and I just loved the name. It flowed; it described what we did, and it was cute.

"I wanted something just as nice for my wedding consulting business. My son tried to help me come up with a name, but we just couldn't agree on anything. So I started to think of my favorite songs, and I came up with 'Only You.' I added 'Wedding and Event Consulting' because I wanted people to understand what I do. It was a very good decision because there are so many vendors listed under 'Wedding Consulting' in the phone book (florists, photographers, DJs, etc.) so a client has no problem picking my company out."

In 1999 she took a well-deserved sabbatical, then decided to reopen the business under a new name that started with the letter "A." The reason? "I'm now first in the phone book," Dolores says.

Not everyone can be listed in that coveted first spot, but you can choose a unique name that's distinctive and evocative of what your business does. To help you get started, check the

> # You need a name that catches the eye and provides instant recognition of what you do.

Yellow Pages for ideas (as well as to avoid duplication). Or you can do what Loreen C., the wedding consultant in Ypsilanti, Michigan, did before settling on a business name. After polling her friends, she came up with a list of about 50 names, which she narrowed down to ten finalists. Then she put those names to a vote before deciding on her highly descriptive name. She knew she made the right choice when she was in the post office one day and a woman who saw her carrying a box with her return address asked if she planned weddings.

"You need a name that catches the eye and provides instant recognition of what you do," Loreen stresses. "That day in the post office proved my business name did both."

We have included a worksheet on page 29 to help you select an appropriate moniker. Once you have picked a suitable name, it's time to move on to the next step: setting up your business structure.

Registering Your Company Name

Most states require you to register your fictitious company name officially to ensure that it's unique. This is usually done at the county level, and is known as filing a DBA ("doing business as") statement. The fee to file is usually nominal (around $30 to $60) and entitles you to use the name for a limited period of time, usually three years. When the time expires, you simply renew the DBA. Before you get your DBA, however, a search is done to make sure your name is unique. If you happen to choose a name that's already being used, you'll have to pick something else, so it's a good idea to have a couple of names in reserve.

Your Corporate Structure

Once you have your DBA in hand, you are considered the proud owner of a legitimate business. So naturally, the IRS will have something to say about the way you run it. (You knew we'd get around to the IRS eventually, didn't you?) Basically, this means the bureaucrats in Washington require that you operate as one of four business entities: a sole proprietorship, a corporation, a partnership, or a limited liability company (LLC).

Name that Business

Establishing a unique business identity is not just important; it's absolutely essential so prospective clients (and, alas, the IRS) can find you easily. Try the following brainstorming exercise to whittle down your choices and find the perfect name.

List the top three things that come to mind when you hear the word "wedding" (such as bride or bouquet). Be creative!

1. _____
2. _____
3. _____

List three unique landmarks or features that characterize the place where you'll do business (such as the sand dunes of northern Michigan or the picturesque caves of Carlsbad).

1. _____
2. _____
3. _____

List three geographical references (such as your city, state, or regional area).

1. _____
2. _____
3. _____

Now, try combining elements from these three sections in different ways:

1. _____
2. _____
3. _____

Did you come up with something you liked? If not, try using alliteration ("Weddings in White") or plays on words ("Altared State") with any of the elements above to create a business name.

Once you've selected a name, put it to the test:

❍ Say it aloud several times to make sure it's easily understood, both in person and over the phone. A name like "Simply Sensational Celebrations" has too many "s" sounds and may be difficult to pronounce, let alone understand on the phone.

❍ Page through your local Yellow Pages directory to make sure someone else isn't already using the name you've chosen.

❍ Check with your county seat or other official registrar to make sure the name is available. Someone may have already claimed the name but may not be using it yet.

❍ Does your name pass the test? Way to go! Now you're ready to register it officially.

Sole Proprietors

Most wedding consultants choose to operate as sole proprietors because it's the easiest type of business to form. All you have to do is file a DBA as discussed above, then open a business checking account in that name. You can use your personal credit card to pay for business expenditures, yet you still get tax benefits like business expense deductions. But there is a downside to the sole proprietorship. You are personally liable for any losses, bankruptcy claims, legal actions, and so on. That can wipe out both your personal and business assets if a catastrophe hits.

General Partnership

If you are planning to join forces with another wedding consultant to open a business, you are forming a general partnership. Partnerships are easier to form than corporations, and you don't have to file any documents to make them legal. But since each partner is responsible for the actions of the other, it's a good idea to have a partnership agreement drawn up by an attorney. That way, you can spell out exactly what each person is responsible for.

Limited Liability Company

A third type of business entity is the limited liability company, or LLC, which combines the tax structure of a partnership, yet protects the business owner from personal liability. This is the type of partnership agreement Marsha B. and Jenny C., the wedding consultants in Dallas, drew up when they started their business. Even though they had known each other for 25 years and brought complementary skills to the partnership that have made it flourish, they recognized how important it was to protect their personal interests.

"I have a sole proprietorship now, but I'm thinking about establishing an LLC in a year or two," says Loreen C., the wedding consultant in Michigan. "I'm still researching the benefits, but I think it's important to have protection so no one can touch my personal property. I wouldn't want anything taken away from my family."

Corporations

The last type of business arrangement is the corporation. It is established as a totally separate legal entity from the business owner. Establishing a corporation requires filing articles of incorporation, electing officers, and holding an annual meeting. Not many wedding consultants choose this route initially because the costs are prohibitive, and the company must pay corporate taxes. On the other hand, a corporation will find it easier to obtain financing, which would be useful if you decided to franchise your business, start a retail store that caters to brides, or expand in a big way.

Incidentally, if you operate under your own name, you can use your social security number when filing your business taxes. But if you adopt another name for your sole proprietorship, or form a partnership or corporation, you are required to have a federal employment identification number (EIN). To apply for one, pick up a copy of form SS-4 at any IRS office, or print one off the Web site at www.irs.ustreas.gov. If you are not sure which business arrangement to choose, talk to an attorney experienced in handling small business issues.

Stat Fact
You have to be at least 18 (or 21, depending on the state) to incorporate a business.

"There are advantages to each kind of entity, and an attorney can help you decide which one is best for your situation," says Daniel H. Minkus, chairman of the business law section of the State Bar of Michigan, and a member of the business practice group of Clark Hill PLC. "If you don't know the people you are doing business with, I'd encourage you to form a single-member LLC or corporation. They're simple to create, and they're invaluable because your clients are dealing with your enterprise and not you personally."

One final note: You can incorporate without using an attorney. It will cost you just $50 to $300 to do it yourself, versus $400 to $1,000 if you have an attorney handle the process. But corporate law is complex and difficult to understand, so it is usually advisable to allow a professional to handle this for you. You'll find information about hiring an attorney in Chapter 5.

The Home Zone

Just when you thought it was safe to test the waters with your new business, you find out there could be a restriction on your activities. That could come in the form of a local zoning ordinance, which prohibits businesses to operate in certain areas like residential neighborhoods. Such ordinances exist to protect people from excessive traffic and noise (as well as to rake in the extra taxes assessed on businesses). But because your business doesn't require signage and you won't have a lot of people coming and going, it's quite likely you can run the business quietly from your home. Still, to be on the safe side, you should check with your local government office to see if any special

Beware!
Zoning regulations are established at the local (city, township, or village) level rather than the state level. A homebased business that's perfectly legal in one city could be verboten in another. The only way to find out is by calling the zoning board in your community.

permits are required. It's better to find out up front, before you go to the expense of printing stationery and obtaining a business telephone line, than to find out later that homebased businesses are prohibited in your area.

It's especially important to check local zoning regulations if you plan to do consultations with prospective clients in your home. You may need to establish a business office elsewhere, as Julia K., the wedding consultant in Oak Point, Texas, did when she rented a 1,500 square foot townhouse and converted it into a business office separate from her home.

Other Licenses and Permits

But wait, there's more! Some municipalities require business owners to have a business license. It's usually available for a very nominal fee and is renewable annually. If by chance you are turned down for a license because of zoning restrictions, you can apply for (and probably receive) a variance from the municipal planning commission so you can get your license.

Then there's the health department permit that's necessary from the county where you do business, if you provide any of the food at your weddings. A permit is also necessary if you bake the wedding cake yourself, says Donna H. An experienced baker who started out in the wedding industry by baking cakes for military personnel on a local base, Donna doesn't trust the job to anyone else. So she dutifully pays for her health certificate every year so she can continue her personal tradition of baking for her brides.

To find out whether you need other special permits or licenses, you can contact:

- *Small Business Administration (SBA)*. See the federal listings in your phone book, or go to www.sba.gov.
- *Small Business Development Center (SBDC)*. Reachable through the SBA, or by logging onto www.sba.gov/gopher/local-information/small-business-develop ment-centers for a list of local offices.
- *Service Corps of Retired Executives (SCORE)*. Go to www.score.org. This non-profit organization is an SBA partner and has hundreds of chapters throughout the United States.

Getting Down to Brass Tacks

There's still one more task you have to complete before you can leave this chapter and plunge into the other uncharted waters that await you. And this is a big one—one that literally can make or break your business.

You have to write a scintillating, compelling, and painfully comprehensive business plan that will guide you though the aforementioned Bermuda Triangle of Business.

Your business plan is like a roadmap. It outlines your plans, goals, and strategies for making your business successful. It's useful not just for applying for credit or attracting investors. It also gives you direction so you can achieve even your loftiest goals as well as measure the success of your business over time.

There are seven major components a business plan should have. Here's how they apply to a bridal consulting business:

Stat Fact

Experts say that a thoroughly researched business plan is about 25 pages long and takes 300 hours to prepare (which includes doing research, compiling financial information, conducting surveys, and writing). This may seem like a drag, but a plan that's too sketchy won't keep you on the right course, nor help you find the financing you may need.

1. *Executive summary.* In this section, which summarizes the entire business plan, you'll want to describe the nature of your business, the scope of the services you offer (including brief details about the various wedding packages you'll offer, additional services like retail goods sales and so on), the legal form of operation (discussed earlier in this chapter), and your goals. If you plan to use the business plan to seek financing for your company, you should include details about your future plans for the business, too.

2. *Business description.* In this section, you'll want to describe both the bridal industry and your target market. You'll find general statistics about the bridal industry in the guide you're holding. But for even more information that can prove helpful in establishing the viability of your business, check the Small Business Development Center Web site at www.sba.gov/gopher/local-informa tion/small-business-development-centers.

3. *Market strategies.* Here's another place where all that market research data will come in handy. In this section, you'll want to analyze exactly what you'll do to reach prospective brides and how you'll pull it off. Focus, too, on the things that make your company unique, from your personal experience in event planning, to specialized business know-how or other factors. You'll find more information about marketing plans in Chapter 3.

Smart Tip

Tip...

The SBA has numerous publications available to guide you through the development of your business plan, including publication MP 21, *Developing a Strategic Business Plan*, and publication MP 15, *Business Plan for Homebased Business*. They're available free at local SBA offices, or by visiting their Web site at www.sba.gov/library.

Foundation Essentials for Your Start-Up

Be sure to address these essentials when getting your business started.

❏ Select a business name and apply for a DBA.

❏ Consult with an attorney regarding the best legal form for your business.

❏ Apply for an employer identification number (Form SS-4), if you're forming a corporation.

❏ Check local zoning regulations to determine compliance.

❏ Apply for a business license if required in your community.

❏ Apply for a health department permit if you're planning to serve food or bake wedding cakes.

❏ Write your business plan.

❏ Contact an accountant to discuss the financial and tax requirements related to establishing and operating your business.

4. *Competitive analysis.* If you have done your homework well, you already know how many wedding consultants are in business in your target market area. But in this section, you should also consider other potential competitors, such as general event planners who also coordinate weddings and banquet facilities that offer consulting services. Analyze their strengths and weaknesses, and contrast them against what you perceive to be your own strengths. Also, don't forget to consider the aspects that make your services unique and special.

5. *Design and development plan.* Here's where you will consider how you will develop market opportunities to help your company prosper and grow. It's helpful to create a timetable of objectives that you can refer to as a benchmark for your successes, like setting a goal for graduating from ten weddings a year to 20 and how much contract help you'll need to accomplish this.

6. *Operations and management plan.* You can use the information in Chapter 2 of this manual, which discusses the day-to-day operations of your business, as a guide for drafting this section. You should keep this section of your marketing plan updated to reflect any new or expanded services you offer.

7. *Financial factors.* Even if you're a sole proprietor with very modest first year expectations, you need to forecast the success of your business. This will help keep your business on track and help you avoid nasty surprises later on. Probably the most important document in this section is your balance sheet, which will provide a running tally of how well your business is doing.

Constructing such a detailed business plan may sound like a lot of nonessential work, especially since you're probably operating out of your den or from your dining room table. But embarking on a new business without a clear-cut plan is like sailing for Europe without a navigational chart or a compass. Without a plan, you won't have any idea whom you're selling your services to or what they're even interested in. So take the time to formalize your business plan now, then refer back to it periodically for both inspiration and direction.

Getting
Professional Help

Just as a busy bride will turn over the details of planning her wedding extravaganza to you, so you will want to relinquish some of the details of running your business to other professionals who have the expertise to do the job right. Even if you have the know-how to do your own taxes or review a real-estate lease, this isn't necessarily a good use of your time. It's almost always better to spend the lion's share of your working hours on the activity you do best—wedding planning—and rely on other professionals to keep your business humming along behind the scenes. This chapter will give you insight into why you should consider hiring an attorney, an accountant, and an insurance agent, as well as look at what you can expect them to do for you.

The Legal Eagle

You're reliable and prompt, conscientious and professional. So you couldn't possibly ever have to worry about being sued by one of your sweet, blushing brides or the members of her family, right?

Wrong. Unfortunately, whenever a job involves working with the public, the potential to be sued exists. The lawsuit could be over a matter that you couldn't possibly have controlled, like a sudden torrential downpour that flooded the streets and trapped the caterer in her car on a low-lying street, so the mostaccioli didn't arrive until after the guests did. Or it could be over something more unthinkable, such as having one of your contract workers show up tipsy and unruly, and fall face-first into the cake.

So it makes sense to retain an attorney before anything ever goes wrong so you have someone to turn to for advice and guidance when the time comes. The main reasons a wedding consultant might have for hiring an attorney include:

- Wanting to form a partnership or a corporation
- Finding the language in a contract difficult to understand
- Signing a contract for a large sum of money or one that will cover a long period of time (such as a long-term lease on an office site)
- Being sued or having someone threatening to sue
- Needing help with tax planning, loan negotiations, or employee contracts

"But above all, protecting yourself from liability is one of the most important things you must do as a small business owner," says Daniel H. Minkus, chairman of the business law section of the State Bar of Michigan, and a member of the business practice group of Clark Hill PLC. "An attorney can help you assess your risk for being party to a lawsuit and help you minimize it."

As we discussed in the last chapter, establishing an LLC or a corporation is a good way to limit the liability on your personal property. Limiting your financial liability when hiring an attorney is just as important, especially when you're just starting out, and your cash flow is modest. Minkus says that because you don't need a litigator (someone who will defend you in court against lawsuits) to handle your legal work at the outset, you can keep the cost down by hiring an attorney in a one- or two-person practice.

Attorneys' hourly rates typically run from $100–$450, with the higher rates being charged by senior partners and those who work at larger firms. Other factors that influence cost include geographic location, the experience of the attorney, and the attorney's area of expertise.

You may be required to pay an initial consultation fee, so it's important to ask about this before you ever set foot in the lawyer's office. In addition, you may have to pay your attorney a retainer upfront, which he or she will draw against as work is completed. Others work on a contingency basis, which means they will take a percentage of any lawsuit settlement that's reached. Still others charge a flat fee for routine work, such as filing incorporation papers.

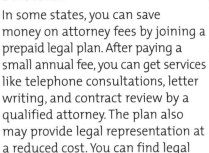

Dollar Stretcher

In some states, you can save money on attorney fees by joining a prepaid legal plan. After paying a small annual fee, you can get services like telephone consultations, letter writing, and contract review by a qualified attorney. The plan also may provide legal representation at a reduced cost. You can find legal networks in the phone directory.

Choosing the Right Attorney

Just as every wedding consultant differs in terms of his or her personal style, temperament, and experience, so attorneys (and indeed, all business professionals) differ from one another. The trick is to find a lawyer who meets your personal needs and expectations, and whose strong communication skills make him or her easy to talk to. Here are some general questions to ask that can be helpful in determining whether your attorney-to-be is one you want "to have and to hold":

○ What's your background and experience?
○ What's your specialty?
○ How long have you been practicing?
○ Do you have other consultants or small business owners as clients?
○ Have you ever represented a wedding consultant before?
○ Will you do most of the work, or will a paralegal or other aide help out?
○ Is there a charge for an initial consultation?
○ What do you charge for routine legal work?
○ Do you work on a contingency basis?

Another way to keep your legal costs reasonable is simply by being organized. "Do your own legwork to gather the information you need beforehand, then limit the number of office visits you must make," Minkus advises. "You also should limit the number of phone calls you make to your attorney, because you'll be charged for those, too."

Many attorneys offer start-up packages that are often more affordable for the small business owner. While you usually can tailor such packages to meet your needs, they typically include an initial consultation, as well as all activities related to the LLC or incorporation process, including the filing of paperwork with your state and other corporate formalities. You can expect to pay approximately $500 if you're establishing an LLC, or $900 if you're setting up a corporation. A payment plan may be available to help you handle the cost.

Locating an attorney you like and respect is often as simple as asking friends or relatives for a referral. In any event, Minkus says that process is much more reliable than just opening the Yellow Pages and picking someone at random. Another way to find a lawyer is through attorney referral services, which are located in many counties throughout the United States. You could also call the American Bar Association at (312) 988-5522, or go online and check out Find an Attorney at www.findanattorney.com or the Martindale-Hubbell Law Directory at www.martindale.com.

Money Managers

It's usually easier to convince a new business owner that he or she needs an accountant over other business consultants, like attorneys. Most people are either admirably adept or totally clueless when it comes to budgeting, bookkeeping, and other financial matters. But even those who feel comfortable cranking out their personal taxes annually or investing online may blanche at the thought of creating profit and loss statements and other complex documents. That's usually a pretty reliable sign that you need to "book" the services of a professional accountant.

An accountant can help you establish an effective record-keeping system, help you keep expenses in line, and monitor cash flow. He or she can also advise you on tax issues, which is crucial because tax law is very complicated and changes frequently. (The IRS alone issues new tax rulings every two hours of every business

Smart Tip

If you're comfortable doing your own bookkeeping and just need tax help, you could hire an enrolled agent instead of an accountant. In addition to preparing your tax return, enrolled agents can represent you before the IRS. They can be found in the Yellow Pages or through the National Association of Enrolled Agents (www.naea.org).

Bright Idea

A Simplified Employee Pension Plan (SEP) is a must for self-employed individuals. It has a higher contribution limit than a traditional IRA (up to 15 percent of business income, depending on your tax situation), and your funds grow tax-deferred. An accountant or financial planner can help you with the paperwork necessary to set up this important retirement savings tool.

day!) Tax issues that might be relevant to a wedding consultant include the amount you can deduct annually for business expenses including travel and entertainment, and office equipment; and the amount of money you can deposit to your simplified employee pension plan (SEP) annually.

Like an attorney, an accountant experienced in handling small business tax issues can also advise you whether you should incorporate your business. In addition to protecting your personal assets, incorporating can cut your tax bill, allow you to put more money into your personal investments, and offer other useful benefits.

There are two types of accountants. Certified public accountants, or CPAs, are college-educated and must pass a rigorous certification examination in the state where they do business in order to put those coveted letters after their names. Public accountants aren't certified and don't have to be licensed by the state. While they may be perfectly capable due to their experience, they usually can't represent you before the IRS like CPAs can, if you're called in for an audit.

There's also a plethora of accounting software on the market that can help you crunch the numbers and manage your business accounting. Intuit QuickBooks is the choice of many small business owners. Keep in mind, however, that some packages may not satisfy IRS requirements for record-keeping. It's probably wiser to rely on a professional to handle accounting matters whenever you need to do anything more complex than record credits and debits, or informally tally up business expenditures.

To find an accountant, ask your attorney, banker, or other professionals in the wedding industry for a referral. The American Institute of Certified Public Accountants branch in your state can also refer you to a qualified number cruncher, or you can go to their Web site at www.aicpa.org. It's very important to select someone who has experience either with small business clients in general, or wedding consultants in particular (although this can be a tall order depending on your area of the country). Avoid accountants who specialize in large corporations, since they're not as likely to be as tuned into your tax and financial situation as you'd like.

Accountants charge anywhere from $75 to $125 an hour and up. You can keep the cost down by organizing your financial records and receipts before you meet—overflowing shoeboxes are not considered a viable accounting system! You'll find more bookkeeping strategies and techniques in Chapter 11.

Covering Your Assets

The other business professional you should have on your side is an insurance agent. Although you could use one of the services that guide you to discount insurance brokers via the Internet, it's probably better to find an agent in your own community instead (or at least at the time of start-up; you can comparison shop and switch later). This will allow you to discuss the particulars of your own business with an agent to make sure you're covered against all potential pitfalls. Face-to-face interaction really is the best way to accomplish this.

Working personally with an agent is also the only reliable way for you to get adequate coverage. An experienced agent will be familiar with the risks you might encounter in your business and can recommend exactly how much coverage you need to protect yourself against those risks.

Locating an insurance agent who can help you with your business needs can be as simple as contacting the person who currently insures your home, apartment, or automobile. However, you should be aware that not all insurance companies (including some of the largest ones) insure homebased businesses. If your insurance provider doesn't offer business insurance, try contacting industry associations for referrals, or simply consult the phone book under "Insurance." Important note: You may find that an independent insurance agent is the best choice for small business insurance. A number of the larger companies we contacted immediately directed us to such agents when we phoned for information.

Dollar Stretcher

If you find you need several different types of business insurance, you might want to look for an independent insurance agent or an insurance broker who can shop around for the best rates on each one. Agents who are aligned with just one company will be locked into its rates, which may be higher than what the competition charges. Check your state's insurance department for a list of reputable brokers.

Insurance Riders

Most insurance companies offer a broad spectrum of insurance plans that can be tailor-made for a homebased business owner. In some cases, supplemental insurance policies can be attached to your existing insurance as riders, or addendums to your main policy. Because they "ride" along with the main policy, they don't require the rewriting of your policy.

If you already have standard homeowner's insurance, you may have a certain amount of general liability insurance already built in so you won't need a rider. For instance, AAA of Michigan includes $2,500 of business equipment replacement insurance in its standard home insurance policy, rather than offering a rider. But if this isn't enough coverage (and it may not be if you have very expensive equipment or will be warehousing retail merchandise in your home), it's usually most affordable to add an insurance rider that offers computer and other business equipment replacement coverage, since most standard homeowner's policies will only cover a fraction of the replacement cost of equipment that's damaged or destroyed. The other type of insurance rider you should consider is one for general liability that protects you and any employees or contractors you hire against business-related personal injury claims.

Riders are generally quite inexpensive; they can be as low as $20 per year for each rider, depending on where you live and do business, and how much insurance you need. Companies that offer riders for homebased businesses include Allstate and Hartford.

Riders generally only protect businesses with less than $5,000 in sales, which is often enough for a wedding consultant who is just starting off in the business. But if your business is more successful, you will need a home business insurance policy instead. This type of insurance provides general liability as well as income loss protection when you can't work. Rates can vary widely depending on where you do business and which company provides the coverage. For example, a general in-home liability policy with State Farm will cost $125 for $300,000 worth of insurance, $5,000 of which is earmarked specifically as business property insurance. On the other hand, an independent insurance agent we contacted offers a $500,000 general liability policy (with a $5,000 limit for home contents, including computer equipment) for just $150 per year.

> **M**ost standard homeowner's policies will only cover a fraction of the replacement cost of equipment that's damaged or destroyed.

Business Owner's Insurance

When you start calling around for insurance, you may discover that many general liability policies are available for homebased businesses only if you are running a low traffic business. If you plan to conduct bridal consultations in your home frequently, or if you will hire many independent contractors who will actually work at your home, you are likely to need business owner's insurance instead. This type of insurance provides coverage against physical injuries to your customers and employees, damage to the property of others while on your property (such as damage to a bride's car when it's parked in your driveway), and other situations. This kind of coverage is separate from your homeowner's policy and can cost $350 to $450 per year for $500,000 of coverage from an independent agent, or $150 to $300 for $300,000 from a company like State Farm.

Finally, if you decide to establish your wedding consultant business in a location away from your home, you'll need commercial business insurance. The amount of insurance you will need depends on the type of business you run (and generally speaking, liability for a service business like wedding consultation is low), as well as state or municipal regulations. Your insurance agent can guide you in these matters, but you can also contact your local government to find out what the regulations are.

One final word: Don't even consider operating without some type of liability insurance. Even if you are very careful and conscientious, you never know when you will find yourself a party in a lawsuit, or the victim of a break-in or an act of God like a tornado or earthquake. A low-cost insurance policy could save your business from bankruptcy in the aftermath of any kind of catastrophic loss, either manmade or natural.

The Wedding
Bell Bills

There are just a few businesses around that eager entrepreneurs can jump into backed by just a modest amount of capital, a vision, and lots of enthusiasm. Fortunately, wedding consulting is one of them.

Photo© Adobe Image Library

Because most wedding consultant businesses begin as homebased businesses, start-up costs are relatively low. You don't have the overhead associated with renting an office space. You may be able to use equipment you already own, such as a computer or fax machine. Your dining room table will suffice as a desk, at least initially, and your home telephone can pinch hit as your business line during regular business hours.

Initially, you won't have any inventory to pay for. A word of warning: Don't even think about investing in retail merchandise or props that can be used at weddings until you've been in business for a while. You don't need the extra financial burden when you start out. You don't even have to invest in an extensive business wardrobe as long as you already own attire that would be appropriate for business meetings, bridal consultations, and on-site wedding coordination.

This chapter will help you take a systematic approach to estimating your start-up costs so you'll know whether you need to seek outside financing.

Tools of the Trade

The basics you must have to get your business off the ground will include office equipment (including furniture and business machines like computers) and office supplies. You'll find a worksheet on page 51 with estimates of the equipment start-up costs for two hypothetical businesses.

Office Equipment

One of the largest expenditures you'll make at the dawn of your new career will be on your office furniture. Although you can run your business from a corner of your living room or your dining room table, you'll feel much more productive and professional if you set up a permanent office space in a room or even a secluded corner of your home. That means you'll need an inexpensive desk or computer workstation, a comfortable office chair (preferably one that's ergonomic, since you'll be spending a great deal of time in it), and a sturdy two- or four-drawer file cabinet. You should also consider acquiring a bookcase so you can keep your reference materials conveniently at hand.

Dollar Stretcher

Rummage through your desk drawers before heading out to the office supply store. You'll probably find all the pens, paper, and paperclips you need there to get started. The only things you'll need that you won't have hidden away in a drawer are business stationery and business cards.

Office supply stores like Staples or Office Depot sell reasonably priced office furniture that will set you back only about $200 to $600 for a desk, and $60 to $250 for a chair. A two-drawer letter-size file cabinet costs $25 to $100, while a four-shelf bookcase will cost around $70. In addition, you can often save a substantial amount of money on your desk or computer workstation by purchasing furniture that must be assembled (known as KD or "knock down") or by scouring the want ads for used furniture.

Dollar Stretcher

Build your own desk inexpensively by laying a sheet of sanded and stained plywood on top of a pair of two-drawer file cabinets. The desk will be exactly the right height for most people and will provide plenty of storage space and room to work. A sheet of tempered glass with beveled edges (available from replacement glass companies) also makes a snazzy desktop.

Personal Computers

Some wedding consultants, like Donna H. in Austin, Texas, still like to keep their records the old-fashioned way, using a typewriter, paper spreadsheets, and a well-loved pen. But for most of us, personal computers are now pretty much a necessity for doing business. Desktop computers offer speed, convenience, and compatibility with other users. They use sophisticated, yet user-friendly software packages to crunch numbers, churn out your billing statements, figure your taxes, and connect you to the Internet. Best of all, this efficiency and accuracy is now available at a cost that's reasonable enough even for a fledgling small-business owner—usually around $2,000 to $4,000 for a complete Pentium-based system that includes the hard drive, monitor, mouse, modem, and printer.

In order to run the most common event planning and business software packages, your system should have a speed of at least 433 MHz with at least 10GB of hard-drive space and 64K RAM. It should come equipped with no less than a 24X CD-ROM (so you can load most software packages), as well as internal fax and modem cards.

Dollar Stretcher

You can save yourself some money on your computer by buying used. As long as the CPU isn't ancient (like more than a year old), you can upgrade the memory and bring it up to speed for considerably less than buying new.

If you have a little more money to spend, other useful add-ons include: a scanner (which will cost you in the range of $150 to $400, depending on the resolution); a CD-RW (for CD Rewritable) drive, which allows you to download data onto CDs ($300 to $400); a Zip drive ($100 to $200) for long-term data storage of records from past

In Your Pocket

Just about anything you purchase for use in your business is deductible on your federal income taxes, provided you have the proper written documentation (like receipts and packing slips). The section 179 expense deduction will currently allow you to deduct up to $20,000 a year for equipment costs including computers, office furniture, telecommunications equipment (phones, answering machines, telephone headsets), and fax machines. Other incidentals needed to run your business, like office supplies and professional journals and trade magazines, are also deductible. If any of these items are used for both business and pleasure (like your kids using the PC to research dinosaurs for a school project), you can only deduct the amount of time the computer is actually in service for the business. The IRS recommends keeping a log showing business versus personal usage.

Happily, other costs typically incurred by wedding consultants, including professional fees for attorneys and CPAs, advertising and marketing costs, business equipment repairs, voice mail, seminars required to improve business skills, trade show and conference fees, and bank fees, may be written off against the business taxes.

weddings and photo files; and a digital camera ($400 to $700), which allows you to download photographs directly to your computer. The camera will come in handy if there's some element of a wedding you'd like to preserve in your digital memory, such as a room layout or perhaps an especially unusual custom cake.

Software

Your software is the engine that makes your computer go. Most of the wedding consultants we spoke to use two basic software packages for conducting business: Microsoft Office and Intuit QuickBooks. Microsoft Office is a bundled package that includes word processing, spreadsheet, database management, e-mail, presentation, and scheduling programs and retails for about $600. QuickBooks is an easy-to-use accounting package that not only keeps your financial records but can manage your business checking account and print checks. The 2001 Pro version retails for around $250.

By now it should be obvious that attention to detail is one of the most important personal traits a wedding consultant must have. And one of the most important tools you'll need is a good planner to help you keep appointments and activities straight and on schedule. A Franklin planner or other notebook-style planner will work just fine. But if you're computer-proficient, you might consider using a PC-based calendar or scheduler program instead. Microsoft Office, which has become the industry standard in workplace software, gives you three options for setting up a personal schedule: the calendar template in Microsoft Word, Microsoft Excel spreadsheets, or Scheduler+ for detailed schedules. Other scheduling programs that may be useful include Affordable Event Planning Software (Certain Software, $495) and ScheduleEZ Pro (Software2020, $95).

There are also a number of specialty bridal consulting software packages on the market that can be used to manage the details of the weddings you oversee. Most of them are geared toward the bride, but may be useful for consultants as well. A few packages include The Wedding Workshop (MicroPrecision, $29.99), which helps you manage guest lists, track expenses, and set up a budget; WedPlan: The Wedding Planner (altreality Inc., $33.95); and iBride, which offers shareware general wedding planning spreadsheets and tips. See the Appendix for information on where to buy these software products.

Wedding consultant Julia K., in Oak Point, Texas, who has a business background, is currently working on a sophisticated bridal consulting software package that should be available by fall 2001. It will allow users to create and track the wedding budget, track client preferences, recommend qualified vendors, track wedding party members, and track wedding vendors. She will also be able to custom-tailor the software to meet a wedding consultant's specific criteria. For more information, see the Appendix or e-mail Julia directly at goc@iglobal.net.

Fax Machines

Although most new computer systems today come with a fax card already installed, you might find it more practical to have a separate fax machine on a dedicated telephone line. That way, your computer doesn't have to be running for you to send or receive a fax, plus today's fax machines do much more than just transmit or receive data—they also serve as scanners, copiers, and printers. A standard plain paper fax will cost $100 to $250, while a multi-function machine ranges from $250 to $800. If you opt to install your fax on a dedicated line, the installation fee will run $40 to $60; then there's a regular monthly service charge. But if you're on the phone a lot, which is a given for wedding consultants, a separate fax line makes good sense.

Telephones, Answering Machines, and Pagers

Speaking of phones, you should buy the best one you can afford since you'll be using it constantly. A standard two-line speaker phone with auto-redial, memory dial, flashing lights, mute button, and other useful features will run $70 to $150, while a top-of-the-line model can cost $250 or more. A great source for high-quality phones is Hello Direct (see the Appendix), which carries the Polycom line of professional business telephones. And while you're at it, consider purchasing a phone with a headset for hands-free calling, so you can prevent the discomfort caused by cradling the receiver between your neck and shoulder.

No wedding consultant worth his or her salt can afford to miss a call during those times when they're away from the office.

Your answering machine is another must-have. No wedding consultant worth his or her salt can afford to miss a call during those times when they're away from the office. An answering machine is also useful when you're at the door signing for an express delivery, sitting down for a well-deserved (and possibly delayed) lunch, or shooing the kids out the door so you can do some work without interruption.

Today's answering machines often come as part of a cordless phone unit and have plenty of bells and whistles. One of the most useful features allows you to call in from a remote location and pick up your messages. A stand-alone answering machine may cost $40 to $150, while a cordless phone/answering machine combo will run $50 to nearly $200.

Cellular phones have become a necessity for wedding consultants, who use them to follow up on details or make wedding arrangements while en route to appointments or events. If you play your cards right, you'll receive a brand-new phone at no charge at the time of service activation. Otherwise, you can expect to pay up to $200 for a reliable wireless phone.

Office Equipment and Supplies

Below are the office equipment and supplies costs for two hypothetical wedding consulting businesses: "Weddings by Jamie," a homebased company, and "Cherished Moments in Time," a start-up based in a commercial office space. The owner of "Weddings by Jamie" already had a basic computer system (not including a printer) and selected items to fit a limited start-up budget. The owner of "Cherished Moments in Time" decided to go with top-of-line equipment and furniture to outfit her office.

	Weddings by Jamie	Cherished Moments
Office equipment		
Computer, printer	$500	$4,000
Scanner	$0	$300
Software		
Microsoft Office	$600	$600
Intuit QuickBooks	$250	$250
Wedding software	$0	$30
Zip drive	$100	$200
Surge protector	$0	$35
UPS (or battery backup)	$0	$125
Digital camera	$0	$500
Fax machine	$0	$250
Copy machine	$0	$800
Phone	$70	$250
Voice mail	$6	$0
Answering machine	$0	$70
Postage meter/scale	$0	$25
Calculator	$15	$50
Office furniture		
Desk	$200	$600
Chair	$100	$250
File cabinet(s)	$100	$200
Bookcase	$0	$70
Office supplies		
Letterhead, envelopes, business cards	$200	$300
Miscellaneous supplies (pens, folders, etc.)	$50	$50
Computer/copier paper	$25	$50
Extra printer cartridges	$25	$80
Extra fax cartridges	$0	$80
Zip disks	$25	$50
3.5-inch floppy disks	$7	$12
Mouse pad	$0	$10
Total	**$2,273**	**$9,237**

▲

> ### Bright Idea
>
> Play soft, tasteful music in the background when you record your answering machine message. Some classical selections that will give your message ambience: Canon in D by Pachelbel, or Air on a G String by Johann Sebastian Bach.

Finally, pagers are a handy way to allow nervous brides and conscientious suppliers to contact you no matter where you are. (Keep in mind that this will include when you're in the bathroom, at your son's pre-school graduation, in the frozen food section at the grocery store, etc.)

As with cellular phones, paging service providers often throw in a basic pager when you activate the service. If you prefer to buy one of those snazzy models that come in vibrant colors and have features like digital messaging, you can expect to shell out around $70. Typical costs for pager service are in Chapter 12.

Copy Machines

No one says you have to have a copy machine right in your office, especially when quickie print shops like Kinko's or Speedy Printing are so conveniently located all around the country. But you can't beat the convenience of having your own copier right at your side, especially now that they cost as little as $500 to $800 for a standard business machine. Today's versatile models can reduce and enlarge, sort and collate, and produce double-sided copies. They use toner cartridges that are readily available from your local office supply store and sell for around $10 to $15. Check your local Yellow Pages directory for the names and numbers of dealers in your area.

Postage Meters and Internet Postage

Talk about a huge time-saver! Postage meters have eliminated those annoying trips to and from the post office (not to mention the long waits in line), and the process of licking and sticking stamps on envelopes and packages. That adhesive does contain calories, you know!

You actually have a couple of options when it comes to buying postage. You can lease a standard postage meter, which requires you to pay an annual mailing fee of about $100 and pay for postage upfront at the post office. Or you can forgo leasing the equipment altogether by buying your postage online from providers like Pitney Bowes (see Appendix). For a modest fee (usually no more than $4.95 per month) above the actual cost of the postage, you can download software that allows you to print your postage directly onto labels. You can charge the cost of the postage to any credit card.

Of course, you'll need a postal scale to make sure you're affixing enough postage to your outgoing mail. Some of the online companies will provide you with a postal scale free or for a nominal charge. Otherwise, you can expect to pay $10 to $25 for a mechanical scale (which is useful if you mail 1 to 12 items per day), or $50 to $200 for a digital scale (if you're sending 12 to 24 items per day). If you plan to send more than 24 items per day, or use priority or expedited mailing services on a regular basis, you should consider purchasing a programmable electronic scale, which will run $80 to $250.

Office Supplies

You'll find that your costs in this category will be far more modest, but the office supply products you will buy are just as important to the functioning of your business as the equipment you purchase. Take your stationery and business cards, for example. These tools represent you and make a statement about you in your absence. For that reason, buy the best stationery you can afford. Print shops like Kinko's and office supply stores like Office Depot can whip up professional-looking coordinated stationery for you at a reasonable cost (about $80 for 250 one-color premium sheets, $85 for 250 envelopes, $35 for 250 business cards). There are also a number of mail order printing companies like Amsterdam Printing & Litho Corp. and Mark Art Productions (see Appendix) that can offer you a wide selection of standard paper, and printing styles and colors to choose from. As a general rule, you should stick with stationery in white, cream, or gray for an elegant, conservative look.

If you're operating on a real shoestring budget, you could purchase blank stationery materials from an office supply store and make your own on your office printer. This stationery runs under $6 for a package of 100 sheets of stationery, under $8 for 50 envelopes, and under $7 for 250 business cards. As far as other office supply costs go, you should figure on spending about $150, which will buy pens, pads, copy paper, file folders, and the like.

Bright Idea

Raised letter printing (known as thermography) or gold foil stamping may cost a little more, but they add an elegant touch to your stationery and business cards. For the very best look, have your stationery printed on laid bond paper. It has the smoothest surface of all printing papers and produces the crispest printed images.

Adding It All Up

If you've been keeping an eye on all the estimated costs on the work sheet on page 51 as you read this chapter, you can get a pretty clear idea of how much capital it will take to cover equipment and supplies for your new business (use the work sheet on page 56 to figure your own expenses). Now take a look at the work sheet on page 55 for a tally of all the start-up costs it will take to get our two hypothetical wedding consultant businesses off the ground.

53

"Weddings by Jamie" is a homebased company with an office set up in the corner of the den. The owner financed the start-up with her personal credit cards. "Cherished Moments in Time" has a 500-square-foot office in a commercial building. This business has top-of-the-line equipment and furniture, and employs a contract person to help out with weddings, at a cost of $100 per wedding. "Weddings by Jamie" is projecting an annual gross income of $12,000 (12 weddings at $1,000 each), while the owner of "Cherished Moments in Time," which is located in an area where weddings average $2,500, expects to earn $37,500 (15 weddings at $2,500 each). Each business owner takes a percentage of the net profits as income.

From the hypothetical expenses we've outlined in the chart on page 55, you can get an idea of what your start-up costs may look like. We've already covered the costs associated with market research (refer to Chapter 3); licenses and permits (Chapter 4); and hiring an attorney, and an accountant and buying insurance (Chapter 5). In Chapter 8, we'll look at the cost of certification, training, subscribing to publications, and joining professinal organizations. Advertising costs will be addressed in Chapter 9, and online service and Web site design and hosting will be covered in Chapter 10. Tally up the start-up costs that you anticipate for your new business, using a form similar to the one we've provided in our example, or another of your choosing.

In addition to the costs listed here, you will also have ongoing monthly expenses once your business is up and running. See Chapter 12 for a discussion of these costs, as well as some advice on approaching bankers and obtaining financing.

Start-Up Expenses

Here are the start-up expenses for our two hypothetical wedding consultant businesses:

	Weddings by Jamie	Cherished Moments
Start-Up Expenses		
Rent (security deposit and first six months)	$0	$3,500
Office equipment, furniture, supplies	$2,273	$9,237
Business licenses	$150	$150
Phone (line installation charges)	$90	$115
Utility deposits	$0	$150
Employee wages (first six months)	$0	$800
Start-up advertising	$100	$500
Legal services	$375	$525
Insurance (annual cost)	$125	$450
Market research	$500	$1,000
Certification/designation training	$340	$2,000
Membership dues (professional associations)	$150	$290
Publications (annual subscriptions)	$22	$47
Online service	$20	$20
Web site design	$800	$2,500
Web hosting	$20	$20
Subtotal	**$4,965**	**$21,304**
Miscellaneous expenses (add roughly 10 percent of total)	$500	$2,100
Total Start-Up Expenses	**$5,465**	**$23,404**

Your Office Equipment and Supplies

Office equipment	
Computer, printer	$
Scanner	
Software	
Microsoft Office	
Intuit QuickBooks	
Wedding software	
Zip drive	
Surge protector	
UPS (or battery backup)	
Digital camera	
Fax machine	
Copy machine	
Phone	
Voice mail	
Answering machine	
Postage meter/scale	
Calculator	
Office furniture	
Desk	
Chair	
File cabinet(s)	
Bookcase	
Office supplies	
Letterhead, envelopes, business cards	
Miscellaneous supplies (pens, folders, etc.)	
Computer/copier paper	
Extra printer cartridges	
Extra fax cartridges	
Zip disks	
3.5-inch floppy disks	
Mouse pad	
Total	$

7

Establishing
a Supplier
Network

One of the things that will make you valuable to your customer is your knowledge of the bridal industry. As a consultant, you are expected to be the font from which all knowledge about the industry flows. That means knowing things like which wedding gown styles or decorating schemes are in vogue and which are passé, or whether it's inspired or gauche to use silk flowers in the bride's bouquet.

But perhaps even more importantly, your clients will count on you to recommend reliable suppliers that offer the best quality and value for their money. So it's your job to research bridal service providers in your target market area to find the best possible sources for the products or services you'll require. From this research, you should compile a list of preferred vendors you can either share with the bride during a consultation, or use yourself if you're in charge of all the planning.

Although this process can be rather time-consuming, it's essential for your own future success. Every time you recommend a vendor, you're putting your own reputation on the line, so you'll want to make sure your suppliers have impeccable credentials and excellent reputations.

General Rules of Engagement

The easiest way to identify potential service providers is by asking friends and business acquaintances for recommendations. Other useful sources of information include the Internet, your local Yellow Pages, and the chamber of commerce. The Better Business Bureau can also be useful for helping you steer clear of businesses whose reputations are less than sterling.

In this initial fact-finding stage, don't limit yourself to locating a certain number of vendors. Rather, identify as many potential sources as possible so you'll have several to choose from when the time comes to make a recommendation to a bride. Keep in mind, too, that you should locate vendors in the low, medium, and high price ranges to accommodate all budgets.

Then once you have compiled your list of sources, pick up the phone and make appointments to see their facilities and products in person. Since business owners are generally pleased to grant you a personal interview and show off their services as a way to secure future business, those who balk should be removed from your list.

Go to each interview armed with a list of specific questions concerning the company's scope of services, prices, delivery schedules, terms, and so on. Don't rely on your memory to keep the details straight; eventually there will come a point when you've talked to or seen so many vendors you won't remember who's who. Instead, try creating a simple questionnaire or form on your home computer that you can fill out as you interview your potential sources. In addition to noting contact information, hours of operation, and location, be sure to ask for the company's Web address.

"Business licenses, appropriate insurance, contracts, health permits for food providers, years in business, number of weddings worked on, and the ability to work well with other professionals should be at the top of your list when gathering information about vendors," says Robbi Ernst of June Wedding Inc.

Once your inspections are completed, evaluate providers in each category against one another and rank them based on quality, value, timely delivery, and so on. Finally, check their business references to verify both their reputation and their reliability. The top-ranked vendors become your preferred suppliers, although you can always add to this list as you hear about other promising vendors. Identifying numerous vendors in each category has another advantage: You'll always have someone prescreened and ready to go when your top choice is already booked.

As you get your business established, you should expect your supplier list to change. You'll probably add new vendors as well as remove those that don't live up to your expectations.

"I constantly shop for vendors to add to my library, so I have a large resource library that enables me to refer vendors based on the bride's preferences, personality, budget, and vendor availability," says Paula L., the wedding consultant in San Clemente, California.

Major Suppliers

As a wedding consultant, you will need to locate and coordinate with several types of vendors including reception facility managers, caterers, florists, DJs, photographers, limousine companies, and others.

The Host with the Most

A substantial part of the bridal budget is devoted to the reception, which is traditionally held in a banquet hall. When meeting with a reception site manager, be sure to inquire about the number of people the facility can accommodate, the cost per person, the number of hours the facility can be rented for, and the type of food it provides. Ask, too, about any restrictions there may be on the wedding party and their guests (such as a lack of handicapped facilities or a ban on smoking). Keep in mind that many banquet facilities offer full-service packages that include food, a wedding cake, a photographer, and even a videographer, so you might be required to select from the facility's own preferred vendor list. If you prefer to use your own sources, you should take your reception business elsewhere.

Finally, ask for permission to visit the facility during a wedding to observe the wait staff and the management in action, as well as the general operation of the business. You should also ask to sample any food provided for a typical wedding dinner.

Smart Tip

When researching reception sites, don't limit your prospect list to traditional wedding banquet facilities. Hotels, country clubs, historic sites (like Henry Ford's Fairlane Manor in Dearborn, Michigan), and resorts make lovely sites for weddings, and provide a wider range of price choices for the bride.

These days, more and more bridal couples are choosing nontraditional sites for both their nuptials and receptions. According to Gerard Monaghan of the Association of Bridal Consultants, alternative locations like gardens are quite popular, as are luxury hotels where the ceremony and reception can be held in the same place. The trend to hold weddings in unusual locales also continues.

"There are now so many scuba weddings that two companies are now manufacturing white wet suits," Monaghan says. "You name it, someone is doing it."

Contact your local chamber of commerce or county seat for a list of places (like restaurants and parks) that allow weddings on their facilities. Remember that a permit may be required, and alcoholic beverages and loud music may be restricted.

Fanciful Feasts

As mentioned previously, many reception halls have their own caterers, but it's still a good idea to establish your own network of caterers, especially for weddings in nontraditional settings. As with banquet facilities, you will want to talk to prospective catering sources about menus, specialties, and price ranges. You'll also want to find out if they can fulfill special requests (such as preparing kosher or vegetarian cuisine), and whether they provide linen, china, and glassware. Then ask permission to drop in on a function they're catering to sample the cuisine and observe the service.

Floral Fantasies

Flowers are an integral part of a wedding, so it's essential to select florists who can deliver floral designs that are both beautiful and innovative. Toomie Farris, American Institute of Floral Designers, American Association of Florists (AIFD, AAF), president of En Flora in Indianapolis, and an FTD Association Master Florist, says the best florists are the ones who take the time to understand the bride's vision for her special day, then translate that feeling into a coordinated floral display.

"I never let a bride or her consultant jump immediately into details like picking which bouquet she wants," Farris says. "It's more important to understand the entire event and the overall feel of the wedding, based on the bride's personal taste and the way she expresses herself."

Toward that end, when you interview florists, ask them about their approach to

Bright Idea

Many florists provide a wide range of rented add-on products to give a wedding extra pizzazz. These might include graceful floral arches, cloth aisle runners, chuppah frames (which support the canopy used for Jewish ceremonies), fancy pedestals, and urns. Many even rent flowering plants, shrubs, topiaries, and trees that can create a charming garden look indoors.

designing a coordinated wedding package. Although flowers make up a large chunk of the bridal budget (ranging from $300 to $1,000), a good florist can work wonders even on a budget. For example, Farris says a simple table arrangement consisting of a large monstera leaf sprayed with metallic paint and accented with bear grass and a few sprigs of fern has a high-style look, yet costs just $15 to create.

Florists can usually show you portfolios of their work to give you an idea of what they can do, but it's also a good idea to take a peek in the cooler to check the freshness of the

The Language of Flowers

Why is it considered perfectly acceptable to use white lilies in a bridal bouquet, while yellow lilies are *verboten?* Because the latter symbolizes "falsehood" in the language of flowers—the charming Victorian practice of assigning meanings to blossoms. Here are the secret messages of love attached to some commonly used wedding flowers:

○ *Alstoremeria:* devotion
○ *Baby's breath:* pure of heart
○ *Calla lily:* beauty
○ *Camellia:* excellence, beauty
○ *Carnation, white:* perfect loveliness
○ *Chrysanthemum, white:* truth
○ *Daisy:* innocence
○ *Delphinium:* open heart and deep attachment
○ *Gardenia:* refinement
○ *Lily of the Valley:* return of happiness
○ *Magnolia:* magnificence
○ *Lily, white:* sweetness and purity
○ *Orchid:* love and beauty
○ *Ranunculus:* radiant with charm
○ *Rose, red:* I love you
○ *Rose, white:* purity and love
○ *Rosebud, red:* pure and lovely
○ *Stephanotis:* happiness in marriage
○ *Tulip, red:* love
○ *Violet:* faithfulness

Sources: FTD, USA Bride

floral product. Note particularly whether the water in the buckets is crystal clear, which indicates the flowers have been processed properly for maximum freshness.

Farris says that traditional romantic weddings á la Martha Stewart are still very much in style, although brides are starting to mix colors like celery with fairly aggressive colors like burgundy, wine, and rust in their attendants' bouquets and reception designs. In addition, since magazines like *Architectural Digest* began showcasing design accents like fruits, foliages, berries, and pods, these elements also are beginning to creep into floral design. So it's likely today's chic bride will ask for some of these more unusual designs, as well.

For the traditionalist, roses are still very popular, but sophisticated garden flowers such as hydrangea, peony, colored minicallas, and tulips are becoming much more prevalent in many wedding designs.

And just as a side note: Balloons are definitely out. Farris says they're tacky and belong at baby showers, not elegant weddings.

A Joyful Noise

Unless you are a real audiophile who keeps up with the latest tunes and musical trends, you should seek the help of a professional entertainment consultant to find bands that provide reception music. These consultants often have audition tapes on file to make the job of selecting musicians easier, but it's usually wiser to see the band perform live so you're not unpleasantly surprised by either the quality of their work or their physical appearance on the big day. Other sources for recommendations are hotel banquet managers, and anyone who works on site with bands, such as photographers and caterers, whose opinion you respect.

Ideally, your "play list" should consist of several bands that can pull off everything from Big Band music to rap. But it's more realistic to expect your musicians to specialize in certain types of music. Generally speaking, a band that can play both rock and easy listening music will be suitable for most audiences.

A less expensive and potentially more versatile musical choice is a disk jockey. You can easily find DJs listed in the Yellow Pages under "Bands," "Music," or "Weddings," or you can ask friends and acquaintances for recommendations. There are also sites on the Internet that can steer you toward a DJ. Two to try are 1-800-DISC JOCKEY at www.800dj.com and the American Disc Jockey Association at www.adja.org, phone (301) 705-5150.

A good DJ will come prepared to handle special requests in many categories. Ask potential vendors for a list of the music he or she typically brings to a reception.

Say Cheese

Good photography is truly an art, so you'll want to screen prospective photographers very carefully. To locate photographers, try the Yellow Pages or an online search. The

Professional Photographers of America Inc. at (888) 786-6277, or e-mail csc@ppa.com, can also provide you with potential sources, but keep in mind that these are just leads, not recommendations. Banquet facilities also may be able to refer you to experienced shutterbugs.

When reviewing a photographer's portfolio, note the settings and lighting conditions under which the snapshots were taken. Some photographers are more adept at interior photography than garden settings, for instance, just as some are more skilled at taking candids versus portraits. Each type of photographer has his or her place on your list.

Fun Fact

In the South, it's customary to display wedding photos of the happy couple at the reception. So there must not be anything to that old wives' tale that it's bad luck for the groom to see the bride before the wedding, or most brides in the South would be in big trouble!

You'll also want to assess the photographer's people skills, since he or she will be interacting constantly with the bride and groom. Look for someone who is professional, yet warm and friendly, and be sure to ask what he or she wears while working. Formal weddings require formal attire for vendors like the photographer, too.

Lights, Camera, Action!

As with photographers, you must view a videographer's work before adding him or her to your list of preferred suppliers. It's important to ascertain whether the sample footage you see was actually shot by that person or by an assistant. It's a good idea to ask for recommendations from people who regularly use videographers, such as banquet facility managers and even other vendors. You want a professional who will be discreet and won't interfere with either the ceremony or reception. Above all, this means no bright lights and no pushy behavior to get just the right angle.

Finally, determine whether the videographer shoots just raw footage, or whether he or she will edit it and add an appropriate musical score. Obviously, the latter is more time-consuming and expensive, and requires more expertise.

A Little Slice of Heaven

Locating a good baker certainly will be one of the tastier aspects of your vendor search. You can ask reputable caterers for leads, or contact the International Cake Exploration Societé at www.ices.org. Additional sources include the pastry chefs at upscale restaurants and banquet facilities themselves, which may even do the baking right on site.

Pore over prospective vendors' portfolios of cake designs, then sample the offerings. Inquire, too, about the availability of cake accessories like toppers, pedestals, and fountains, all of which give the cake a custom look.

In some parts of the country (notably the South), a groom's cake is a charming tradition. The groom's cake is generally richer and denser than the bride's cake, and is often sliced and wrapped in ribbon-tied boxes so guests can carry pieces home to enjoy later. Another charming southern tradition calls for the baker to hide charms attached to ribbons in the cake. Before the cake is cut, each bridesmaid pulls a ribbon to remove a small token like a four-leaf clover, which is a symbol of good luck, or a ring, which signifies the next to marry. Keep in mind, however, that some states have laws that prohibit the baking of inedible objects in cakes, so be sure to check state regulations before you offer such a service to a bride.

Smart Tip

One way to get leads on vendors is to ask each vendor you interview who he or she likes to work with. When you start to hear the same names over and over, you can assume those vendors are reliable and will provide consistent service.

Wedding Wheels

A bride's special day calls for the special transportation provided by a limousine service. Limousines are usually rented by the hour (with a three hour minimum) and often provide amenities like champagne. It goes without saying that it's important to locate a reputable limousine company because the safety of your clients and their families are at stake. In addition, Packy B., the wedding consultant in Ohio, warns that limousine companies are notorious for not holding up their end of the contract.

"A family member once used a limousine company that brought in an out-of-town driver to help with the summer crush of weddings," she says. "The driver didn't have a clue where he was going, plus it was 90 degrees that day, and the air conditioning was broken. Obviously, this couple didn't ask for any referrals from their sister-in-law, the wedding consultant!"

Bright Idea

Horse-drawn carriages and vintage trolleys make charming conveyances for the bridal party. An added benefit: They can be used as a backdrop or "prop" for wedding photographs. As a special gift to the bride and groom, stock them with gourmet chocolates, champagne, and special hors d'oeuvres so they don't arrive hungry at the reception.

To avoid this kind of problem, contact the National Limousine Association at (800) 652-7007 or www.limo.org for a list of preferred service providers. You should actually inspect the company's vehicles to assess their general condition, upkeep, and size.

8

Certification and
Professional
Development

Flip open the course catalog for any major university in the United States and you'll see degree programs that teach people a wide variety of skills, including how to package and move objects, perform open heart surgery, and run corporations. What you won't find there is a curriculum that specifically teaches a person how to become a wedding consultant.

Dollar Stretcher

Many of the wedding consulting associations offer a wide range of membership benefits, including the use of the organization's logo in literature and advertising, merchant credit card acceptance programs, discounts on bridal show booth space, group rates on insurance, and even discounts on rental cars.

Yet wedding consultants need many of the same business skills that other professionals routinely acquire at universities and colleges. These are skills they use every day for project management, personnel administration, financial planning, even logistics. That's why, over the years, the denizens of the wedding consultant industry have created their own professional certification and training programs. No doubt this was done to combat the misconception that wedding consultants were merely bored housewives or terminally perky people who planned their own weddings and loved the experience so much they just had to start businesses of their own.

"These people are 'dabblers' who simply appropriate the title of 'professional,'" says Robbi G.W. Ernst III, president and founder of June Wedding Inc. "Many of today's consultants have experience in wedding-related businesses such as catering or event planning, and it's that kind of experience that makes them successful wedding consultants."

While a college business degree is definitely a plus for anyone planning to start a small business, it's not an absolute necessity. After all, it's not uncommon for business owners of all kinds to hire professionals like accountants or public relations officers to handle tasks they don't have experience with. You can do the same thing. In the meantime, your own common sense and innate intelligence can help to make you successful in the bridal consulting industry. Then you can take professional development courses and certifications to fill in any gaps in your knowledge.

"The wedding consultant is the expert, and if you are going to be an expert in this industry, you have to know as much as possible on all levels," says Packy B., the wedding consultant in Broadview Heights, Ohio. "I suggest you take as many courses as you can afford."

Here's a look at some of the certifications, professional development programs, and associations available to help you excel in your new chosen profession.

Making It Official

Founded in 1981, the Association of Bridal Consultants (ABC) is an international trade association with 2,400 members worldwide. It offers members three professional designations (these are not certifications): Professional Bridal Consultant, Accredited Bridal Consultant, and Master Bridal Consultant. It takes at least six years to reach the senior level. Training begins with a five-part home-study Professional Development Program with coursework in etiquette, sales and marketing, the wedding day, related services, planning, and consulting. The cost of the five-part home-study program is $340; it's also possible to take each course individually at a cost of $85 (plus $90 for the start-up manual). Membership dues are $215 annually (with a $30 one-time application fee), although most new consultants can qualify for the $140 novice rate. For contact information, see the "Associations" section in the Appendix.

Stat Fact

Only one university in the United States offers a degree program with specific application to a career in wedding consulting. George Washington University in Washington, DC, has a certificate program in event management. Master's degree credit is available for those who take the course of study. Alternately, general business administration coursework is considered valuable for wedding consultants.

The Path to Success

Robbi Ernst, president of June Wedding Inc. (JWI), knows the value of wedding consultant education and certification, having been a wedding consultant himself for more than two decades.

"The information that's imparted in these courses is information that really works in real life situations," Ernst says. "An advantage of JWI's course is that it's not just a correspondence course. There are three telephone consultations in the program so the student has genuine human interaction with an instructor and can ask questions or ask for clarification right away rather than having to wait for an e-mail or a written critique sent through the mail. They can also get ongoing follow-up technical support and help at no charge as long as they remain a member in good standing."

Ernst points out that the wedding industry has changed significantly over the years, so the need for professional development has changed, too. "When I started out in this industry, wedding consultants were not much more than people who sold invitations, did calligraphy, wrapped almonds in tulle, and such," he says. "I founded JWI because I had a different vision. I saw the need for a true professional and intelligent consultant who knew how to give good guidance to a bride. What the JWI home-study course has done for the industry is to create consistency. You can call a JWI-trained and certified consultant in Boise, Chicago, New York, or Dallas and get a similar professional response from each of them."

▲

Smart Tip

Tip...

Community colleges often will allow business entrepreneurs to take a few classes without having to enroll in a formal degree program. It's sometimes even possible to audit a class for no grade (although this also means your class work won't be evaluated). Opt for entry-level management and accounting classes to help hone your business skills.

ABC holds a major international meeting each November, as well as one- and two-day educational seminars at locations around the United States and Canada. Two popular seminars include "New Horizons" for individuals interested in a career in the wedding industry, and "Expanding Horizons" for beginners and those who wish to increase their skills. The organization also publishes a wide range of materials for its members including the *Ethnic & Specialty Wedding Guide*, the *Retail Resource Directory*, the *Bridal Show Planner's Handbook*, and *Weddings as a Business*.

Based in San Jose, California, the Association of Certified Professional Wedding Consultants (ACPWC) offers a personalized five-day course and a home correspondence course. The personalized course is presented by certified instructors and is held three times a year in Los Gatos and West Hollywood, California, and in Atlanta, while the home-study program is self-directed. The program covers everything from setting up a wedding consulting business to specifics like selecting vendors and wedding protocol. The fee is $795 for the five-day program or $650 for the home-study program. The same materials and assignments are used in both programs. You become eligible for membership in the organization after successful completion of one of the programs.

ACPWC certification is awarded after completing the coursework, working for two years as a consultant, coordinating 12 weddings, and obtaining 14 letters of recommendation. A certification project is also required. For contact information, see the Appendix.

June Wedding Inc., An Association For Event Professionals, is a Las Vegas-based membership organization that awards the "JWIC" (June Wedding Inc. Certification) professional certification to consultants who complete the two-part JWI Consultant Training & Certification Home Study Course. The home-study components include "Designing and Running a Successful Wedding Consultant/Event Coordination Company," and "Continuing Education for the Advanced Wedding Consultant." The tuition for each seminar is $1,000. The organization also offers courses in the field periodically to further consultants' education. A recent offering was "How to Become a Professional Wedding Consultant," which was presented at a cost of $479 (plus a $35 materials fee). Annual dues in June Wedding Inc. are $150 for small business/sole proprietors (contact information can be found in the Appendix).

"We have done surveys that show that wedding consultants who are formally trained and certified can get higher fees from the onset of their business if they are

Stat Fact

Bride's magazine and *Modern Bride* have circulations of 441,000 and 400,000 respectively. Their readership is estimated to be 4.3 million.

professional and know what they're doing," says Ernst. "My strongest advice to anyone starting in this business is to seek out the best and most competent professional training in the industry. The experts can teach you how not to make the mistakes they made, which can save you a small fortune."

Wedding consultant Donna H., who started her career 25 years ago by baking $15 cakes for military personnel, founded the Wedding Career Training Program. She is still an active wedding consultant who coordinates 60 to 75 weddings per year. Her training program offers a full range of coursework covering bridal consulting, ceremony and reception design, floral design, cake decorating, and catering. Additional training is available in bridal show promotion and booth design, and in retail topics like bridal store design and staff training. Individual classes are priced from $65 to $4,500. The entire training program is a substantial $20,000, and would be most appropriate for the entrepreneur who wishes to go beyond general wedding consulting services into full-fledged event management.

The National Bridal Association is an organization of more than 1,200 independently owned businesses, including wedding consultants, which serves consumers of wedding industry products and services. It offers the Weddings Beautiful Worldwide home-study training program (www.weddingsbeautiful.com) for consultants who are interested in starting a business or who wish to augment their knowledge. The program consists of 18 specialized assignments. Upon completion of the coursework, students receive a certified wedding specialist certificate. The course costs $495 and includes review and grading of assignments by a Weddings Beautiful specialist.

Industry Publications

Another way to get educated and stay current on news, information, events, and trends in the wedding industry is by subscribing to publications that serve both the consultant and the consumer. Here's a brief rundown on some of the best-known publications that can keep you plugged into this volatile industry:

Trade Publications

- *Vows magazine.* This publication, which comes out six times a year, is available only to the bridal trade and provides information that runs the gamut from industry trends, to customer service and business techniques. The subscription cost is $25 per year (published by Grimes & Associates).

Consumer Publications

- *Bride Again.* An online publication for "encore" brides over the age of 30 whose readership has a median household income of $61,500 per year. Second-time brides tend to be older and established in a career, which makes them prime prospects for wedding consulting services. Visit www.brideagain.com.

- *Bride's magazine.* One of the two premier wedding guides for brides that's instantly recognizable thanks to its doorstop-sized issues, some of which have more than 1,000 pages. This magazine is published six times a year by Condé Nast and covers everything from relationship issues to dreamy dresses and other wedding day fripperies. The subscription price is $11.97, or two years for $21.97. It's a must read. In addition, the publication has a Web site called WeddingChannel.com that features the best of the magazine.

- *Modern Bride.* The other heavy hitter in the consumer bridal market. It's published six times a year by Primedia Network for 20s-something women. Like its competitor, it emphasizes the romantic fantasy of weddings, yet also offers brides useful tips on wedding planning, beauty, fashion and style, relationships, and other provocative issues. This magazine is another must for the wedding consultant because it's what your customer is reading. A one-year subscription is $9.95. *Modern Bride* also publishes 16 state editions twice a year (with names like *Michigan Bride*) that have specialized coverage of every aspect of bridal planning in that state.

- *Wedding Pages Bride & Home Magazine.* This semi-annual publication of Weddingpages Publishing serves the Washington, DC, area and 60 other cities in the United States and Canada. It offers advice on wedding products and locations with editorial geared specifically to the geographic market it serves.

Event Planning Publications

- *Expo.* Wedding consultants often find general event planning publications helpful as idea-starters and information wellsprings. One of the best-known publications in this category is *Expo*, which is published by Atwood Publishing LLC for exposition and convention industry professionals. It's useful for wedding consultants because it taps into tradeshow topics of importance to exhibitors. A one-year subscription is $48.

- *Exhibitor magazine.* This publication of the Exhibitor Magazine Group also serves trade show and event marketing professionals. A one-year subscription to this magazine costs $68.

9

Spreading
the Word

What do catchphrases like "We love to see you smile," "I can't believe I ate the whole thing," and "Moving at the speed of life" have in common?

They're all memorable advertising slogans created to increase awareness and name recognition for a specific product. And while you don't have to dream up a catchy tagline or jingle that people will be humming from coast to coast, you do need to devise a carefully crafted advertising plan that can help boost your business and create a positive image.

Many of the wedding consultants we spoke to rely on word-of-mouth (WOM) advertising and Yellow Pages listings as the basis of their advertising efforts. Often, these strategies alone are enough to fill a consultant's calendar comfortably. But there are many other easy and inexpensive things you can try that you may find especially effective for your particular region and situation. In this chapter, we'll examine the full range of techniques you can use to market your business and make it the top-of-mind choice for brides who are looking for a creative and responsive wedding consultant.

Your Marketing Plan

Before you start dropping dollars on advertising of any kind, it's wise to create a basic marketing plan. This plan doesn't have to be complicated, but it should be detailed enough to serve as a roadmap that keeps your business on track and your marketing efforts on target. In addition, it should be updated periodically as market conditions change so you are always in touch with the needs of your customers.

Your marketing plan can be a part of the business plan you've already written. (Refer to Chapter 4 for information about business plans.) It should describe your target market and the competitive environment you are operating in (this is where your market research comes in—refer back to Chapter 3), as well as address how you're going to make your customers aware of your business. Information relating to pricing, industry trends, and advertising also has a place in your marketing plan.

SWOT Analysis

An integral part of the marketing plan is your SWOT analysis. SWOT stands for:

- *Strengths.* Characteristics that make you special and set you apart from the competition.
- *Weaknesses.* Things you need to overcome or work on that your competitors could take advantage of.
- *Opportunities.* Anything you can do that might benefit your business either now or in the future.
- *Threats.* Anything that can harm your business.

Putting these characteristics on paper will give you a snapshot of your business's prospects.

SWOT Analysis

The following chart is an example of what a SWOT analysis might look like for a new wedding consultant business that will be operating in a medium-sized market of at least 25,000 people.

Strengths
- ❏ My strong business background (crucial expertise in business development!).
- ❏ My experience with event planning for conventions with 1,000 attendees.
- ❏ My strong communication skills (including writing).

Weaknesses
- ❏ No experience with advertising, marketing.
- ❏ Can't travel outside of immediate area because of husband's work schedule and child-care needs.

Opportunities
- ❏ No other consultants located within five-mile radius.
- ❏ New condo community nearly completed is geared toward middle-aged empty nesters that may have marriage-age offspring.

Threats
- ❏ Banquet facility at corner of Cleophus Avenue and Ferris has just added a wedding consulting package.
- ❏ Rumors that city is changing zoning to disallow homebased businesses.

Take a look at the SWOT analysis above to see what one might look like for a new wedding consultant in a medium-sized market of at least 25,000 people. Try creating your own SWOT analysis using the blank form we've provided on page 74. You can also use the SWOT approach to analyze the strengths and weaknesses of your competition to see how you stack up against them. Once you've created your SWOT analysis, refer to it often as a guide for addressing the weaknesses you've identified and as a benchmark against which you can judge your successes.

Julia K., the wedding consultant in Oak Point, Texas, found out firsthand the benefit of doing a SWOT analysis. "We wrote a formal marketing plan using a SWOT analysis because

Smart Tip

When writing your marketing plan, think about every time you'll interact with your customers. This includes everything from personal contact during consultations, through e-mail, and even the invoices you'll send. Each contact should be considered to be a potential marketing opportunity.

SWOT Analysis Worksheet

Use the following worksheet to do a SWOT analysis for your own business.

Strengths

1. _____

2. _____

3. _____

Weaknesses

1. _____

2. _____

3. _____

Opportunities

1. _____

2. _____

3. _____

Threats

1. _____

2. _____

3. _____

we wanted to make sure that the business was going to be profitable considering that I was going to make it replace my current income and supplement my partner's income," she says. "What we determined from the analysis and market research was that, had we done what we originally intended, we would have failed miserably. I can say that with all confidence because there is another consultant doing what we were going to do and she is failing.

"What we learned was that our market area was too small and too far removed from the places where the big money was being spent. We were planning to begin in a small town and move toward Dallas. Instead, we took a little longer to get our ducks in a row and began right in the heart of Dallas."

Read All About It

Another important part of your marketing plan is your promotion strategy. Every wedding consultant, from the "one-man band" who coordinates just a handful of weddings annually to the person who needs a large staff to help handle the workload, must advertise to get new business.

The types of advertising that are most effective for wedding consultants include Yellow Pages advertising, magazine ads, brochures, business cards, and word-of-mouth. Each method is discussed below.

Let Your Fingers Do the Walking

Without exception, the wedding consultants who we spoke to said that their Yellow Pages ad was a low-maintenance, low-cost workhorse that returned great value for their advertising dollar. There are two types of ads to choose from. The first is the line ad, which is the basic listing that's published under a heading like "Wedding

---

Five Biggest Mistakes

Barbara Koch, author of *Profitable Yellow Pages*, says you can make your display ads more effective by avoiding these common mistakes:

1. *Selling the category, not your business.* If a bride opens the phone book to the wedding consultant listings, she doesn't have to be convinced that she should hire a consultant. So sell yourself in your ad to make her choose you over the others who are listed. Emphasize what's special about your business and tell her something she needs to know that sets you apart from your competition.

2. *Selling products, not benefits.* Of course you handle catering, flowers, and other wedding day services. So instead, emphasize what makes your business special and how in turn you can make the bride's day special.

3. *Emphasizing nothing.* This has more to do with the appearance of the ad than the content. If everything in the ad is visually the same (same typeface, same type size, etc.), nothing seems important. At the very least, use a larger type size for your header, and consider adding color to make the ad stand out.

4. *Using tired phrases.* Terms like "full service," "number one," and "highest quality" are so overused they've lost their meaning. Instead, use action verbs and powerful language, like "making dreams come true," to convey your message.

5. *Using your business name as your header.* Putting your company name at the top of the ad doesn't grab attention or tell the reader anything about your business.

Bright Idea

There are many privately published, special interest phone directories that serve specific groups, like ethnic groups or members of a particular faith. If these people live or do business in your target market, you should be listed in these directories.

Consultants" or "Wedding Services." Line ads normally contain only the business name, address, and telephone number, and are provided to you free of charge when you turn on your phone service. These days, some directories will also list your Web address for an additional fee, which is usually worth the cost.

Some directories also allow you to place an expanded line ad that gives you room for additional information. One wedding consultant in the Southwest pays a modest $60 a month for her one-by-one-inch in-column ad. She feels the money is well spent and plans to add color for an additional charge to give it more emphasis.

The second type of ad is the display ad. It's usually boxed and is much larger than a line ad. As a result, a display ad can contain far more copy, including details about the services you offer, your hours of operation, and even a piece of clip art that relates to your business—like a bridal bouquet or a pair of stylized wedding bells. Display ads are sold by the column width and the depth in inches. Most directories have their own standard sizes, so you'll have to inquire about both the size and the cost.

Often, a line ad is enough to attract calls from interested brides, as Donna H., the wedding consultant in Austin, Texas, can attest. She has coordinated nearly 8,500 weddings in a career that has spanned 25 years and does little advertising outside of her line ad. But if you do decide to buy a display ad, examine the directory listings carefully to make sure there's an appropriate category heading that brides can find easily. Also, check to see if your competition places display ads. If not, that's a pretty strong indication that it's not necessary to spend the money to attract callers.

You might think that placing a display ad when everyone else has a line ad would be a great way to grab attention. But that's not necessarily the case, according to Barbara Koch, author of *Profitable Yellow Pages*.

"Many small business owners buy more ad space than they need," Koch says. "Yellow Pages ads are effective because advertisers have a captive audience who have already made a decision to buy. But that's also what makes it unnecessary to buy a display ad in most cases. The real role of your ad is to get the customer to choose you over someone else, and factors like your location may be what actually causes them to call you."

Overall, Yellow Pages advertising is a cost-effective technique for attracting business. But it does have a few disadvantages. For instance, let's say your local directory is published in April, but you didn't start your business until May. A full year will go by before your ad ever appears in the directory. On the other hand, Directory

Assistance callers will be able to request your telephone number, but only if they know the exact name of your business.

Another disadvantage is that if the name of your business begins with a letter at the end of the alphabet, you'll be at the bottom of the list of wedding consultants. If the list isn't very long, that isn't much cause for concern. But if you're operating in a large city that has many wedding consultants, you could be overlooked by starry-eyed, busy brides.

A third disadvantage is that unless you buy a big display ad, your ad may be placed in the gutter, which is the space formed by the adjoining pages in the book. This can make it harder for customers to find your ad, especially if the directory is large and doesn't lie fully flat when opened. Unfortunately, you have no control over the placement of your ad in the directory. The best you can hope for is that the design of your ad or the use of color will make it stand out.

To place a Yellow Pages ad, or for more information, call the publisher of the directory you wish to be in.

Magazine Display Ads

In magazine publishing, a 60/40 advertising-to-editorial ratio is considered the Holy Grail, which means there's plenty of room for your paid advertisement in practically any magazine you choose to advertise in.

It's best to advertise only in consumer publications that cater specifically to brides since, at any given time, only 1 percent of the population is considering marriage. The "biggies" in the bridal industry are *Bride's* and *Modern Bride*, but there are many others in the field (see the Appendix for a list). In addition, many cities have their own monthly bridal magazines, which are excellent vehicles for your ad. (One to try: *Modern Bride*, which publishes a regional magazine in numerous U.S. markets.)

Advertising in these publications can be expensive. To get the best possible rate, run what's known as a schedule of ads, since the per-insertion rate is reduced when you repeat the ad over a set period of time. Another bonus: Studies show that ads that are repeated regularly tend to generate the most interest among consumers. It's really not beneficial to advertise only when you need business, so save your money if you can only afford one or two insertions.

> **Tip...**
>
> **Smart Tip**
> Photographs can make your business cards and brochures more interesting. But that doesn't mean you should use your picture on the front. Instead, choose a photo that represents some aspect of your business, like a headshot of a happy bridal couple, which spotlights your services rather than you. Your customers will be more interested in what you can do for them than who you are.

Bright Idea

Cable TV is another place where your marketing dollars will go far. Since cable systems serve relatively small, local markets, placing an ad on the local cable station's "bulletin board" practically guarantees it will be seen by precisely the people you're trying to reach. Call the system's sales department for advertising rates before you pay to produce an ad.

If you have some imagination and access to a publishing software program like Pagemaker or Quark Xpress, you can try your hand at designing your own ad. But since you'll be spending a lot of money running that ad, which has the potential of being seen by thousands of readers, you probably should have it professionally designed. You don't have to go to a big advertising agency to get the job done. It's far more cost-effective to find a freelance artist through your local Yellow Pages, professional advertising association, or university art department. Even the Internet can be a viable source. Using a search engine, type in keywords like "commercial artist" or "graphic designer" to locate prospects.

Like your Yellow Pages display ad, your magazine print ad should be eye-catching and informative. Focus on the unique things your business does best, and be sure to give full contact information, including your telephone number (and toll-free number, if applicable), and your Web site and e-mail addresses. You may also wish to have a special logo developed for use in your ad, as well as on your stationery and business cards. Whatever you do, don't use a logo from your art or word processing program's clip art library. Chances are, someone else is already using that logo in his or her advertising. Always go for custom-designed logos that reflect your personal taste and style.

Incidentally, newsletters also often accept advertising at a cost that's considerably less than that of a magazine ad. If your regional bridal newsletter accepts advertising, it could be a very good place to spend your marketing dollars.

Brochures

A brochure is a great tool for reaching brides-to-be in the places they're likely to frequent, like bridal shops, bakeries that specialize in wedding cakes, and so on. The cover should prominently feature your company name and have a meaningful graphic that represents your business (such as a happy bride, a bridal bouquet, or entwined wedding rings). Other elements the brochure should include are:

- A detailed list of your services
- Testimonials from satisfied customers ("ABC Bridal made my wedding a wonderful day to remember!"—Constance Zebracki, Detroit Lakes, Minnesota)

- Contact information (your address, phone number, fax number, e-mail address, Web site address)

Brochures can take many forms. The most common are the two- and three-panel brochures that, when folded, will fit into a number ten envelope. Stationery and office supply stores sell brochure stationery and envelopes that can be used in a laser or ink jet printer. But for a more professional look, have your brochures designed by a professional artist and printed on a high quality paper stock to reflect the high quality your customers can expect from your business.

Your brochure is a powerful marketing tool that works for you day or night, even when you're not there. For this reason, you'll want to distribute it widely. Start by making arrangements with local bridal and florist shops to display your brochure, either for a small fee or a promise to recommend them to the brides who engage your services. Be sure to provide a small literature holder with the brochures to keep them neat and tidy on the counter. (These acrylic racks are available for about $2.99 each through office supply stores like Office Max and Staples.)

Display Ad

Every bride needs a fairy godmother…
Yours has just arrived!

You've got the groom, the dress and high hopes for a wonderful future. So why spend the happiest time of your life worrying about food and seating charts?

Instead, let Fit for a Princess Celebrations handle all the details needed to create a beautiful and memorable wedding day. We're specialists in making magic happen, no matter what your dreams or budget may be.

Our packages are custom-tailored to meet your needs and expectations, from full event coordination to wedding day-only services.

Don't spend another minute on the phone with florists, printers or caterers. Call 800.555.0856 today to arrange a convenient consultation.

Fit for a Princess Celebrations
Where dreams do come true

Ad Courtesy: Diane Apfel

You'll also want to consider mailing your brochure to prospective brides in the geographical area you serve. Many publications sell their mailing lists and can segment the names by ZIP code or other criteria you choose. Refer back to Chapter 3 for more information on how to find and purchase mailing lists.

Regional bridal shows often compile their own mailing lists and make them available for sale. These are extremely effective lists because they are "hot lists," or compilations of likely buyers. Contact the show's public relations office a few weeks after the show (to make sure they have time to finalize their list) to determine whether you will be allowed to buy it. Finally, carry a supply of brochures in your briefcase so you'll always have one available to hand out with your business card when any conversation turns to matters matrimonial.

Business Cards

Here's a great way to advertise at a very low cost. Your business card is not only your calling card; it reminds a prospective bride, or her parent(s), that you're only a phone call or an e-mail away. As a result, you should distribute your card freely wherever you go. The sole exception: Don't ever give out business cards at a wedding you are coordinating, unless you are specifically asked for one. There's nothing less professional or tackier than placing a neat little pile of business cards on the cake table or—horrors!—handing out unsolicited cards to the unmarried guests in attendance.

Increasingly, wedding consultants are choosing folded business cards that can accommodate a large amount of information, like certifications and a list of special services. Because these cards fold along the top, it's possible to put your logo and perhaps a special tag line on the outside, and the rest of your message (including contact information) on the lower panel on the inside. And while a script typeface may look elegant, avoid using too much of it on your cards. Some people find it difficult to read.

Business cards are usually designed to match your business stationery, and it's generally more cost-effective to print the whole order at the same time. As mentioned in Chapter 6, you should use the highest quality paper stock you can afford, as well as thermographic printing, since these give your printed materials an expensive look that reflects well on your business.

Word-of-Mouth Advertisting

Whoever said there's no such thing as a free lunch must have overlooked word-of-mouth (WOM) advertising. Not only is the price right, but WOM praise is one of the most powerful advertising vehicles you have at your disposal. One of its major advantages is that you often don't have to do anything special to garner this kind of freebie publicity. All you must do is perform your job to the best of your ability, and people will talk favorably about you and your willingness to do whatever it takes to satisfy the customer.

Alexander Hiam, author of *Marketing for Dummies* (1997, IDG Books Worldwide Inc.), says the key to getting good WOM is influencing what your customers say about you. You can do this a number of ways. Some wedding consultants call their clients a few weeks after the wedding to get feedback and verify their satisfaction. Doing this projects a positive image of you and your company because it's so rare for businesspeople in service industries to follow up after the sale. You might also get a referral or two from the satisfied bride during the conversation, which you can turn into a WOM opportunity by using her name when you call the person to whom she referred you.

Beware!
Bad word-of-mouth advertising can be devastating for a start-up business. Experts say that a dissatisfied customer might not complain to you, but will tell six to seven other people about the bad experience. So if you suspect that a client isn't happy with you, do whatever you can to find out why, and fix the problem. The future of your business could depend on it.

Another way to influence WOM is by doing something positive and visible in your community or on the wedding business circuit. For example, you could host a complimentary hour-long, do-it-yourself wedding workshop for low-income brides and invite the local media to attend. Any coverage you get is bound to focus not only on your benevolence, but also on the services you offer. That can lead to new business.

A third way to influence WOM is by becoming involved in local business organizations, like Rotary International or the chamber of commerce. As you may know, many people have the perception that wedding consultants are "dabblers," who like to attend weddings and have turned that interest into a little side business. Although thankfully this perception is changing, you can establish yourself as a professional by networking at meetings of these local organizations. The members, in turn, are likely to use your services themselves, or recommend you to others in need of a wedding coordinator.

10

The World
Wide Wonder

Ah, the Internet. Whatever did we do without it? How did we research market trends, locate specialty items, learn about new products, touch a mouse without screaming, and buy and sell '70s memorabilia without its powerful capabilities?

Photo© PhotoDisc Inc.

There's no doubt that the Internet and the World Wide Web have revolutionized the way America does business. For many companies, being connected to the Internet through an ISP (Internet service provider) has become just as important as having electricity or a telephone (both of which you need to access the Internet).

In fact, being online is no longer an option; it's an economic necessity. What the Internet has done for us (outside of giving us access to cheesecake photos of Brendan Fraser, and showing us "live cam" shots of stuff like the Kilauea volcano erupting at night) has been to give us the world. Quite literally, in fact, since at the click of a mouse, we can now communicate 24/7 with people and businesses in the far-flung outer reaches of planet Earth.

It has also given us the ability to reach an extraordinary number of people. Among people aged 18 to 34, there were 64 million who went online in 1999, according to the online statistical resource eMarketer. An additional 81 million people aged 35 to 54 (who are likely to be the parents of the happy couple, or who may be remarrying themselves) were surfing the Web that same year. eMarketer also reports that 46 percent of the Internet users in 1999 were women, which is significant for you because the majority of the consumers seeking out wedding consultants are women.

All this accessibility opens the door to new and exciting business opportunities for you. It also means that, as a fledgling wedding consultant, you cannot overlook the power of the Internet, both as a resource for your own business and as an electronic pathway for your customers. That bears repeating. You must be online these days because consumers have become so used to having information whenever they want it. Many of these consumers will surf the Net to find answers and leads to products and services. So if you're not out there when they're looking, they definitely will go somewhere else.

"I get a lot of hits on my Web site, and probably 50 percent of my business comes from those leads," says Packy B., the wedding consultant in Ohio. "This percentage is high and probably should not be expected by most wedding consultants. It happens because I have links from some very high traffic areas, and I keep track of and update them whenever I make any changes."

Stat Fact
What is now known as the Internet was first developed in the 1960s as a project of the Defense Advanced Research Projects Agency (an agency of the U.S. Department of Defense). It was primarily a tool for academics until 1989, when Tim Berners-Lee developed the World Wide Web while working at the European Laboratory for Particle Physics (CERN) in Switzerland.

This chapter will not teach you the basics of surfing the Web. We will assume that you know how to log onto an ISP, use a search engine, and send and retrieve e-mail. Instead, we will discuss the ways you can use the Internet to help you run your business and capture new customers at the same time. But if by chance you're Internet illiterate, you must learn to use this valuable resource right away. Community colleges and adult education programs are excellent places to learn about this amazing tool. There are also many books and software packages on the market that can walk you through the basics of e-mail, surfing, and Web site development.

Now, let's start surfing...

A Phenomenal Resource

One of the most important uses you'll have for the Internet is as a resource. As you establish your business, you can turn to the Web for everything from advice on sticky business matters, like collections problems, to locating vendors that can provide services your brides will need. You can do market research and investigate local zoning ordinances and tax implications. And you can accomplish all of this any time of the day or night, and all without leaving the comfort of your home office.

You can also find small business opportunities and advice on the Internet. Although there are only a few chat rooms and bulletin boards specifically for wedding consultants (like the chat room at www.junewedding.com, and the discussion board at www.ultimatewedding.com), there are many other sites out there where small business

Stat Fact

The U.S. Commerce Department reports that online purchases made between October and December 2000 topped $8.7 billion. It was the first time ever that online sales amounted to more than 1 percent of total retail sales.

owners can find ideas to help them do business better. One to check out is *Entrepreneur* magazine's site at www.entrepreneur.com.

There's no charge for all the wisdom out there, beyond the cost of the phone call you place to connect to the Web. But remember: You get exactly what you pay for. Just as you can't always believe everything you see in print or on the evening news, you shouldn't necessarily believe everything you read on the Internet. Everyone and anyone, from your half-baked neighbor Ernie to the president of the Rubber Band Association of America, can create a Web site and post seemingly accurate information on it. So as the saying goes: Caveat emptor, or "Let the buyer beware." Always consider the source when searching for information, and stick with reliable and reputable people or companies. For instance, if you're looking for help with writing your business plan, you know you can trust a source like the Small Business Administration's Web site, rather than one featuring "Jason's 12-Step Plan for Making Big Bucks."

As mentioned previously, the Internet is also an excellent place to start your search for suppliers you can use to provide the products and services you'll need to do your job. Although not every company has its own Web site, there has been a huge proliferation of new Web sites in the past few years. As a result, it's likely you'll find the larger service companies, such as banquet facilities, florists, and bridal shops, out in cyberspace at your beck and call.

When you start researching vendors, you can expect their Web sites to provide information like their location, hours, and descriptions of their products or services. What you often won't find (unless the company is selling retail products) is pricing information. Generally it's omitted because companies prefer to discuss pricing with a real live person who can be persuaded to buy. But you can still accumulate enough useful data to know whether a lead is worth pursuing.

Yet another useful purpose for the Internet is as a tool to fulfill the bridal party's unusual requests. Does the bride want an Elvis impersonator to serenade her like hound dog at the reception? Search on the keywords "celebrity impersonators," plus the name of your city, to see what pops up. Or maybe she remembers seeing charming replicas of 18th century tussy mussy holders in a magazine and insists on using them for her bridesmaids' bouquets. Try searching on "tussy mussy" and see where it leads you.

Still another invaluable function the Internet serves is as a communication medium. In addition to staying in contact with vendors concerning wedding day timetables and delivery schedules, you can keep in touch with your brides. This is especially important when you're handling arrangements for an out-of-town bride, or a career woman who's short on time.

Important Web Addresses at a Glance

Here are some Web sites you can use to do business better, find useful (free) advice, or just get a giggle:

- ○ *Amazon:* sells books, CDs, and videos (www.amazon.com)
- ○ *Dilbert:* the famous cartoon strip antihero goes interactive (www.unitedmedia/comics/dilbert)
- ○ *Entrepreneur:* the premier source for small-business advice (www.entrepreneur.com)
- ○ *e-Organizer:* a free service that e-mails reminders about important dates, chores, etc. (www.eorganizer.com)
- ○ *Federal Express:* an expedited delivery service (www.fedex.com)
- ○ *FindLaw:* for legal resources (www.findlaw.com)
- ○ *Internal Revenue Service:* premier source for tax tips and advice (www.irs.ustreas.gov)
- ○ *Mapquest:* online driving directions in the United States (www.mapquest.com)
- ○ *National Association for the Self-Employed:* offers advice, group insurance, and more (www.nase.org)
- ○ *National Association of Enrolled Agents:* a source for locating accountants (www.naea.org)
- ○ *National Association of Home Based Businesses:* tips and information for homebased businesses (www.usahomebusiness.com)
- ○ *National Association of Women Business Owners:* resource, networking, and advocacy group (www.nawbo.org)
- ○ *National Small Business Network:* interactive resource for home-office and small-business owners (www.businessknowhow.net)
- ○ *Small Business Administration:* the small-business owner's best friend, with extensive FAQs and advice (www.sbaonline.sba.gov)
- ○ *Small Office:* a site with articles and advice for small businesses (www.smalloffice.com)
- ○ *Travelocity:* a site for airline and hotel reservations worldwide (www.travelocity.com)
- ○ *United Parcel Service:* an expedited delivery service (www.ups.com)
- ○ *U.S. Census Bureau:* the official government Web site for statistics and demographics (www.census.gov)
- ○ *ZIP code look-up:* helps you find any ZIP code in the United States and its possessions (www.usps.gov/ncsc)

"I often work by e-mail with my clients," says Packy B. "It's much easier to send off an e-mail than to write a letter, and it's cheaper than a phone call. I may also receive an answer back the same day. You cannot beat e-mail for efficiency."

Your Cyber Salesperson

Just as you can access other companies' Web sites for information about their products and services, you'll want prospective customers to find you in cyberspace, too. That means establishing your Web site should be a high priority on your list of things to do as you start your business.

This is particularly important if you live and work in a city that is a known tourist destination. It's not unusual for couples to travel to exotic places like Hawaii or cosmopolitan cities like New York for their nuptials. Disney World is another hot spot for weddings, and the resort capitalizes on this by offering its own wedding packages. So if you are willing to handle long-distance arrangements (which is easier than ever today thanks to e-mail), you need to get that Web site up as soon as possible.

You don't necessarily have to be an information technology whiz or a computer programmer to get the job done. There are many do-it-yourself Web page kits on the market, though you may want to consider hiring a Web page developer to create one for you. Before we start the exciting process of building your cyberspace corporate identity, let's start by looking at the Web site development process.

Back to Basics

Because your Web site is virtual advertising that's available on demand 24 hours per day, it's important to spend a fair amount of time considering what it should say. Before approaching a Web site designer, consider the questions you think your customers would have when searching for a wedding consultant. Here are examples of the kinds of questions your customers might have:

- How can I set up a reasonable budget?
- What is the average amount I can expect to spend on my entire wedding?
- Can you plan my entire wedding?
- How can you help me on my wedding day?
- Can you coordinate my honeymoon arrangements?
- Can you help me find a good florist (or caterer or DJ or baker)?
- Can we correspond by e-mail, or must we meet in person?
- Is there a charge for the initial consultation?
- What do your services cost?

- How will I pay you? Do you have a payment plan?
- Do you have references?
- How can I reach you?

Armed with these questions, you should next consider how you want the site to look. You want it to be user-friendly, yet elegant so it reflects the tastes of your customers. You can do this by keeping the Web page design clean and uncluttered, and the copy succinct. This doesn't mean you can't say what you need to say. But you don't have to tell readers every detail related to your business. You just want them to have enough information to make an informed decision about whether hiring a wedding consultant fits well with their plans—and their budgets.

You'll also want to keep the copy brief because many people find it annoying to have to keep scrolling down as they read. In addition, if the text runs onto too many screens, it's harder for the customer to print material from your Web page—material that you hope will induce them to call you for a consultation later.

Building a Better Web Site

The next decision you must make relates to the type of Web site you want to build. A simple option is the online business card, which is no more than a single screen that gives your company name and contact information, like your address, phone number, and fax number. This type of Web site is actually quite easy to build, even for those who don't know a byte from a baud. There are a number of how-to Internet books available in bookstores, or from online retailers like Amazon.com, that can guide you through the process of creating your own page. However, the disadvantage of this kind of Web page is there's not much room for information. If you have a lot to say (and a sales pitch to make), you should consider creating an online "brochure" instead.

Online brochures are the choice of many wedding consultants precisely because they can accommodate more information. Not only can you answer the types of questions addressed above, you also can provide links (electronic connections) to your preferred vendors, your online retail store (if you plan to sell items like invitations and champagne flutes), your e-mail inquiry form, and other pertinent information. This is also a good place to discuss the details of the various packages you offer so customers have a clear idea of the scope of your services.

> **Tip...**
>
> ## Smart Tip
>
> Portals are electronic entryways into the Internet. When you access a portal like AltaVista, Excite, Yahoo, or Google, you are tapping into a complex "Web" of indices that can connect you to the sites you wish to visit. The indices are divided into categories to make surfing easier and can be accessed by typing as little as a single keyword.

Loreen C. in Ypsilanti, Michigan, relies heavily on her online brochure to promote her business. Working with a Web designer, Loreen gave her site a Hollywood flair, complete with graphics, like director's clappers and studio chairs, as well as snappy copy that evokes the feeling of a professional production (she uses terms like "box office hit" and "It's showtime!"). She also has a lead screen with blanks the bride (or other interested surfer) can fill out and e-mail back for further information.

Home Sweet Home Page

By now you've probably realized that because your expertise lies in event planning and organization, you'll want to hire a professional Web designer to create your Web page. As mentioned above, you can design it yourself using a how-to book. But unless you're well-versed in both HTML language and graphic design, it's probably more trouble than it's worth, especially when there are professionals who are awaiting your call.

Because Web designers are often also graphic designers, you can find them in the same places already discussed in Chapter 9. You should expect to work closely with your designer to make decisions about copy placement, colors, typefaces, and so on. Don't just dump the project into his or her lap. The Web page should reflect your style and taste, so you should be involved in all stages of its development. But do rely on the designer's best judgment when it comes to level of interactivity, navigation tools, and artwork.

The wedding consultants we spoke to paid anywhere from $800 to $4,000 for Web site design. Part of this cost is based on the number of pages on the site. The more complex the site is, the more it will cost.

If you really think you can handle HTML and Web site development on your own, try using a Web page layout program like Dreamweaver 4.0 by Macromedia (which retails for about $300, at www.macromedia.com) or Microsoft FrontPage 2000 (which retails for $150, available from www.compusa.com). Microsoft Word also has an HTML conversion feature that can translate your prose into computer-ese.

Name that Domain

Like your company, your Web site has to have a unique name that will be used on the server it resides on. This is called the domain name, or URL. Examples of domain names used by some of the wedding consultants we spoke to include "everafterweddings.com," "goc.com" (an acronym for "Grand Occasions"), and "Designmywedding.com." In the bridal consulting business, using your business name as your domain name is usually your best bet, but do keep in mind that domain names must be unique, and someone else might already be using the name you've chosen.

Domain names must be registered for a minimum of two years, after which you can renew them. The cost to register a name for two years is approximately $70.

There are several companies that handle registration, but the best known is DOMAIN.com, which also allows you to register your name for five- or ten-year periods. The cost for these longer registrations is $30 and $25 per year, respectively.

Your Web Host

You're now just one step away from having a live Web site. That last step involves selecting the Web host site where your site will reside so users can access it 24 hours a day. Examples of well-known Web hosts include Microsoft Network and Prodigy, but there are many, many smaller hosts around the country. Before selecting a host, ask other business people for recommendations.

Stat Fact
Close to half of engaged couples that have Internet access use the Web to plan their wedding, according to a study by the market research firm NPD Group Inc. The most visited site, at 37 percent, was WeddingChannel.com, with TheKnot.com and ModernBride.com running close behind at 35 and 34 percent, respectively. (These figures add up to more than 100 percent because respondents often visited more than one site.)

You'll want to know how often the site goes down and how long it takes to fix it; whether it has reliable customer support; how many incoming lines the server has (so users don't get a busy signal when they call); whether it has experience with high traffic sites; and how big it is.

A caveat is in order here. Remember that loony neighbor we mentioned earlier? Even he can be a Web host if he has the right computer equipment and telephone trunk lines installed in his dusty old attic. Unfortunately, if you take a chance with a lesser-known host you run the risk of having it go out of business or disappearing in the night, which will not inspire confidence in your customers.

As you probably expected, there is a cost for Web hosting. The price of Web fame starts as low as $14.95 per month for 100MB of disk space. Some of the hosts will also allow you to register your domain at the same time. Web hosting is very competitive, so it pays to shop around. You'll find the names of a few companies you can investigate in the Appendix at the end of this manual.

Generating
Positive Press

In Chapter 9, we talked about the benefits of advertising your business. But advertising costs money—something that may be in short supply when you first start your bridal business.

Fortunately, there are many low-cost marketing and public relations tools you can use to generate positive publicity for your business. Among these tools are news releases, feature articles, newsletters, bridal shows, and networking. Here's a rundown of what they entail and how they can help you.

News Releases

News releases (also called press releases) are like little advertisements for your business. But they're subtler than ads, and possibly more credible to the reader because when they appear in print they look like news stories rather than advertisements. To appreciate the difference between the two, think of a 30-second TV commercial touting a popular sports drink and a longer infomercial lauding the benefits of a new exercise machine. An infomercial sounds more like a news program even though there's a sales pitch at the end. That's the same impact a well-written news release can have.

News releases differ from ads in another important way: There is no cost to run your releases in newspapers, magazines, or other print sources. But there's also no guarantee that what you write will ever appear in print. That's because editors sometimes use news releases as "idea starters" that can be developed into related or more detailed stories. They also use releases as filler material or when they have room on a page with editorial content relating to the same topic you've written about.

But even though it's not a given that your news release will be picked up, you should still send them out faithfully and regularly. News releases are one of the most economical ways you have to promote your business, and a steady stream of releases sent to a publication will increase the chances that at least some of them will appear in print.

The news outlets that are most likely to use news releases about your bridal business are newspapers, magazines, and business publications. If you have a local talk radio station or cable TV station, you might want to put those on your news release list, too. Always call to find out the name of the appropriate person to send the release to. Releases addressed to "Editor" or, worse yet, just the name of the publication, are far less likely to get into print.

Bright Idea

Packaging your news release in a novel way (like sending it rolled up in a champagne flute, or securing it with a lacy garter) will definitely spark an editor's interest. Save this technique for really special news, like when you announce your business start-up, or if you've been hired to coordinate a celebrity or other important wedding.

Wedding Consultant News Release

NEWS RELEASE
For Immediate Release

Date: April 13, 2001
Media contact: Marie Masters
Telephone: (714) 555-0197

Wedding Consultant Makes Matrimony Into an Art Form

LOS ANGELES—Marie Masters is weeping copiously into a soggy tissue for the second time this week. But weddings always have that effect on her, so this certified wedding consultant good-naturedly sees the tears as part of her job.

"I always get a little misty-eyed when one of 'my' brides walks down the aisle," Masters says. "We work together so closely to plan her special day that I can't help being just as happy and proud as she is."

Masters is the owner and founder of *A Vision in White*, a wedding consultant business based in Chino Hills. Her task is to coordinate the seemingly insurmountable mountain of details that go into planning the perfect wedding, from securing the banquet hall to picking the menu, ordering the flowers, coordinating the newlyweds' hotel reservations, and handling everything else in between.

"And of course, the real trick is to get everything to come together correctly and on time," she says with a laugh. "Brides love turning over all those details to me."

Bridal industry statistics show that more and more women are relying on wedding consultants to coordinate the wedding of their dreams. And no wonder. Masters earns each client's trust by consulting with her every step of the way to ensure her satisfaction. She charges a flat fee for her services based on the number of tasks she's asked to coordinate. For a consultation appointment, call *A Vision in White* at (714) 555-0197.

▲

The first news release you'll want to write will announce the opening of your new wedding consultant business (see example on page 95). But you can write a news release about nearly anything newsworthy that relates to your business including:

- New services you're offering
- A move to a new location
- An expanded service area
- Special discounts (i.e. discounts for weddings in the off-season)
- Addition of new staff members
- Your wedding consultant certification
- Special events or seasonal information (such as Valentine's Day packages)

You can also write what's known as a "backgrounder," or a news release that gives general information about your services, hours of operation, and contact information. Be sure to include biographical information about yourself (like educational background and pertinent experience) that emphasizes your qualifications. The hope is that an editor's interest will be piqued by the details about your business, and he or she will want to interview you further for a feature story.

A Successful Strategy

Julia K., the wedding consultant in Oak Point, Texas, is adept at promoting and advertising her services. She uses several tools to spread the word about her business, but finds that two of them are the most effective: the full-page ad that she runs regularly in a local Dallas bridal publication, and her in-column Yellow Pages ad.

"I would say that 95 percent of our initial business came from those two sources, with the other 5 percent coming from begging our friends to spread the word," Julia says. "Now I would say that 50 percent comes from those sources and 50 percent from prior clients and vendors recommending us."

One issue Julia deals with in her primary market is that there are expensive semi-annual publications and inexpensive monthly publications to choose from. Most of the clientele reading the inexpensive monthly publications are hosting inexpensive weddings and thus are not candidates for the level of services she offers. She has found that booking just one wedding off the expensive publication pays for the cost of the advertising there, and, as a result, most of the calls she receives are from well-suited potential clients.

Writing the Release

A good news release will answer the five "W" questions (who, what, where, when, and why) and the "H" question (how). Put the most important information first, since editors tend to cut copy from the end of a release if it's too long to run in its entirety. In any event, try to keep the release short and to the point. It should be no longer than two 1.5-spaced or double-spaced pages. If the release does flow to a second page, use the word "more" at the bottom of page one to indicate that it continues. Use three pound symbols (# # #) to indicate the end of the release.

Stat Fact

Ninety percent of news releases never get into print—often because they're incomplete, late, or full of errors. To increase the likelihood that an editor will print your release, check it carefully for typos, time it to arrive while the news is still fresh, provide interesting details that will catch his or her interest, and include a photo whenever possible.

To alert editors that what they're reading is a news release, use the format shown in the sample release on page 95. Some of the elements this format includes are:

- *Release information.* Unless your release shouldn't be published right away, it will always say "For Immediate Release" at the top.

- *Contact name.* Your name and phone number go here so editors can call you for further information, if needed.

- *Headline.* This is a succinct description of what the release is about. Center this line over the text of the release. Using bold type will make the headline stand out.

- *Dateline.* This is the city from which the release originates. For example, if your business is located in metropolitan Seattle, the first word before the text of the release begins should be "SEATTLE," in uppercase type.

- *Text.* This is the body of the release with all the pertinent details, including the five Ws and the H.

You don't have to be a journalist to write a release. But if writing is not your strong suit, consider using a freelance public relations writer to produce your releases. His or her rate can vary, but you can expect to pay $25 to $150 for a one-page news release, depending on the experience of the writer and the area he or she serves. You can find freelance writers through the Yellow Pages, local professional advertising organizations, your local chamber of commerce, and university journalism departments. You could also use a public relations firm. But most firms work on retainer, and that can be pretty expensive for a new business owner.

Producing the Release

Once you've finalized your copy, you're ready to send your news release out to the companies on your mailing list. Print the release on your company letterhead using a high quality laser or ink jet printer. Standard size (8.5 by 11) white bond paper is preferred. Alternately, you can photocopy the text onto your stationery. But if your personal photocopy machine doesn't produce extremely high quality copies, consider using a quick print shop like Kinko's or American Speedy Printing, which charge around eight cents per copy. If the release runs to a second page, staple the pages together. Then mail the finished releases in your company's imprinted number ten envelopes for the most professional look.

> **Bright Idea**
>
> Thanks to the Internet, it's a breeze finding the names and addresses of editors whose publications you'd like to send your news releases to. To make the mailing process faster and easier, create a label file using your word processing software, then print out a new set of labels to affix to your business envelopes. Be sure to update the list periodically (maybe twice a year) to make sure the information is always current.

Promoting Your Cause

Your job isn't finished once the envelopes are stamped and in the mail. About a week after the releases have been mailed, call each editor personally. Introduce yourself, and politely inquire whether he or she has received your release and whether it's likely to be published. Be sure to ask, too, if there are specific types of information he or she is more likely to use. Make a note of these preferences so you can refer to them the next time you're drafting a release.

Feature Articles

Like news releases, feature stories are an excellent way to garner publicity for your business. What makes these articles such powerful and effective tools is the fact that they can be used to position you as an authority in your field. This is a great way to gain credibility in your field while building a solid reputation as a savvy businessperson.

Feature stories can run the gamut from informational articles to how-tos to profiles about your services. The slant you take depends on the type of publication you're planning to send them to. For instance, a story on "The Top Ten Reasons to Hire a Wedding Consultant" might be perfect for the features section of your daily newspaper. On the other hand, an article about your entrepreneurial talents, or your successful business start-up, might be more appropriate for the business section of your paper or a specialty business magazine.

Don't overlook the value of sharing your knowledge and insight with readers. The idea is to "wow" them with your creative ideas so they immediately think of you when they're ready to engage someone to coordinate their wedding celebration. So write articles giving tips for creating a beautiful wedding. Share stories about wedding disasters and how they can be averted or fixed. Or report on the spectacular wedding you coordinated for the daughter of a leading citizen in your town. The possibilities are endless.

Although feature articles can run anywhere from 800 to 2,500 words, depending on the publication, a reasonable length is 1,200 to 1,500 words. As with news releases, you can use a freelance writer to "ghostwrite," or produce the articles under your byline. You can expect to pay a freelance ghostwriter $350 to $750 for a 1,200-word article.

> ## Smart Tip
>
> **Tip...**
>
> Human interest stories about your brides and the funny, poignant, and unexpected things that happen at their weddings can be turned into great feature articles. But do ask for the bride's permission to use her name in such feature stories. If she demurs, offer to change her name to protect her identity.

Submitting Your Manuscript

The article manuscript should be on 8.5- by-11 white bond paper with one-inch margins on all sides. Editors also appreciate receiving a floppy disk of the article saved in "text" or "rich text format" at the same time. Send the article with a pitch letter that briefly describes what the article is about and why it would appeal to the readers of the publication. Always remember to give information about how and where you can be reached. Mail the article to the appropriate persons on your news release list, then follow up by phone as described above to increase the chances that the article will be published.

Newsletters

If you're like most people, your mailbox is probably overflowing with newsletters from everyone from your state senator to your local nursery. There is a good reason for the proliferation of these pithy little news vehicles. They're inexpensive to produce, they are easy to create, and they're a very effective way to spread the news about any product or service you offer.

The main reason you'll want to produce a newsletter is to "upsell," or suggest other fee-generating ways you can help the bride. Say, for example, you've accepted a consulting job that consists of coordinating wedding day basics only, such as arranging for the church, setting up the reception, hiring a disk jockey, and reserving a limousine. You might be able to generate additional work—and income—by sending a newsletter with articles focusing on your honeymoon planning services, tuxedo pick-up and delivery services, and so on. You could also include checklists (such as "Things to Do One Month Before the Wedding") and useful information about things like wedding software and marriage traditions.

You don't have to send a lot of newsletters to get the bride's attention. Rather, to keep the newsletter process manageable, plan on creating a single "stock" newsletter, or a generic piece that can be mailed to each new client as she engages your services. Time the delivery of the newsletter for a couple of weeks after the consultation, as a way to jog the bride's memory about the many ways you can help. Put your fee schedule and the lead time you need to complete additional projects right in the newsletter.

The newsletter itself should be written in a concise, journalistic style no matter whether the intent of its articles is to inform or solicit business. You can use one

Dollar Stretcher

Printing your newsletter in no more than two colors will help keep costs down. If you have a very high quality laser printer and just a small quantity of newsletters to print, you might consider printing them yourself. But remember that printing takes valuable time, and unless the newsletter is printed on a high quality paper stock, it might look chintzy. Generally, you should opt for professional printing (or at least speedy printing) instead.

of the numerous affordable software packages available to create the newsletter yourself. A good one to try is Microsoft Publisher 2000 Deluxe (which retails for approximately $130). It's perfectly fine to design your newsletter with all words and no artwork. But clip art is now so inexpensive and easy to use that it makes sense to buy an all-purpose clip art package that includes wedding art. A good one to try is ClickArt Premiere Image Pak 300,000 from Broderbund, which retails for under $30. In addition, Microsoft Office 2000 includes a very small selection of wedding clip art. If you feel daunted by the task of designing your newsletter, hire a freelance designer.

The standard size for a newsletter is 8.5 by 11 inches, and it's usually produced in multiples of four pages (although two pages—one sheet with type on the front and back—is also appropriate and easy to produce). A newsletter that's two or four pages will easily fit into a number ten envelope, which is the easiest way to mail it.

Bridal Shows

For sheer numbers, there may be no better place to gain quick exposure for your business than a bridal show. These events attract hundreds, or even thousands, of brides-to-be—women who will definitely be consumers of the services you offer.

Bridal shows are generally held in convention centers in large cities. For a fairly reasonable price (anywhere from $600–1,300, on average), you can rent booth space in these shows. Then it's up to you to chat up prospective customers, cheerfully hand out your business card and brochure, and otherwise lay the groundwork that will result in new business.

Although it's possible to make a professional impression using just the 10- or 12-foot skirted table that's usually provided with your space, you can also personalize your display area. Since you'll be competing with other companies that offer the same kinds of products and services, strive to be innovative. Use a dressmaker's mannequin to display a lovely vintage wedding gown. Artfully display large photographs of weddings you've coordinated on lace-festooned easels. Or invest in a pre-fab booth that can be set up quickly right in your space.

These ten-foot high booths have a steel skeleton that's covered with fabric panels that can support signage, photographs, and other visuals. This kind of display is set up at the back of your booth as a backdrop. There's a wide variety of styles to choose from including single-unit panels with custom designs, or triple-units. The multi-unit displays usually require lighting to give them pizzazz.

> **Smart Tip** — *Tip...*
>
> Don't just exchange pleasantries and business cards when you network at professional business organization meetings. Plan a follow-up meeting with people whose interests mesh with yours, or those who might even be potential clients. Just be sure to make a notation on the back of their cards so you'll remember why you're pursuing the relationship.

These booths are easy to assemble and tear down. But while such booths are very eye-catching, they can run from $795 for the single panel model up into the stratosphere. They also don't usually include the graphics, which you'll have to have created separately by a graphic designer. The halogen lights recommended for these displays run about $139 each. You will find sources for trade-show booth distributors in the Appendix.

A more cost effective way to exhibit is by using a tabletop display. As the name implies, it sits right on the table, leaving you space to display brochures or other handout materials. These displays come in several configurations and run about $1,100, excluding the cost of the graphics.

This probably sounds pretty pricey, especially for a start-up operation. But if you're planning to attend many bridal shows, the investment is worth it in terms of the professional image you'll project.

Another way to attract show attendees to your booth is by holding a drawing for a wedding-themed gift. For instance, you might invite visitors to fill out an entry form for a chance to win a pair of champagne flutes or a floral arrangement for the rehearsal dinner. One lucky winner will take home a gift (or a promissory note in the case of flowers), and you'll take home a bowl-full of entry forms with the names and addresses of prospective clients. These prospects should immediately go on your mailing list so you can send them a newsletter you've developed especially for this purpose.

Packy B., the Ohio wedding consultant, says she has found that bridal shows aren't always the best possible venue for attracting new business, but they still serve an

▲

> ## Bright Idea
>
> Some wedding consultants package all their promotional and sales materials in a media kit, which can be given out to business prospects. Some of the items in the kit (usually organized in a pocket folder) may include a letter thanking the client for his or her interest, a "backgrounder" and other news releases, a brochure, and the owner's biography and photograph.

important purpose. "Bridal shows give you visibility with the public, even if they don't generate a lot of business," she says. "They also give you a chance to meet and network with a lot of vendors all in one place."

Julia K., the wedding consultant in Oak Point, Texas, concurs. She says, "Bridal shows are great—and I mean really great—for building credibility among vendors. We set up our booth an hour or two early before the other vendors, then go around and offer snacks and assistance to those who are scrambling to finish in time. They would get a chance to see first-hand how we can make their lives easier the day of the wedding and would begin recommending us without actually having worked with us at a wedding before."

Some of the major bridal shows in the United States include Bridal Show Producers International, Brides-To-Be, and The Great Bridal Expo. You'll find contact information in the Appendix at the back of this book.

Networking

You know the old saying: It's not what you know, but who you know. Well, it holds true. The more people you know in this business, the easier it will be to locate and land new business.

Two extremely valuable networking sources are your local chamber of commerce and Rotary Club. These organizations consist of both small- and large-business owners, and encourage their members to exchange ideas, support each other's businesses, and barter services. The cost to join either organization is reasonable, and you can quickly build a reputation as a caring and reputable business owner by becoming involved in the groups' public service activities.

You might also consider joining other professional business organizations in your area, such as economic clubs or women business owners' groups. Then get involved in the leadership of the group. That way, your name will be top of mind when one of the members is looking for or knows someone who needs a wedding consultant.

Finally, professional wedding consultant organizations are a good place to meet other planners and share tips and techniques. Many of the national organizations have regional chapters that hold regular meetings. See the Appendix for contact information.

Here Come the Finances

By now, you should be pretty jazzed about becoming a wedding consultant and feel like you're ready to take on the world. But there's one itty bitty little thing you still have to work on because it can mean the difference between startling success and abysmal failure. We're talking, of course, about financial management.

Alas, this is the point where many people turn pale and cast their eyes skyward in supplication. But maybe you're one of the lucky ones. Maybe you excelled in math and accounting in school, so you're not phased by the thought of balance sheets and cash-flow statements. Or maybe you earned a bachelor's degree in business administration in a previous life and find the real challenge in this job to be soothing weepy brides or dealing with prima donna vendors.

But if you're like many wedding consultants, who are long on enthusiasm, creativity, and common sense and perhaps a wee bit short on financial acumen, don't despair. Help is available. You just have to know where to look for it.

> ## Smart Tip
> Three measures of your business's ability to make a profit are the gross profit margin, operating profit margin, and net profit margin. Bankers will look at these ratios to determine how profitable your business is because without profits you're not considered a good financing risk.

Income and Operating Expenses

In Chapter 5, we mentioned the value of a good accountant to help you through the wonders of corporate bookkeeping. But you must still know enough about your own business situation to understand what he or she is doing to keep you honest in the eyes of the IRS and your creditors.

One tool you will need is a simple monthly income/expenses statement like the one on page 107 that will help you estimate your operating costs and project your earnings. The statement on page 106 shows the operating costs for our two hypothetical wedding consulting businesses: one that's homebased, and another that operates out of a small commercial space. While not all of the expenses we'll discuss will apply to you, here's a rundown of the typical expenses a homebased wedding consultant can expect to incur.

Telephone Calls

If you have a business telephone line, you should note the total cost of the bill, including both zone and long-distance calls. Your cellular phone bill should be included in this amount if the phone is used strictly for business.

If you're still using your home phone as your business line, estimate only the cost of the zone and long-distance calls made for business, since Uncle Sam won't allow you to deduct the entire phone bill on your business tax return. A word of advice: Keep a handwritten log of telephone calls that you can compare against your phone bill every month. The IRS usually requires written records for any expenses you deduct, and it will be much easier to figure which calls are legitimate business expenses if you have a log to refer back to.

Telephone charges are likely to make up the lion's share of the service fees you'll pay on a monthly basis. Thanks to the deregulation of the phone company a number of years ago, these charges vary regionally, but it's reasonable to estimate a cost of $25 per line. Useful features you'll want to consider adding to your basic service include voice mail ($6 to $20 per month), call waiting (approximately $5 per month), and caller ID (around $7.50 for number identification, and an additional $2 for name and number identification).

Your cellular phone is billed at a totally different rate. There are many great usage deals around right now, ranging from $4.99 a month for a no-minute basic package (minutes are charged separately at a rate of 25 to 45 cents each), to $39.99 for 600 minutes or more. Because these high-end packages are so reasonable, you might want to opt for one right off the bat, since you'll be locked into a certain rate plan for a pre-determined number of years anyway. What's really great is that many of these package plans offer thousands of minutes of calling time free on the weekend—which will probably be your peak calling time. You can also expect to pay an activation fee of around $30 if you don't sign up for a three-year contract.

Pagers are another option and are probably the best value around for keeping in touch. Many rate plans cost $60 or less for a full year of service that's billed upfront, either annually or quarterly.

Office Supplies

This includes all the paper clips, stationery, business cards, and other supplies you need to do business every day. Obviously, some expenses like business printing won't be incurred every month, so use the figure you found when you priced your stationery and business cards, and divide by 12. This number is added to the other costs you estimate for the month.

Postage

You will be mailing contracts to clients, confirmation letters to vendors, and possibly direct mail pieces to prospective clients. If you anticipate having monthly shipping charges, include those, too.

You may choose to rent a post-office box, or a box at a mailing center like Mail Boxes Etc., as a way of keeping your business mail separate from your personal mail. This service fee will run around $10 to $20 per month.

Wages

This is what you'll pay the contract or temporary employees who will help you with on-site wedding day management, clerical tasks in the office, and so on. Many wedding consultants pay their helpers $10 to $15 per hour, while some pay a minimum of $100 for a daylong event. Try hiring college students or young adults right

Sample Income/Operating Expenses

Here are sample income/operating expenses statements for our two hypothetical wedding consulting businesses that reflect typical operating costs for this industry. "Weddings by Jamie" is the homebased business that averages 12 weddings per year. "Cherished Moments in Time" handles 20 to 30 weddings per year and operates out of a small space in a commercial building. You can compute your own projected income and expenses using the worksheet at right.

	Weddings by Jamie	Cherished Moments
Projected Monthly Income	$1,000	$3000
Projected Monthly Expenses		
Rent	$0	$500
Phone (office and cellular)	$40	$65
Utilities	$0	$50
Postage	$50	$50
Employee payroll/benefits	$0	$200
Advertising	$60	$125
Maintenance	$0	$50
Accounting services	$0	$100
Transportation	$0	$50
Loan repayment	$0	$125
Online service	$20	$20
Web site hosting	$20	$20
Miscellaneous expenses (stationery and other office supplies)	$25	$50
Total Expenses	(-$215)	(-$1,405)
Projected Monthly Net Income	$785	$1,595

Income/Operating Expenses Worksheet

Projected Monthly Income $ _____

Projected Monthly Expenses $ _____

    Rent $ _____

    Phone (office and cellular) $ _____

    Utilities $ _____

    Postage $ _____

    Employee wages $ _____

    Advertising $ _____

    Insurance $ _____

    Maintenance $ _____

    Accounting services $ _____

    Stationery and office supplies $ _____

    Transportation $ _____

    Loan repayment $ _____

    Online service $ _____

    Web hosting $ _____

Total Expenses   (- $ ——————)

Projected Monthly Net Income $ _____

Unless you hire full-time employees, you aren't required to pay any benefits or withhold federal taxes from paychecks.

out of high school (any younger and you'll have to worry about them trying to make the altar boys laugh during the blessing of the rings, or staging an impromptu toga party using the Battenberg lace table linens). Young adults are usually ecstatic to accept even the low-end wage, since jobs in fast food or retailing pay much less.

In general, it's best to do your own hiring rather than using an employment agency to provide temporary or leased employees. Agencies tack a hefty service fee (as much as 40 percent) onto the basic hourly rate you'll pay, which can quickly erode your profits. Instead, try placing a brief want ad in your local community newspaper. Since most people love weddings, you should get a respectable number of responses, which will give you a nice pool of applicants to choose from.

Also, don't overlook stay-at-home moms or retirees as prospective employees. Retirees in particular make wonderful employees—they're usually very happy to help out however they can. Just make sure they have the stamina to be on their feet for long periods of time. By the same token, make sure any moms you hire have a reliable babysitter so you're not left to juggle the demands of a nervous bride and 500 hungry guests all by yourself some Saturday night.

Fortunately, unless you hire full-time employees, you aren't required to pay any benefits or withhold federal taxes or FICA from workers' paychecks. The contractors themselves are responsible for ponying up with the Feds. However, the IRS requires you to file Form 1099-MISC for every contractor whose annual wages exceed $600.

> ### Smart Tip
> Community newspapers are an excellent tool for unearthing prospective employees. Not only are their classified rates quite reasonable; they're also read by people who live right in the area where you do business. Their familiarity with your market area is a plus, and their proximity to your work site increases the chances they'll always be on time.

Insurance

In addition to the rider on your existing homeowner's insurance policy, or your business owner's insurance policy, you should include the cost to insure the primary vehicle you'll use to travel to weddings and business appointments. As with the phone expenses, you should only note business-specific expenses. So if you use your vehicle to transport the kids to soccer or to go shopping, you'll have to estimate what percentage of the car is actually used for your business, then apply that to your insurance cost to arrive at a useable number. One reliable way to do this that the IRS will find acceptable is to keep a simple mileage log. Office supply stores sell mileage logbooks that are small enough to stash in your glove compartment or a pocket of your visor.

Transportation

You're allowed to deduct mileage on your business tax return each year, but in the meantime, you have to spring for gas money, windshield wiper fluid and other travel-related costs. If you work in a metropolitan area like New York, you will also have public transportation costs that can be penciled in on your income/expenses statement.

Online Service Fees

This one is easy to predict since you will sign up for service at a set price when you sign on for the first time. You will incur a monthly charge billed in advance to your credit card to connect your computer to the Internet. You normally have four service choices. The least expensive service is delivered by an Internet service provider (ISP), which charges $20 to $25 per month for unlimited usage and uses the modem that comes with your computer. For faster connection and transmission of data, you can choose an ISDN (Integrated Services Digital Network) line, which

> **Dollar Stretcher**
>
> Choose an Internet service that gives you multiple mailboxes so you can keep business and personal e-mail separate. Remember, though, that the IRS will only let you deduct the percentage of the ISP cost that's directly related to the business. To simplify bookkeeping, get a separate account for business e-mail and surfing.

processes at speeds up to 128K. This connection requires a setup fee of $200, a terminal or modem that costs $250, and a monthly fee of around $50.

For faster service yet, you can choose a DSL (Digital Subscriber Line), with speeds up to 384K. The setup fee for a DSL line is $100, while the terminal or modem will cost $250. Your monthly fee will be $40 to $60 for basic service.

Finally, cable modem service is available at speeds up to 2,000K. It requires a setup fee of $100, a modem priced at $200 to $300, and a monthly fee of $50.

Other Miscellaneous Expenses

Don't forget to add up the cost of your dry cleaning (you have an image to uphold!) and the cost of any food, snacks, or incidentals (like hairspray, panty hose, etc.) that you provide to the bridal party.

Receivables

At last, here's the good part! If all is right with the world, the money you receive from your clients will offset all the operating expenses you just read about. Hopefully, you'll have a little change to jingle in your pocket after paying all the bills. But the only way you'll know where you stand is if you keep careful records of your receivables.

You can either design your own sheet for receivables or customize a standard accountant's columnar pad available at any office supply store. These pads come with two to 12 or more columns to keep your accounting tidy. Usually, a six-column pad will do the job nicely. It's low-tech, but it works for people who are not computer-literate. If you decide to invest in an accounting software package (discussed in further detail below), you can log your receivables right on your computer and always have a running total available.

Paying the Piper

Of course, to obtain all that lovely remuneration, you have to bill your clients regularly. You'll find a sample invoice you can adapt to your specifications on page 111. Most of the wedding consultants we spoke to bill incrementally. Typically, they require payment for the consultation on the spot, then expect monthly payments for weddings that are planned over a very long period of time (like nine months to a year). Weddings that have a shorter lead-time may be billed in two installments: one at the time of the contract, and a second final payment 30 days after the event.

Cancellations are not uncommon in this business, and Loreen C., the consultant in Michigan, tries to keep hers to a minimum by refunding just half of the deposit if the cancellation occurs within seven days. After that, the deposit is forfeited.

"I have to do that because I might have turned someone else down for the same date," she explains.

Some of the wedding consultants we spoke to have merchant accounts, which allow them to bill their clients' credit cards. Julia K. points out that credit card fees can be very high for the merchant (that's you), but they're a necessary expense if you wish to be paid on a timely basis. But if you haven't been in business very long, a merchant account probably isn't necessary just yet.

Smart Tip

Tip...

Always provide a written contract that spells out your responsibilities and payment terms, since under the Uniform Commercial Code, contracts for the sale of services or goods in excess of $500 must be in writing to be legally enforceable. Even if your bill will be under $500, it's a good idea to have a written contract just in case a dispute arises.

High-Tech Bookkeeping

Remember that financial help we talked about at the start of this chapter? It's available in the form of affordable user-friendly accounting and business software you can buy at nearly any office supply or computer store. The hands-down choice of the wedding professionals we interviewed was QuickBooks by Intuit. The 2001 Pro version (which costs around $250) allows you to create invoices, track receivables, write checks and pay bills, and more. It also interfaces with Microsoft Word, Excel, and other software. Another plus: Data from QuickBooks can also be imported directly into income tax preparation packages like Turbo Tax, if you're brave enough to do your own business or personal taxes (not recommended if your tax situation is complex).

Invoice for Wedding Consultant Business

Cherished Moments

25771 Waterloo Drive
Lake Buena Vista, Florida 00003

September 28, 2002   Terms: Net 30

Sold To:

Susan Pfeiffer
49855 Petrucci Drive
Clinton Township, FL 00003

Full service "Wedding Extravaganza" consulting/coordination package $3,000

Pfeiffer/Roberts Nuptials

September 15, 2002

TOTAL $3,000

Thank You!

Another popular accounting package you might like to try is Peachtree Complete Accounting Release 8.0. It retails for about $270 and is available online from computer stores like Comp USA (www.compusa.com).

One of the best reasons to use accounting software is to prevent inadvertent math errors. All you have to do is put in the right numbers, and, voilà, they're crunched correctly.

Where the Money Is

Now you have all your ducks in a row, and they're ready to quack. Your business plan is exemplary, and you have solid evidence that your community or metropolitan area has the well-heeled economic base necessary to support your fledgling business. So financing should be a snap, right?

In your dreams. Small-business owners sometimes find it's pretty hard to find a bank willing to work with them. This is usually because the mega rich banks are far more interested in funding large companies that need large amounts of capital. They're also leery about dealing with one-person and start-up companies that don't have a long track record of success. So you may have trouble finding banking services like financing and merchant accounts that meet your small business needs.

One way around this problem is to shop around to find the bank that will welcome the opportunity to work with you. "Small business owners usually do better by selecting a bank with a community banking philosophy," says Robert Sisson, vice president and commercial business manager of Citizens Bank in Sturgis, Michigan, and author of *Show Me the Money* (Adams Media Corp.). "These are the banks that support their communities and function almost as much as a consultant as a bank."

You probably already have a pretty good idea who the smaller banking players are in your community. Start by checking out their annual reports (which you can usually find at branch offices) for clues about their financial focus and business outlook. Important clue: Institutions that support minority- and women-owned businesses as well as small businesses are likely to be more willing to help your business. Next, look for information about the number of loans they make to small companies. That's a pretty good indicator of

Stat Fact
According to the Small Business Development Center, all banks use certain key factors to determine a business' credit worthiness. These criteria include: collateral (assets to secure the loan), capital (owner's equity), conditions (anything that affects the financial climate), character (personal credit history), and cash flow (ability to support debts, expenses).

Self-Financing Made Easy

Financing your wedding consulting start-up with your personal credit cards can save you both the hassle of applying for a bank loan and the hefty costs that can be associated with it. Of course, the downside is that you'll probably pay interest rates of as much as 24.9 percent. So if you decide to use plastic, use a card with the lowest interest rate.

If your credit is good, you may be able to obtain a separate small-business line of credit through your credit card company. This allows you to borrow as much as $25,000, with no cost other than an application fee, and at a rate that's probably a lot less than what your bank would charge for a similar line of credit. American Express is one company that offers such a small-business line of credit.

Tapping into the equity in your home is another good way to secure funding. Banks now offer up to 125 percent equity loans. Just remember that your house is the collateral for the loan, and if the business doesn't do well and you can't make the payments, you could lose your home.

their community commitment. Finally, study their overall business mix and the industries they serve.

While it's not impossible to find a big bank that will welcome you into the financial fold, it's actually far more likely that warm welcome will come from a smaller financial institution.

"Small banks traditionally are better for small businesses because they're always looking for ways to accommodate these customers," says Wendy Thomas, senior business consultant at the Michigan Small Business Development Center (SBDC) at the One Stop Capital Shop in Detroit. "Small banks are simply more willing to deal with small business concerns and are more sensitive to issues like the need for longer accounts receivable periods."

Uncle Sam to the Rescue

Even if you do find a bank friendly to small businesses, you may still have trouble establishing credit or borrowing money as a start-up business. Banks, both large and small, are always more reluctant to part with their cash when the business owner doesn't have a proven track record of success.

That's where agencies like the Small Business Administration (SBA) can help. The SBA offers tons of free services to small business owners, including counseling and training seminars on topics like business plan or marketing plan development. The

▲

idea is to help the owner understand what the bank will want from him or her before ever setting foot inside the front door, thus improving the chances of being approved for a loan or other financial services.

The SBA also offers a number of different loan programs, counseling, and training. For more information, check the SBA's Web site at www.sba.gov, or call the answer desk at (800) 8-ASK-SBA.

Do-It-Yourself Financing

Even with all the financing options out there, some newly established wedding consultants prefer to whip out their plastic to buy office equipment, pens, staplers, and the other goodies that make the business go. Others rely on loans from friends and family. But no matter what you do, make sure the process is handled in a professional, businesslike way. If you borrow from loved ones, sign a promissory note that details repayment terms and an equitable interest rate. Nothing can break up a tight knit family faster than a broken promise of repayment, or a misunderstanding of how the repayment will be handled. Your new business is important, but your family is precious. Protect it just like you would protect your business assets.

If you use your personal credit cards, watch your expenses closely. You can easily put yourself thousands of dollars in debt if you are not careful. Start out with the bare minimum whenever possible so your business will have a chance to grow and prosper without the specter of debt hanging over it.

13

Happily
Ever After

In Chapter 1, we mentioned how wedding consultants make dreams come true for happy couples. We know you have your own dream: the dream of owning a successful business that allows you to do something you love. It is our hope that all your plans and hard work pay off, and you enjoy both happiness and longevity in your newly chosen career. But

Photo© PhotoDisc Inc.

while we wish you the best as you embark on this exciting new venture, we must acknowledge that every new business owner faces pitfalls that could threaten his or her company.

According to studies by the Small Business Administration (SBA), there are 25 million small businesses (defined as having fewer than 500 employees) in the United States, and they employ more than half of the private work force. What's more, 60 percent of all new businesses begin as homebased businesses, according to the U.S. Department of Labor.

Sounds promising, doesn't it? But let's do a reality check here. According to Dun & Bradstreet, the average rate of business failure in the United States is 13 percent, while the U.S. Census Bureau says that 99.9 percent of business closures occur among small companies. In fact, many small businesses don't make it through the very first year.

Why Businesses Fail

Surveys by organizations like the Small Business Administration have shown that the reasons for these failures are numerous. Business failures can be due to market conditions (such as competition or increases in the cost of doing business), financing and cash flow problems, poor planning, mismanagement, and a host of other problems.

Wedding consultants in particular are susceptible to additional difficulties fostered by poor communication, bad vendor relations, personal or family illnesses, and under-priced services.

This is why we strongly recommend that you hire professionals like attorneys, book-keepers, accountants, and contract employees to assist you in the proper management and operation of your business. Because no matter how enthusiastic, knowledgeable, and bright you may be, you're probably not an expert in every field, and your time will only stretch so far. In the beginning, it can be pretty hard to part with the cash to pay those professional fees, but in the long run, it's worth it because this kind of help will allow you to focus your attention on the things you do best.

And by the way, the outlook for success in a new business isn't completely bleak. Statistics suggest that the longer you're in business, the better your chances of staying afloat. Dun & Bradstreet reports that 70 percent of small businesses are still in business eight and a half years later. That's not a bad outlook considering the capricious nature of both consumers and the economy.

Hindsight Is 20/20

Nearly every wedding consultant who agreed to be interviewed for this book readily admitted there were things he or she would do differently if it were possible to start again. For instance, Julia K., the wedding consultant in Oak Point, Texas, says she would have selected a partner who was more committed.

"Specifically, I ran the daytime activities, and she ran the evening activities because she chose not to give up her daytime job," Julia says. "That meant she was working way too many hours in total, and I felt compelled to take more and more of her work so that she could have some downtime every week. If I did it over, I would insist that both my partner and I were equally committed to doing only the wedding consulting so neither of us was too overworked."

Paula L., a wedding consultant in San Clemente, California, thinks she started out meeting the vendors in the industry too slowly, and if she had to start over, would speed up that process since that's the way to get a handle on the industry.

Lisa M., in Bozeman, Montana, would have advertised more, something she didn't do much of in the early days because of the constraints

 Beware!
Try to avoid dealing with vendors who are friends or family of the bride or groom. As Julia K., the wedding consultant in Oak Point, Texas, says, "Many family and friends offer assistance or services out of the goodness of their heart and see the service as a favor or gift to the couple. Favors and gifts do not rank very high on the commitment level of most people."

of her initial budget. She also would have revamped her prices sooner, something she did (with much success) after she realized that people who came for the free introductory meeting didn't book her because her prices didn't fit the area she serves.

But even though every wedding consultant can identify something he or she could have done better, in every case these intrepid entrepreneurs used creative thinking, hard work, and good old-fashioned determination to meet whatever challenges faced them. Obviously, this is a strategy that works. These consultants survived that scary first year, and some of them have been prospering for decades.

Was it a miracle they persevered in the face of economic uncertainties and other pressures? Definitely not. It's due more to having the right stuff and knowing how to use it. It's also due to being willing to go the extra mile, which often results in acquiring a reputation as a miracle worker when it comes to solving the crises that can crop up in the course of planning and executing a dream wedding fit for a princess.

Wedding Stories to Learn From

Being able to think fast and execute plans on the spot can mean the difference between an ecstatic bride and one who is inconsolable.

Saving the Day

Julia K. earned her wings as a wedding day angel when she came to the rescue of a bride whose bower of flowers didn't materialize. The bride, who hired Julia to coordinate a wedding for 500 guests, insisted on using a florist friend to do the flowers. Because the bride was a liquor distributor, she bartered with the florist to provide $300 worth of liquor in exchange for the wedding day flowers. All of this was done without the benefit of a contract.

Two weeks before the wedding, Julia learned that the florist had gone out of business and someone else had taken over the business. Of course, the new owner knew nothing about the floral order. So even though she wasn't officially in charge of the floral arrangements, Julia sprang into action and persuaded the new owner to design the bouquets and reception arrangements without charge, using flowers, glassware, and floral

Smart Tip
Always draw up a contract for your clients outlining the services you've agreed to provide and what they will cost. Your attorney can help you draw up a standard contract that will cover most exigencies. You can also find preprinted forms for sale online at The Wedding Source, www.weddingspecialist.net, or phone (520) 453-6000.

containers donated by two of her regular florist suppliers. Julia donated candles from her own stock, so the caterer could create decorations for the tables using donated rose bowls and hurricane lamps. All of the product was delivered right to the reception site, and everything was completed in time for the reception.

"The amazing thing about all this was the original florist showed up before the wedding with a bucket of cheap leatherleaf greenery and started putting it into our arrangements," Julia says. "We yanked it all out after he left."

Julia credits her relationship with her vendors, her staff, and her own experience for being able to pull off such a feat on such short notice. She believes that if the client would have tried to solve this problem herself, the story probably wouldn't have had the happy ending it had for all concerned—even Julia herself, who says, "This woman has sent us more referrals than anyone else I've worked with."

The Case of the Disappearing Guests

It's not unusual for summer showers or winter flurries to put a damper on a carefully planned wedding. But Lisa M. had to fight the forces of nature to pull off the nuptials on one memorable summer day.

Lisa was engaged to coordinate wedding day activities for a ceremony that was scheduled to take place on U.S. Forest Service land. Unfortunately, three days before the wedding, the Forest Service closed all the parks in the state of Montana because of the extreme threat of fire danger. The bride managed to locate an alternate site on private land about five miles up the road, but there wasn't enough parking to accommodate all the guests. So Lisa had to make arrangements to bus the guests to the new site instead.

"Apparently there was some confusion about where the new place was because, at 5:15 P.M., we still had no guests for the 5:30 P.M. ceremony!" Lisa says. "I had brought my husband along to assist me that day, so I sent him up the road to look for the bus. The driver had gone about a mile past the turn and was starting to wonder where he had gone wrong. The guests were so happy to be rescued, they started applauding. I was glad I was there to worry about the guests so the bride and the mother-of-the-bride could enjoy the day."

Butterflies Aren't Free

Imagine having $2,000 worth of insects in your foyer—on purpose. That's what happened to Packy B., in Ohio, when a bride (who happened to be a family member) asked her to arrange for a butterfly release after the ceremony.

"That's why brides hire you—to give them ideas that are different and to choreograph everything," Packy says. "So I suggested the butterflies and had them delivered to my house before the wedding. I would never send them to the church because

▲

Fun Fact

Despite the expense, butterflies are becoming more popular with brides who want an alternative to rice, which can cause a disastrous slip-and-fall accident, or birdseed, which attracts wedding "guests" that leave behind unwanted "gifts." Even rose petals are a no-no at many churches and banquet facilities.

someone could put them by the heat and kill them. Luckily they come boxed in small triangle-shaped packets and are shipped on ice because I didn't want to touch them!"

Head Over Heels

Loreen C., the Michigan wedding consultant, always takes a tool kit with personal supplies for the bride, and a utility kit full of tools for herself to every wedding she coordinates. But one of the things she didn't used to pack was super bonding glue. That is, until a mishap with a cake brought the omission to her attention.

"While we were setting up for a reception, the DJ hit the cake table with a cord," Loreen says. "The cake topper fell off the cake, and the groom's head came right off. I bring a lot of extra things with me, but I never have a back-up cake topper. I also didn't have any super glue."

But the quick-thinking wedding consultant did have nail glue in her purse, so while her assistant smoothed out the frosting on the top layer of the cake, Loreen reattached the groom's little head and no one was the wiser. "I sure never said a word about it!" she says.

Speaking of coming to the rescue, that's the idea behind the tool kits Loreen brings along on wedding days. Some of the things in her tool kit (besides super glue) are a hammer, nails, screwdriver, tape, tape measure, decorator straight pins (for tasks like attaching lights to tablecloths or pinning ivy), wire cutters, extension cord, glue gun, rope (presumably not to use on a reluctant groom), and office supplies. The bride's customized kit contains things of a more personal nature, such as Tylenol, antacid, ginger ale, panty hose, mints, face powder, body lotion, lip gloss, makeup, perfume, hairspray, and a small water cup.

"I have each bride fill out a little survey in advance so I know her preferences and sizes when I put her kit together," Loreen says.

Ants for the Memory

Julia K. had her own close encounter with a wedding cake when she was supervising a rehearsal at an old mansion, while a reception for a different wedding was being set up in another room. "I happened to look into the empty room, when I passed by and noticed the cake," Julia says. "From a distance, it looked like parts of it were moving, so I went in for a closer look and saw it was covered with thousands of ants."

Neither the caterer nor—luckily—the bride were anywhere in sight. So even though she was not coordinating that particular wedding, Julia calmly removed the top layer of the cake, which mercifully was untouched by the bugs, sprayed the rest of the layers with bug spray, and blew off the dead insects. She then made arrangements with a local grocery store to provide sheet cakes free of charge that could be served instead of the ruined cake.

"In the South, the cake is usually cut in front of the guests, but this time it was wheeled into the kitchen so no one ever knew a thing," Julia says. "This kind of problem with insects actually is more common in the South than you might think because of the heat and humidity. I just insisted the facility spray for bugs the next day so I didn't have problems, too."

Your Formula for Success

It's easy to see that the kind of flexibility exhibited by Julia and the other consultants mentioned here is one of the hallmarks of being a professional in this field. "You

---

Signs of Success

You now know about the red flags that can signal a business failure. So what are the signs that your wedding consulting business will be successful?

1. You are providing a useful service at a price the market can bear.
2. Your local business market has enough customers to support your business.
3. You have enough savings or financing to weather the three-year make-or-break period.
4. Your business and marketing plans are sound, and you know where to go if you need help implementing them.
5. You have a good team of support service providers.
6. Your top priority is providing great customer service to your brides.
7. You keep careful records and always know where your business stands financially.
8. You're always aware of what your competition is up to.
9. You're flexible enough to change your business strategy when the situation warrants it.
10. You truly love your job and can't imagine doing anything else!

Beware!

The SBA reports that too many small business owners in financial straits don't call for help until it's too late to salvage their company. Don't fall into this trap. If you ever need help, call the SBA, which can provide advice and direction, or act as a loan guarantor. There's no charge for this service, and it could save everything you've worked so hard for.

can't be a dramatic person in this business," Julia stresses. "You also can't let the bride see that you're upset. You have to smile when you're upset, or when you're dressing down a vendor, or when you're worried because a car hit a utility pole and knocked out the power two hours before the reception. You have to be fast on your feet and even faster than the bride."

You also have to be very committed to making your business a success. "We don't go on vacation," says Jenny C., a wedding consultant in Texas. "Everyday is an adventure as it is."

Organization and mediation skills rank high on Loreen's personal list of required skills. "A lot of times you have to step in and keep the peace because the family wants something one way, while the bride and groom want it another way," she says. "Other times you have to put your foot down and stand firm so everything goes right."

Success in this business also comes from taking advantage of every opportunity that comes along. For instance, Loreen had magnetic signs the size of bumper stickers made up that say, "Planning a Wedding?" and that give her Web site address. She affixes them to the bumper of her car whenever she goes out for a spin, and at $19 each, they are a very inexpensive way to advertise her services. Incidentally, she chose to give her Internet address instead of her phone number because she thought it would be easier for drivers on the road to remember later.

Loreen also hands out her business card lavishly as a way to generate new leads. "If I go to the bank and the teller is wearing an engagement ring, I give her a card," she says. "I'm always looking at women's left hands."

Finally, patience is a virtue that every consultant we spoke to cited as critical for success. "You have to be patient, both with your clients and your business, because each wedding you're hired for will require different things of you," Lisa M. says.

And it is exactly that variety, that challenge, and that desire for excellence that makes the wedding consulting business so vital and exciting. May you enjoy great success in your new venture, and may all your dreams come true!

Appendix
Wedding Consultant Resources

They say that you can never be rich enough or young enough. While we could argue with those premises, we do believe you can never have enough resources. Therefore, we present you with a wealth of sources to check into, check out, and harness for your own personal information blitz.

These sources are tidbits; ideas to get you started on your own research. They are by no means the only sources out there and should not be taken as the ultimate answer. We have done our research, but businesses tend to move, change, fold, and expand rapidly. As we have repeatedly stressed, do your homework. Get out and start investigating.

As an additional tidbit to get you going, we strongly suggest the following: If you haven't yet joined the Internet Age, do it! Surfing the Net is like waltzing through a library, with a breathtaking array of resources literally at your fingertips.

Associations

Association of Bridal Consultants (ABC), 200 Chestnutland Road, New Milford, CT 06776-2521, (860) 355-0464, www.bridalassn.com

Association of Certified Professional Wedding Consultants (ACPWC), 7791 Prestwick Circle, San Jose, CA 95135, (408) 528-9000, www.acpwc.com

June Wedding Inc. (JWI), 1331 Burnham Ave., Las Vegas, NV 89104-3658, (702) 474-9558, www.junewedding.com

National Bridal Service, 3122 West Cary Street, Richmond, VA 23221, (804) 355-6945, www.nationalbridalservice.com

Attorney Referrals

American Bar Association, Service Center, 541 N. Fairbanks Ct., Chicago, IL 60611, (312) 988-5522

Find an Attorney, The Trenton Group, (888) 544-9800, www.findanattorney.com

Martindale-Hubbell Law Directory, 121 Chanlon Road, New Providence, NJ 07974, (800) 627-8463, fax 908-464-3553, e-mail: listings@martindale.com, www.martindale.com

Bridal Shows

Bridal Show Producers International, (800) 532-8917, www.bspishows.com

Brides-To-Be, 40700 Hayes, Clinton Twp., MI 48038, (810) 228-2700, fax: (810) 228-7210, e-mail: info@brides-to-be.com

The Great Bridal Expo, 510 Montauk Highway, West Islip, NY 11795, (800) 422-3976, (631) 669-1200, fax: (631) 669-1680, e-mail: sales@greatbridalexpo.com, www.great bridalexpo.com

Business Software

Affordable Event Planning Software, Certain Software Inc., One Daniel Burnham Court, #330C, San Francisco, CA 94109-5460, (415) 353-5330, fax: (415) 353-5335, www.cer tain.com

QuickBooks Pro 2001, (888) 246-8848, www.quickbooks.com

Peachtree 2000, Peachtree Software, 1505 Pavilion Place, Norcross, GA 30093, (770) 724-4000, www.peachtree.com

ScheduleEZ Pro, Software 2020, 2845 Soft Sun Circle, Las Vegas, NV 89128, (888) 528-0939, (702) 228-7764, fax: (702) 228-3844, www.software-2020.com

Butterfly Farm

Florida Monarch Butterfly Farm, P.O. Box 48966, St. Petersburg, FL 33743-8966, (727) 381-1932, e-mail: adverweb@adver-net.com, www.floridamonarch.com

Certifications and Professional Designations

Association of Bridal Consultants, 200 Chestnutland Road, New Milford, CT 06776-2521, (860) 355-0464, www.bridalassn.com

June Wedding Inc., 1331 Burnham Ave., Las Vegas, NV 89104-3658, (702) 474-9558, www.junewedding.com

National Bridal Service, 3122 West Cary Street, Richmond, VA 23221, (804) 355-6945, www.nationalbridalservice.com

Demographic Information

American Demographics, P.O. Box 10580, Riverton, NJ 08076-0580, (800) 529-7502, www.demographics.com

U.S. Census Bureau, www.census.gov

Disc Jockeys

American Disc Jockey Association, 10882 Demarr Road, White Plains, MD 20695, (301) 705-5150, fax: (301) 843-7284, www.adja.org

1-800-DISC JOCKEY, www.800dj.com

Employee Issues

U.S. Department of Labor, www.dol.gov

Limousines

Limos.com, P.O. Box 51113, Phoenix, AZ 85076, e-mail: service@limos.com, www.limos.com

LimousinesOnline, www.limousinesonline.com

National Limousine Association, 2365 Harrodsburg Rd., Suite A-325, Lexington, KY 40504, (800) 652-7007, fax (859) 425-5077, www.limo.org

Office Equipment (Phones)

Hello Direct, (800) 444-3556, www.HelloDirect.com

Office Supplies, Forms, and Stationery

Amsterdam Printing & Litho Corp., Amsterdam, NY 12010-1899, (800) 833-6231, fax: (518) 843-5204

Mark Art Productions, www.business-stationers.com

Office Depot, www.officedepot.com

Office Max, www.officemax.com

Rapidforms, 301 Grave Road, Thorofare, NJ 08086-9499, (800) 257-8354, fax (800) 451-8113

Staples, www.staples.com

Online Information Sources

The Knot, www.theknot.com

Ultimate Wedding, UltimatePublishing.com Corp., 6345 Balboa Boulevard, #165, Encino, CA 91316, (818) 776-2920, fax: (818) 776-2905, www.ultimatewedding.com

Online Postage

Pitney Bowes, ClickStamp support, (800) 390-0297, e-mail: support@pitneyworks.com, www.pitneyworks.com

USPS, www.usps.com

Photographer Referrals

Professional Photographers of America Inc., 229 Peachtree St. NE, #2200, Atlanta, GA 30303, (800) 786-6277, (404) 522-8600, fax (404) 614-6400, e-mail: csc@ppa.com, www.ppa.com

Publications

Advertising Age, 965 E. Jefferson, Detroit, MI 48207, (800) 678-9595, www.adage.com

Bridal Guide Magazine, Globe Communications Corp., 3 E. 54th St., 15th Fl., New York, NY 10022, (212) 838-7733, fax: (212) 308-7165, www.iarelative.com/wedding/b_guide.htm

Bride Again Magazine, 1240 N. Jefferson, Ste. G, Anaheim, CA 92807, (714) 632-7000, fax: (714) 632-5405, www.brideagain.com

Bride's, The Condé Nast Publications, 4 Times Square, New York, NY 10036, (212) 286-2860, www.brides.com

EXPO, EXPO Magazine Inc., 11600 College Blvd., Overland Park, KS 66210, (913) 469-1185, fax: (913) 469-0806, www.expoweb.com

Exhibitor Magazine, Exhibitor Magazine Group, 206 South Broadway, # 745, Rochester, MN 55904, e-mail: webmaster@exhibitornet.com, www.exhibitornet.com

Grace Ormonde Wedding Style, Bridal Promotions Inc. and Elegant Publishing Inc., P.O. Box 89, Barrington, RI 02806, (401) 245-9726, fax: (401) 245-5371, www.Bridalpro motions.com

Michigan Bride (one of 16 state magazines published by *Modern Bride*), 2955 Coolidge Hwy., # 112, Troy, MI 480084-3202, (248) 614-0065, www.michiganbridemagazine. com

Modern Bride and Modern Bride Connection, 249 W. 17th St., New York, NY 10011, (212) 462-3472, fax: (212) 367-8342, www.modernbride.com

Today's Bride, Family Communications, 37 Hanna Ave., #1, Toronto, Ontario M6K 1W9, (416) 537-2604, fax: (416) 538-1794, www.todaysbride.com

WEDDINGBELLS, Weddingbells Inc., 50 Wellington St. E., # 200, Toronto, Ontario M5E 1C8, (416) 862-8479, fax: (416) 979-1214

Wedding Pages Bride & Home Magazine, Weddingpages Publishing Inc., 1924 Hillside Dr., Falls Church, VA 22043, (703) 356-7586, fax: (703) 506-4611, www.wedding pages.com

Vows, Grimes & Associates Inc., 522 Kimbark St., Longmont, CO 80501, (303) 776-3103, fax: (303) 776-3798, e-mail: petergrimes@idcomm.com, www.vowsmag.com

Publishing Software

Microsoft Publisher 2000 Deluxe, available from Comp USA retail outlets or www.com pusa.com

Small Business Development Organizations

Small Business Administration (SBA), SBA Answer Desk, 200 North College Street, Ste. A-2015, Charlotte, NC 28202, 800-UASK-SBA (800-827-5722), e-mail: answerdesk@sba.gov, www.sba.gov (You can also check the federal government listings in your telephone directory for an office near you.)

Small Business Development Centers (SBDA), SBA Answer Desk, 200 North College Street, Ste. A-2015, Charlotte, NC 28202, 1-800-UASK-SBA (1-800-827-5722), e-mail: answerdesk@sba.gov, www.sba.gov/SBDC

SCORE, SCORE Association, 409 3rd Street SW, 6th Fl., Washington, DC 20024, (800) 634-0245, www.score.org

Tax Advice, Help, and Software

Internal Revenue Service, www.irs.ustreas.gov

Intuit TurboTax for Business, 2535 Garcia Ave., Mountain View, CA 94043, (650) 944-6000, www.intuit.com

Training and Professional Development

Association of Certified Professional Wedding Consultants, 7791 Prestwick Circle, San Jose, CA 95135, (408) 528-9000, www.acpwc.com

National Bridal Service, 3122 West Cary Street, Richmond, VA 23221, (804) 355-6945, www.nationalbridalservice.com

The George Washington University Event Management Certificate Program, 2121 Eye Street NW, Washington, DC 20052, (202) 994-0043, www.gwu.edu

Training Forum, A Division of Interactive Training Inc., 100 Cummings Center, Ste. 457J, Beverly, MA 01915, (978) 921-1755, www. trainingforum.com

Wedding Career Training Program, c/o Elegant Weddings by Donna, 7400 Lunar Drive, Austin, TX 78745, (800) 839-9235, fax: (512) 707-9710

Trade Show Displays

Airworks Displays & Booths, 816 Coronado, San Diego, CA 92109, (800) 900-9247, www.airwork.com

BMA, Booth Management Assistants, 3588 West 1820 South, Salt Lake City, UT 84104, (800) 442-3685, (801) 972-0202, fax: (801) 972-4397, www.bmadisplay.com

Pinnacle Displays, (800) 320-1466, (805) 965-9970, e-mail: Sales@Pinnacledisplays.com, www.pinnacledisplays.com

New World Case Inc., 10 River Road, Uxbridge, MA 01569, (508) 278-5526, (888) 883-0107, fax: (508) 278-5432, e-mail: Sales@PortableBooths.com, www.portable booths.com

Siegel Display Products, P.O. Box 95, Minneapolis, MN 55440-0095, (800) 626-0322, fax: (800) 230-5598, www.siegeldisplay.com

Web Hosting

DOMAIN.com, www.domain.com

Prodigy Internet, http://pages.prodigy.net

Webhosting.com, www.webhosting.com

Yahoo, http://yahoo.com

Wedding Cake Referrals

International Cake Exploration Societé, c/o Mail Boxes Etc., PMB 166, 1740 44th St. SW, Wyoming, MI 49509, fax: (318) 746-4154, www.ices.org

Wedding Consultants

Only You, Packy Boukis, JWIC, 8230 W. Ridge Drive, Broadview Heights, OH 44147, (440) 237-4257, e-mail: packy@clevelandwedding.com, www.clevelandwedding.com

Design My Wedding, Loreen Couch, Ypsilanti, MI, (734) 482-9690, e-mail: info@ designmywedding.com, www.designmywedding.com

Dolores Enos, JWIC, 131 Magnolia Ave., Larkspur, CA 94939, (415) 924-3563, e-mail: russ dee@earthlink.net

June Wedding Inc., Robbi G.W. Ernst III, 1331 Burnham Ave., Las Vegas, NV 89104-3658, (702) 474-9558, e-mail: robbi@junewedding.com, www.junewedding.com

StarDust Celebrations Inc., Marsha Ballard French, JWIC, and Jenny Cline, JWIC, 2728 Routh Street, Dallas, TX 75201, (214) 871-9610, e-mail: mb@stardustcelebrations.com, e-mail: jc@stardustcelebrations.com, www.stardustcelebrations.com

Elegant Weddings by Donna, Donna M. Horner, 7400 Lunar Drive, Austin, TX 78745, (800) 839-9235, fax: (512) 707-9710, e-mail: ELEGANTWBD@aol.com

Grand Occasions Consulting, Julia Kappel, JWIC, CWC, 710 Pearl Cove, Oak Point, TX 75068, (972) 294-1701, e-mail: goc@iglobal.net, www.grandoccasions.com

Champagne Taste, Paula Laskelle, JWIC, P.O. Box 3447, San Clemente, CA 92674, (949) 498-4806, e-mail: champagnetaste@home.com

Ever After Weddings, Lisa Michael, JWIC, 116 S. 9th Ave., Bozeman, MT 59715, (406) 585-8104, e-mail: lisa@everafterweddings.com

Wedding Consultant Supplies

The Wedding Source, 29 S. Acoma Blvd., Lake Havasu City, AZ 86403, (520) 453-6000, fax: (520) 453-3001, www.weddingspecialist.net

Wedding Planning Software

NOTE: Much of the wedding software available on the market is geared toward the bride. The packages listed here have features that are useful for wedding consultants.

▲

Modern Bride Complete Wedding Planner, SierraHome Software, (426) 644-4343, e-mail: support@sierra.com, www.sierrahome.com

My Wedding Companion, iBride, www.ibride.com (shareware)

WedPlan: The Wedding Planner, c/o Kagi, 1442-A Walnut St., #392 PMB, Berkeley, CA 94709-1405, fax orders: (510) 652-6589, e-mail orders: sales@kagi.com, www.altreality tyinc.com

Glossary

Backgrounder: a news release that gives general information about your business that will spur the local media to do a more in-depth story about your company and services.

Brochure: printed sales piece outlining your company's services and capabilities.

Chat room: on the Internet, an electronic "gathering place" for people who share special interests where they can exchange information, comment, or commiserate about topics of mutual interest in real time; see also *real time*.

Contingency fee: payment for legal services taken as a percentage of a settlement (often 25 percent or higher).

Corporation: a separate legal entity distinct from its owners.

Cyber: related to the Internet.

DBA ("doing business as"): refers to your legal designation once you have selected a business name different from your own and registered it with your local or state government.

Dedicated telephone line: a phone line used for a single purpose, such as for a fax machine or Internet data line.

Demographics: the primary characteristics of your target audience, such as age, gender, ethnic background, income level, education level, and home ownership.

▲

Domain name: the address of an Internet network (for example, www.entrepreneur.com); see also *URL.*

Ergonomic: office furniture or equipment designed for comfort and safety (for example, an ergonomic chair).

Executive summary: brief document at the beginning of a report, like a business plan that summarizes its contents.

FAQs: Frequently Asked Questions.

Feature article: an in-depth article that tells a story using dialogue, scene-by-scene construction, and personal opinion.

Freelancer: a self-employed person who works on a project or contract basis to produce written materials or artwork for advertisements, brochures, or other printed materials (including news releases).

Gigabyte: a unit of computer memory; most new computer systems now come with 10 gigabytes (or gigs) of memory, which is sufficient to run most business software.

Gutter: in book publishing, the white space formed by adjoining pages of a book when they're bound together.

Hit: in Internet parlance, a successful retrieval of information from a Web site.

Home page: the gateway to your Internet Web site.

HTML: Hypertext Markup Language; the coding or computer language used to create Web sites.

Icon: a symbol on a Web site that links the user to specific information.

Independent Contractor: see *freelancer.*

Interactive: in computer language, characterized by an exchange of data between the computer user and a host like an Internet Web site.

ISP: Internet Service Provider.

LLC: Limited Liability Company.

Link: a connection on your Web site that ties it to another Web site.

Litigator: an attorney who represents a client in a lawsuit.

Logo (or logotype): an identifying symbol used by organizations (as in advertising).

Media kit: a packet that contains publicity and sales materials about a company and its services.

Navigation: cyber directions given on a Web site to help the user to navigate easily from one page to another.

Newsletter: a marketing vehicle that contains short, newsy articles meant to promote a business.

News release: also called "press release"; a one-to-two page article about some positive aspect of your business meant to generate favorable publicity.

Partnership: a business owned equally by two or more persons, or partners.

Pitch letter: a letter sent to the media to generate interest in your company, product, or service.

Portal: electronic gateways that allow users to "enter" the Internet.

Real time: as it happens; in computer lingo, this means you can respond immediately to a message posted on a bulletin board or in a chat room; also known as "instant messaging."

Resolution: the clarity achieved by a printer, scanner, or monitor; measured in dpi (dots per inch).

Retainer: amount of money paid in advance for services.

Rider: an add-on provision to an existing insurance policy designed to protect against losses not covered by the standard policy; homebased wedding consultants typically add general liability and equipment riders to their homeowner's insurance to guard against property loss or injuries to them or their employees on the premises.

SEP (or SEP IRA): Simplified Employee Pension Plan; similar to an IRA, this tax-deferred savings plan has higher contribution limits (15 percent of business income); considered to be a qualified pension plan.

Server: the computer that controls access to a network or peripherals (such as printers or disk drives).

Shareware: software accessible on the Internet or on disk that is free of charge or available for a very nominal cost.

Sole proprietorship: a business owned by one person.

Tag line: a slogan used to build audience recognition for a product (i.e., "Got milk?").

Telemarketing: using the telephone to generate new sales or leads.

Thermography: a type of raised printing used on stationery and business cards.

Tussy mussy: a small floral nosegay designed in an antique bouquet holder.

URL: Uniform Resource Locator; or the Internet address locator.

Videographer: a person who videotapes an event like a wedding.

Web site: a group of related documents posted in cyberspace, usually accessed through a home page.

Index

A

Accountant
 hiring an, 40–41
 tax and financial advice from, 35,
  104
Accounting
 software, 110–112, 128
Advertising, 75–81
 brochure, 78–80, 89–90
 cable television, 78
 in magazines, 77–78
 in the Yellow Pages, 28, 72, 75–77,
  96
 newsletter, 78
 use of photographs in, 77
Advocate, bride's wedding day, 11
American Demographics magazine, 3
Appendix, 123–130
Association for Wedding
 Professionals International, 3, 11,
 16, 20
Association of Bridal Consultants
 (ABC), 2, 12, 123, 125
 annual international meeting of,
  68
 professional designations of, 66–68

professional development home
  study program, 67
 seminars, 68
Association of Certified Professional
 Wedding Consultants (ACPWC),
 123
 coursework and certification, 68
Attorney
 help in writing contracts, 118
 help with establishing business
  structure, 31
 hiring an, 38–40
 questions to ask before hiring, 39
 referrals, 124

B

Balance sheet, 35
Bands, wedding, 62
Banquet halls, researching, 59–60
Billing, 110–112
Bridal consultant software, 49
Bridal consultations, 9, 10–11
Bridal shows, 124
 booth, 100–102
 displays, 128
 purchasing mailing lists from
  sponsors of, 18, 21, 80

▲

Bride Again Magazine, 70, 126
Bride's Magazine, 70, 126
    advertising in, 77
Brochure
    advertising, 78–80
    Web site as online, 89–90
Bumper sticker advertising, 122
Business
    choosing type of, 28, 30–31
    description, 33
    failure, 116–117
    organizations, involvement in local, 81, 102
    plan, components of, 32–35
    school students, enlisting for help in developing marketing questionnaire, 20
    structuring your, 25–35
Business administration
    coursework, 66, 67, 68
    knowledge of, 9
Business cards, 47, 53, 101
    as advertising tool, 80, 122
Butterflies, 119–120, 124

C

Cable television advertising, 78
Cake, wedding, 63–64, 120–121, 129
Caterers, 60
Certification programs, 67–69, 125
Company name
    in the Yellow Pages, 28, 77
    on the Internet, 90–91
    registering your, 28
Competitive analysis, 33–34
Computer as office necessity, 47–49
Contract help, hiring as-needed, 11, 107–108, 125
Contracts, written, 110
Coordination of total event, industry trend toward, 9
Copy machines, 52
Corporation, 30, 31
Cost, average wedding, 2–3
Credit worthiness criteria, 112
Customer
    contact as potential marketing opportunity, 73
    feedback, 81

D

Daily tasks of wedding consultant, typical, 9–10

Demographic
    data, obtaining free or low cost, 22
    research, 14–17, 125
Design and development plan, 34
Destination weddings, trend toward, 16
Detail business, 10
Digital camera, investing in a, 49
Disk jockeys, wedding, 62, 125
Display ads, 76–78
Domain name, registering your, 90–91. *See also* Company name, Internet, Naming your company, Web site

E

Earnings potential, 3
Economic environment of your target market, researching, 16–17
Entertainment consultants, 62
Entrepreneurial spirit, 4
Essentials, start-up, 34
Event management training, 69
Executive summary, 33
Exhibitor Magazine, 70, 127
Expenses, deducting, 48
Expenses, miscellaneous, 109
Expo Magazine, 70, 126

F

Fairy tales, wedding, 1–2
Fax machines, 50
Federal employment identification number (EIN), 31
Fees
    consulting service, 12
    industry standard, 3
    initial consultation, 10
Financial
    factors, 34–35
    management, 103–114
Financing
    bank, 112–113
    self, 113, 114
    Small Business Administration, 113–114
First-time brides, percentage of, 23
Florists, finding and hiring wedding, 60–62, 119
Flowers, wedding
    trends in, 62
    Victorian messages in commonly used, 61
Full-service package, 11

Furniture, office, 47, 51, 53–54

G

Gatlinburg Tennessee as second most popular wedding destination (after Las Vegas), 11
General partnership, 30, 31
George Washington University certification program, 67
Glossary, 131–133

H

Homebased business
  start-up costs, 45–53
  zoning regulations, 31–32
Hometown wedding, 15
Horse-drawn carriage, 64
Hot lists, 18, 21, 80
Hourly rates, formula for determining, 12

I

Income and operating expenses, 104–110
  statement, 87, 104
  sample of, 106
  worksheet, 107
Incorporating, 30, 31, 40
Industry publications, 69–70, 127–128
Insurance
  agent, hiring an, 42–44
  business, 43–44
  expense, 108–109
  riders, 42–43
Internet, 83–91
  and destination weddings, 16, 88
  as communication medium, 86, 88
  as resource, 85–87, 98, 126
  finding vendors and suppliers on, 86
  postage, 126
  research, 86
  service fees, 109
  wedding planning, 88, 91 (See also Web sites)
Invoice, sample, 111

J

Joys of consulting, 4
June Wedding Inc. (JWI) professional development certification course, 67, 68–69, 125

L

Las Vegas as wedding capital of the world, 11
Legal networks, 39

Liability insurance, 44
Licenses, 32
Limited Liability Company (LLC), 30, 31, 40
Limousine service, wedding, 64, 125
Line ads, 75–77
Logo, company, 78

M

Magazine display ads, 77–78, 96
  sample of, 79
Magazines, writing feature articles for, 98–99. *see also* Publications
Mailing lists
  for news releases, 97–98
  purchasing, 17, 20–21, 80
Market research, 13–22
  firm, hiring a, 21
Market strategies, 33
Marketing
  low-cost, 93–102
  plan, 72–81
Marriages, annual number of, 3
Media kit, 102
Merchant accounts, 110
Mission statement, 22–23
  worksheet, 24
Modern Bridal trade show company, 23
Modern Bride Magazine, 70, 127
  regional editions of, 77
ModernBride.com as second most visited Internet site by engaged couples, 91
Money manager, hiring a, 40–41
Music, wedding, 62

N

Naming your company, 26–28, 29
  for Yellow Page listing at the beginning of the alphabet, 28, 77
  on the Internet, 90–91
National Bridal Association home-study training program, 69, 125
Networking, 3, 102
News releases, 94–98
  "Backgrounder," 96
  sample, 95
  writing your, 97
Newsletter
  advertising, 78
  creating your own, 99–100

O

Office equipment and supplies, 46–56, 125–126
cost comparison of two hypothetical businesses, 51, 54, 55
expense, 105
worksheet, 56
Older brides, targeting, 15
Operations and management plan, 34

P

Packages, wedding
"blueprint," 10
offering a variety of service levels in, 11, 89
party, 11
planning, 11
Pagers, 52, 105
Paperwork, 10
Parents of the bride and groom, targeting, 15
Party "only" package, 11
Permits, 32
Personal computers, 47–49. *See also* Internet
Phone books, advertising in private and special interest, 76
Photographer, wedding, 62–63, 126
Planning package, 11
Postage, 52–53, 105, 126
Press releases, 94–98
writing your, 97
Primary research, 17–21
Problem solving, creative, 9
Production, weddings as staged, 8
Professional
associations, 123–124
development, 65–70
help, hiring, 37–44
office, importance of, 10
women, targeting, 15–16
Profit margins, 104
Promotion strategy, 74–81
Public relations, 93–102
free workshops for low-income brides, 81
Publications
consumer, 70
event planning, 70
list of, 126–127
trade, 69
writing feature articles for, 98–99

Q

Questionnaire, market research, 18–21
Quiz, wedding consultant aptitude, 5

R

Ratio analysis, 104
Receivables, 110
Reception
exotic locales for, 60, 88
planning on the Internet, 88, 91
sites, nontraditional, 59–60
tourist destinations for, 60, 88
Research
demographic, 14–17
Internet, 86
market, 13–22
primary, 17–21
questionnaire, 18–21
secondary, 22
supplier, 58–59
target market, 16–17
tool, survey as most cost-effective, 20–21
venue, 59–60
Resources, wedding consultant, 123–130

S

Scanner, 48
Schedule, providing wedding party and vendors with detailed, 11
Scuba weddings, 60
Secondary research sources, 22
Service coordination, 9
Service providers, researching target market, 58–59. *See also* Suppliers, Vendors
Simplified Employee Pension Plan (SEP), 41
Slogans, 71–72
Small Business Administration, 113–114, 127
Small Business development organizations, 113–114, 127
Software, 49, 78
accounting, 110–112
publishing, 127
wedding planning, 129–130
Sole proprietorship, 30, 31
Start-up
costs, estimating, 45–56
essentials, 34
Stationery, 47, 53, 125–126
Stories from the trenches, 117–122
Success, formula for and signs of, 121–122
Suppliers
establishing a network of, 57–64
Web sites, 86
Supplies, office, 53–54

Surveys
   as most cost-effective research tool, 20–21
   including dollar bill as incentive for return-
      ing questionnaire, 21
SWOT analysis, 72–74
   worksheet, 74

T

Tax
   advice, help, software, 128 (See also,
      Accountant, Accounting, Software)
   deductions, 48
Telemarketing, 21
Telephone
   expenses, 104–105
   headset, necessity of, 10
   system, 50, 52, 125
Trade show displays, 128
Training and professional development, list of
   programs, 128
Transportation expenses/deductions, 109
Trolleys, vintage, 64
Twenty-somethings, targeting, 15

V

Vendors
   avoid hiring bridal party friends as, 117
   coordination of, 9
   vetting potential, 58–59, 64
   Web sites, 86
Videographers, wedding, 63
Vows Magazine, 69, 127

W

Wages, 107–108
Web site
   creating your own professional, 88–91
   hosting, 91, 128–129
Web sites
   list of important, 87
   suppliers and vendors, 86
   wedding consultant chat and information,
      85 (*See also* Internet)
Wedding consultants
   "day of wedding" package, 11
   duties on wedding day, 11
   list of, 129
   resources, 123–130
   stories to learn from, 118–120
   supplies, 129
Wedding Pages Bride & Home magazine, 70, 127
WeddingChannel.com as most visited Internet
   site by engaged couples, 91
Weddings Beautiful Worldwide certified wedding specialist certificate, 69
Word-of-mouth (WOM) advertising, 72, 80–81

Y

Yellow Pages advertising, 28, 72, 75–77, 96
   avoiding mistakes in, 75

Z

Zoning ordinances, 31–32

Start-Up Guides
Books
Software

To order our catalog call 800-421-2300.
Or visit us online at smallbizbooks.com

Entrepreneur Magazine's
SmallBizBooks.com

your personal advisory board

you need more....you'll find it at
entrepreneur.com/money

MONEY

- Tired of looking for financing in your couch's seat cushions?

- Want to write-off more than just your bad date last night?

- Expert answers are just a click away in our Money Channel.

- Can't find what you're looking for? We'll show you where
  to go—e-mail us @ **wheretofindit@entrepreneur.com**

Entrepreneur.com
solutions for growing businesses

THE
DYNA-BAND®
CHALLENGE

HILARY ATKINSON & ANDRÉE DEANE

THE OVERLOOK PRESS
WOODSTOCK • NEW YORK

To my darling daughter Jane, for without her dedicated support and encouraging words, the Dyna-Band adventure would not have begun.

Hilary Atkinson

First published in the United States in 1994 by
The Overlook Press
Lewis Hollow Road
Woodstock, New York 12498

Published in 1991 by Ebury Press
an imprint of Random House UK Ltd
Random House
20 Vauxhall Bridge Road
London SW1V 2SA

Library of Congress Cataloging-in-Publication Data

Atkinson, Hilary
The Dynaband challenge: a fabulous figure in only ten minutes a day / Hilary Atkinson and Andree Deane.
p. cm.
1. Exercise. 2. Physical fitness. I.Deane, Andree.
II. Title.
GV481.A85 1994
613.7'14–dc20

ISBN: 0-87951-562-7

 35798642

Second printing

Printed and bound in Great Britain
by Clays Ltd, St Ives plc.

Dyna-Bands are sold in sportswear and health outlets, or by mail order from Crown World Marketing Ltd. (Telephone U.S.A. 813-951-0767).

CONTENTS

FOREWORD 7

INTRODUCTION 9

CHAPTER ONE
WHAT IS A DYNA-BAND AND WHAT WILL IT DO FOR YOU? 10

CHAPTER TWO
THE DYNA-BAND STORY 18

CHAPTER THREE
CASE HISTORIES 26

CHAPTER FOUR
THE WARM UP 37

CHAPTER FIVE
THE GENERAL CHALLENGE 53

DAYS 1, 3 AND 5: CHEST, ARMS AND ABDOMINALS 56
CHEST PRESS 57
EXTENDED CHEST PRESS 58
SCISSORS 59
PULL DOWNS 60
SEATED ROW 61
LOWER TUMMY TIGHTENER 64
WAIST TWIST 65
STOMACH CURL 66
WAIST WHITTLER 66
STOMACH CRUNCH 67
FOREARM CURL 69
UNDERARM KICK BACK 69

DAYS 2, 4 AND 6: HIPS, THIGHS AND BUTTOCKS 70
SIDE LEG RAISES – BENT KNEE 71
GLUTEAL PRESS 72
INNER THIGH RAISES 73
BUTTOCK SQUEEZES 74
BACK OF THIGH (HAMSTRING) CURL IN 75
BUTTOCK LIFTS 76
TAUT THIGH PUSH 77
CALF AND SHIN STRENGTHENER 78
SUMMARY OF EXERCISES 79

CHAPTER SIX

THE ULTIMATE CHALLENGE 81

DAYS 1, 3 AND 5: CHEST, ARMS AND ABDOMINALS 84

Chest press 84
Extended chest press 85
Pull downs 86
Press ups 87
Lower tummy tightener 88
Crunch curl 89
Bicylce 90
Stomach curl 91
Waist whittler 92
Stomach crunch 93
Dips (triceps) 94
Forearm curl (biceps) 95
Shoulder lifts 96
Arm pull 97

DAYS 2, 4 AND 6: HIPS, THIGHS AND BUTTOCKS 98

Gluteal press 98
Side leg raises – straight leg 99
Inner thigh raises 100
Buttock squeezes 101
Hamstring curl in 102
Outer thigh pull 102
Leg press 103
Buttock lifts 104
Thigh extension 105
Calf and shin strengthener 106
Summary of Exercises 107

CHAPTER SEVEN

COOL DOWN STRETCHES 109

DAYS 1, 3 AND 5: CHEST, ABDOMINAL AND ARM STRETCHES 112
DAYS 2, 4 AND 6: BUTTOCK, THIGH AND LOWER LEG STRETCHES 119

CHAPTER EIGHT

SPECIFIC EXERCISES FOR PROBLEM AREAS 125

Shoulders 127
Upper Arms 130
Chest and Upper Back 135
Abdominals and Waist 140
Thighs and Buttocks 145
Lower Legs 151

CHAPTER NINE

EXERCISES FOR THE YOUNG AND OLD 153

Pre-School Children 155
Five to Fourteen Year Olds 155
Fifteen Year Olds and Over 156
Dyna-Band and the Older Age Group 157

FOREWORD

Dr R B Tovey MBBS, BSc Hons University of London
Medical Practitioner, Hillingdon Hospital

The Dyna-Band Challenge is a simple, quick and effective programme for toning, strengthening and conditioning all the major muscle groups with benefits to the individual which are being increasingly recognised from a physical and psychological point of view. Andrée Deane has constructed a safe and innovative way of incorporating effective exercise into busy daily life. The explanations are easy to follow with pictures for each exercise. The Dyna-Band Challenge allows an individually graded and adjustable workload to suit beginners and experienced exercisers alike with the considerable advantage of being able to work certain muscle groups which otherwise require special equipment and facilities. The Dyna-Band approach could be described as inventive, effective, sensible and flexible as opposed to the so often seen limited gimmicks which rapidly lose favour through obvious shortcomings.

WORD OF CAUTION

If you suffer from high blood pressure or have a history of heart disease, consult your doctor before you perform any exercises with the Dyna-Band.

If you are severely overweight, have any joint disabilities or injuries or are on permanent medication, consult your doctor before undertaking this exercise programme.

This exercise programme is not suitable for women in the first or third trimester of pregnancy.

If you have a history of knee problems, always tie the Dyna-Band above your knee and not over it.

The Dyna-Band is not a toy and supervision is recommended when children are exercising with the band.

9

INTRODUCTION

Would you like to lose inches and achieve a firmer shape in just ten minutes a day? If the answer is 'Yes' then read on as the Dyna-Band Challenge has to be a must for you. If you follow this exercise programme for at least four weeks I guarantee that you will see and feel a change in your shape and posture. You can lose inches off your thighs, buttocks, abdominals, chest and upper arms – the areas that the Dyna-Band Challenge specifically concentrates on.

How can I make you this promise? Because I have seen dramatic improvements in the shape of both men and women who have taken part in the Dyna-Band Challenge. Our case-histories have all lost inches and improved their shape in only four weeks. Most of them carried on with the Dyna-Band Challenge for a further six weeks and the improvements are remarkable as you will be able to see in the photographs.

I am convinced that once you have started the Dyna-Band Challenge you will continue with it. You won't give up as you may have done with so many other exercise programmes as this one is quick, simple and, what's more, effective. You will feel your muscles working against the Dyna-Band and will know that you are achieving something.

The exercises in this programme are based on my considerable experience of teaching men and women in fitness classes. When I have asked them in the past what they would like to see in a home exercise book or video the majority always said that:

- It should be clear, simple and easy to follow.
- The exercises should take minimum time and space, yet produce effective results.
- There should be varying levels to cater for ability differences.
- It should offer the opportunity to progress.

A tall order! I hope that I have satisfied all of these points in the Dyna-Band Challenge – I think I have.

Normally I am very sceptical about new crazes in the fitness industry because, let's face it, there have been many in the past! However, in only a very short time I have become convinced that the Dyna-Band is an exercise product that is not just an overnight wonder but here to stay as a valuable part of our, and I hope your, exercising lives.

Andrée Deane

CHAPTER ONE

WHAT IS A DYNA-BAND AND WHAT WILL IT DO FOR YOU?

A Dyna-Band is a latex rubber strip which works your muscles on a simple but ultra effective principle – that of resistance. Unlike other exercise bands, the Dyna-Band is so versatile that it can be tied or held round any part of the body with ease, depending on which muscles you want to work, and is comfortable whatever your shape, size or ability. In fact, it offers you a complete home gymnasium and yet can be stored away in a drawer, or even your pocket, after use. The concept may be simple, and the product may be small but the effects of the Dyna-Band Challenge on your body, and consequently your looks and confidence, are fantastic!

The exercises will increase the strength and endurance of all your major muscle groups meaning that your body will become firmer, particularly in the hip, thigh, buttock, abdominal and upper arm areas. The best news of all is that results are much quicker than with most other exercise programmes because of the resistance or tension that the band provides. It means less time each day spent exercising and less time to wait before you see visible results in your mirror.

When I was first introduced to the Dyna-Band by Zara Atkinson, an introduction which Hilary tells you about in her Dyna-Band story, I viewed it with caution. I have been in the exercise teaching and lecturing business for over fifteen years and in that time I have seen just about every type of exercise band on the market, as well as a whole lot of other exercise gadgets which have proved to be five-minute wonders. The idea of a resistance band being used for exercise originated from America, and so far none of them had really completely satisfied my requirements.

First of all we had elastic bands that you could buy from your local stationery shop. They were just a much larger version of an ordinary elastic band – the type we used to use to tie our hair up with. These giant elastic bands would last for two or three exercise sessions before they snapped – and when they snapped it wasn't a very nice experience! They would either catapult into the air and give somebody nearby a nasty shock or, sometimes worse still, they might snap in your face. As you can imagine, the possible damage to your eyes was extremely worrying. Whilst exercising you had to keep your face well away from the band which was sometimes inconvenient and restricted the exercise positions that you could get into. Also these elastic bands were quite short, after all they were never made with exercise in mind, and often cut deeply into the skin – particularly if you were on the large side!

I vividly remember going to a huge exercise workshop being taught by an American girl 'specially flown in' from LA. The topic was 'Condition your body with a revolutionary way of exercising – A Rubber Band'. About two hundred of us crowded into a hall ready to devour anything that was new! Everybody raved about it afterwards and elastic bands took British exercise classes by storm shortly after this. However, they didn't last long – the bands cut deeply into your fingers and hands, your ankles and thighs because they were so thin and tight. They only allowed you to make very small movements which meant that, as muscles were not working through a full range of movement, they tired very easily. Also because classes weren't used to holding the bands correctly they used to let go and the bands would fly all over the place!

When the elastic bands became too tight and uncomfortable, there was a new cause for concern – would circulation be restricted? The answer was yes – and this restriction could be particularly dangerous if you suffered from any circulatory disorders or had a tendency towards high blood pressure.

Although the elastic bands weren't very successful most people recognised that the principle was a good one. The rubber provided effective resistance to work against, the band was small and easy to carry around, it was inexpensive and the exercises could be done any time, anywhere. Companies started trying to perfect a safer, more durable exercise band. Several types of resistance bands then came onto the market. They were all better than the first elastic bands but none was perfect. Their disadvantages tended to be that:

- They were never wide enough. The Dyna-Band's width makes it comfortable to work with and provides an even spread of resistance to the area of the body being worked upon.
- They were never long enough. Often you had to tie more than one band together which was time consuming as you didn't always need more than one band for every exercise.
- They were never strong enough. The life of most rubber bands is limited – elastic properties don't go on for ever. The difference with the Dyna-Band is that it will last for at least a year if looked after carefully (see instructions on page 15). Other bands tend to have a much shorter life time and will eventually snap. When this snapping occurs there is always a safety concern – as well as giving you quite a shock when it happens! The Dyna-Band will show wear and tear eventually by gaining tiny tears or splits in the rubber. When this starts to happen you know that it is time to get a new one. Even if you do carry on, the Dyna-Band will only tear and not snap as other bands do.
- Other rubber bands were normally joined, like elastic bands are. This restricted exercise positions – unlike the Dyna-Band which is in one length and offers the choice of being tied or left in one long strip according to the exercise and personal preference.

You can probably see now why I was sceptical when I first saw the Dyna-Band. I'd had plenty of experience with other resistance bands and was beginning to think that the idea was a dead loss as nobody could ever get it right. I had to admit though that this new band – the Dyna-Band – did look a little different from all of the others so I decided to investigate the matter further.

I contacted Hilary Atkinson who sent me the details of a strength study using the Dyna-Band conducted by Professor Richard Mostardi from Akron University. On reading this study I decided that the results were interesting enough to consider the Dyna-Band in a different light to that of all the other bands. The first step was to take a Dyna-Band home and give it a try. As it happened my local gym, of which I'd been a member for the past couple of years, had just closed down, and I had been looking for a quick and easy method of exercising at home. My spare time is limited (I have a husband and three small children), and the last thing I wanted was to travel miles before I could even begin my workout. I began to use the Dyna-Band for just 10 minutes a day along with my usual jogging programme of about 20 minutes three times a week. When the local gym does reopen I will not be re-joining – I don't need to with the Dyna-Band at home!

Firstly I had quickly discovered that it is like no other resistance band that has ever been on the market. It is comfortable, versatile, safe, durable and simple to use. Secondly, the Dyna-Band's effect on muscle tone is tremendous – I could feel my muscles being worked which surprised me as I really am quite strong.

The next step was to introduce the Dyna-Band to the students on my training courses. The response was fantastic! Where can we buy them? Is there a book of exercises? Have you got a video? Can we use them in our exercise classes? By now I was convinced by the bands as – if this was just a small sample of individuals – how would the population at large respond?

You may notice that I talk about all of these other rubber bands in the past tense even though several of them are still on the market today. That's because for me they are the past tense. There is only one safe and effective resistance band that satisfies all of my requirements – the Dyna-Band. But I couldn't understand why nobody had heard of, or used, the Dyna-Band before. As it was so obviously a fantastic product why hadn't anybody recognised its potential? I then discovered that the medical profession had cottoned on to the Dyna-Band over seven years ago. At first the band, called 'Thera Band', was used in physiotherapy units for the rehabilitation of muscles and joints after injury. More recently it has had widespread use in sports injury clinics and departments throughout the country with the orthopaedic profession taking more and more notice. Children with disabilities are also being taught how to use a 'Thera Band'. Now the general public have a chance to experience the incredible effects the Dyna-Band can have on your shape, strength and well-being.

I have devised two workouts – the General Challenge and the Ultimate Challenge. I call them a 'Challenge' because to achieve any real benefits and to see visible improvements you need to push yourself just a little to enable your muscles to respond and improve. This does not mean that the exercises should be painful – the myth 'No pain – no gain!' has long been considered by exercise professionals as rubbish.

Everybody, however fit, should really begin with the General Challenge if only to get used to the technique of using the Dyna-Band. It will be up to you to decide when and if you want to progress to more demanding exercises – I give you advice about this further on into the exercise programme. Both Dyna-Band Challenges have been created to offer effective exercises for all levels of ability. The General Challenge takes only ten minutes a day, six days a week. Days 1, 3 and 5 are upper body and abdominal exercises with leg and buttock exercises on days 2, 4 and 6. In other words, it will take you only one hour every week to achieve noticeable results, often as quickly as four weeks after you have begun the Challenge. You may be only four hours away from a new, more shapely figure.

So why will the Dyna-Band work so quickly and effectively for you? Because the exercises are all carefully designed to work your muscles evenly through a range of movement against tension. The tension provided by the band means that more of your muscle fibres (the microscopic cells that make up muscles) have to be used to overcome that extra resistance. In short, your muscles will have to work hard but will respond quickly under safe conditions. You will achieve a better shape and your muscles will become more clearly defined. Don't worry though – the exercises will not make women become 'muscular'. Women don't tend to develop large and bulky muscles through this type of exercise as they lack the predominantly male hormone, testosterone, which is necessary for developing muscle mass. Your muscles will just become more clearly defined giving your body a firmer, more youthful appearance. The exercises will also mean that your body will become stronger and you will be able to perform those everyday tasks like gardening, decorating and shopping more easily.

WHICH DYNA-BAND IS FOR YOU?

The resistance your muscles will have to work against is determined by the thickness of the Dyna-Band, which comes in four strengths. Any of the four different coloured bands can be used individually or in combination for even greater resistance. You can choose between:

Pink – least resistance. Mainly suitable for the elderly, those recovering from injury, or pre- and post-natal exercisers (NB special exercise programmes are necessary for these groups of people).

Green – medium to low resistance. Mainly suitable for the beginner exerciser.

Purple – medium resistance. Suitable for the more experienced exerciser, perhaps when you have become used to the green Dyna-Band and need to move on.

Grey – greatest resistance. This is an advanced level Dyna-Band which is suitable for those with a good deal of strength. Quite a few men work out with this band as well as people with considerable exercise experience.

Choose a Dyna-Band to suit your level of exercise experience. If you are a beginner I suggest that you start with the green band. You can always move up one thickness once you have become used to the exercises. During your daily Dyna-Band Challenge your muscles should start to feel the effects of the exercise you are performing after about 8–10 repetitions. When you get to the stage where it takes 12–15 repetitions before you feel your muscles working you need to move up to the next strength of Dyna-Band. Make sure though that the Challenge is feeling easier throughout most of the exercises and not just one or two. If you move on to the next Dyna-Band too quickly you will feel tired very quickly, you won't enjoy your workout as much and you could harm yourself. Exercises are often performed incorrectly when you are tired or the movement is too difficult for you and this is where injury to joints and muscles can occur.

If you get to the stage where your progression is so fantastic that you want to use two Dyna-Bands in combination with each other, consider the following suggestions:

- You are on the green band but not quite ready to transfer to the purple. Try combining the pink with the green for a while.
- You are on the purple band but not ready to go on to the grey. Try combining the purple with the green temporarily.
- If you become exceptionally strong and find that the grey Dyna-Band is inadequate, try combining the grey with any of the other colours.

There is no clever technique or secret to using two different Dyna-Bands together – you don't need to tie them or roll them around each other. Just hold their ends together or tie them together where the exercise requires it and they will automatically stick to each other.

CARE OF YOUR DYNA-BAND

I have already said that the Dyna-Band is very hard wearing and will last for ages if you look after it carefully. If you mistreat it, leave it tied up after exercising, crumple it up and leave it squashed in a drawer, leave it lying on the top of your central heating boiler or a radiator then you can't expect it to last long. The special properties of the latex rubber in the Dyna-Band make it long lasting and hard wearing – but not indestructible! If you take note of the following tips you should find that your Dyna-Band will go on for ages:

- Store your Dyna-Band in a box or a bag, or hang in a dark area like a wardrobe or cupboard. Do not store in direct sunlight.

- Sprinkle your Dyna-Band with talcum powder every now and then. It stops the rubber from sticking and it also freshens up the band after you have been exercising with it.
- Remove your rings before you use the Dyna-Band and take care of long, sharp fingernails.
- If you have to tie a knot in your Dyna-Band don't pull it so tightly that you find it difficult to undo. (Advice about how to tie your band comes on page 55 before the description of exercises in the General Challenge.)
- Untie and flatten your Dyna-Band after use and before storing.

THE DYNA-BAND CHALLENGE MODELS

We have used a different model for each section of the Dyna-Band Challenge so that you will be able to recognise the exercises quickly and easily.

CORINNE is the model for all of the chest and upper back exercises. She has a fantastic figure, mainly because she has danced, both professionally and as a hobby, since she was a child. She found the Dyna-Band chest exercises really helped to keep her bust lifted.

LINDA is the model for the buttock and thigh exercises. She offered to do these exercises because it's the area she feels she has to work on the most. Linda has a neat waist and small upper body and if she puts on weight it always goes to her thighs. She has noticed quite a difference after six weeks in her bottom which is tighter and her outer thighs which have slimmed down.

VALDA is the model for the upper arms. She is a trained exercise teacher and I asked her to do the upper arm exercises because it is the part of the body that she is particularly conscious of. Valda is in great shape considering that she is well into her fifties. She didn't really need to improve her shape other than her arms which were beginning to get a little saggy. Valda started off using the pink band and then progressed after 4 weeks to the green band. She has seen a great improvement in the tone of her upper arms.

SANDRA is performing the warm-up exercises. She is a young girl with an amazingly tiny waist and hips. She is naturally slim and doesn't have to work at her figure, but finds that the Dyna-Band exercises are good for toning and for improving her posture and body awareness.

HILARY ATKINSON is the model for the cool down stretches. She wanted to do the stretches because she is very flexible and can get into the positions easily. I have seen a fantastic improvement in Hilary's figure since she has been using the Dyna-Band and the improvements are still being made.

ANDRÉE DEANE – yes, I am the model for the waist and stomach exercises. I am very used to doing these exercises as, having had three children, it's the area that I like to work on most! I find that tummy exercises using the Dyna-Band work really well – better than any I've done before in fact.

CAROLINE is one of our success stories. She is featured in our case histories as she volunteered to take part in the ten-week Dyna-Band Challenge before and after photos. Caroline is modelling the lower leg exercises, something she would never have had the courage to do before her figure was completely transformed by using the Dyna-Band.

All of the models are wearing the same leotards throughout the book so that you can easily recognise them.

CHAPTER TWO

THE DYNA-BAND STORY

HILARY ATKINSON

How this book came into being is a lengthy, but fascinating, story. First let me explain that I'm not a fitness expert, just an average woman with the typical problems of keeping in shape. Like a lot of you, I have an exercise bike that has been relegated to the garage and weights lying in the corner of my bedroom which my husband keeps stubbing his toes on! I've got a shelf full of exercise and diet books which have been read, tried and put back on the shelf again only to gather dust.

I've tried various diets that work if you stick to just eating one particular food all day. These can be extremely boring to follow, and as soon as you begin to eat other foods again – on goes the weight!

I have religiously followed various exercise programmes but my vital statistics have remained unchanged.

By then I had become very cynical about 'latest craze' exercise and diet books, tapes and videos. I had tried the lot – and persevered on most of them – but none of them had worked for me. I didn't have vast amounts of weight to lose. I just wanted to tighten up some of the flabbier bits of me – my waist, stomach, hips and thighs. Surely it was not too much to ask?

THE DYNA-BAND

While visiting Champneys Health Club, I noticed a girl in the gym using a pink strip of rubber to exercise with. She had trapped one end of the rubber in the door and was pulling on the other end. I was fascinated and asked what on earth she was doing! The

American girl explained that she had dislocated her shoulder and that she was using the Dyna-Band to strengthen the muscles surrounding her shoulder to speed up recovery. She spoke very highly of the Dyna-Band but said that she'd had to send to America to get is as it was not available in the UK. She explained that the Dyna-Band was very popular in America, both for strengthening to improve recovery from injury and for toning and conditioning in exercise classes. I was so interested in this new possibility for exercising that I asked if I could borrow one of her Dyna-Bands.

By this time I had started having private lessons with a fitness instructor as I was so desperate to get in shape. When I showed my fitness instructor the Dyna-Band she was apprehensive at first as she had already had experience of working with 'rubber bands'. She had found that the different types of narrow bands on the market were uncomfortable to use and snapped quite regularly. She was constantly worried about the band snapping into her face or that of somebody close by. She tried the Dyna-Band and was impressed by its comfort and versatility and could feel it actually working her muscles. She was keen to introduce the Dyna-Band into her body conditioning classes but the problem was – where to buy it? I decided to start looking. Easier said than done because where do you start looking for a product that nobody seems to have heard of?

I knew that Dyna-Band was a registered trade name so I telephoned the US consulate's commercial library. Unfortunately they couldn't trace anyone under the name of Dyna-Band. Great – a tumble at the first hurdle! I was not to be put off easily though. The American student who had given me her green Dyna-Band had also given me a summary of a strength study on the Dyna-Band which had been conducted at Akron University in conjunction with Akron City Hospital. I rang the hospital in Akron and their medical library referred me to the Hygenic Corporation. The Hygenic Corporation had a European distributor based in Belgium – but they didn't have a UK distributor. At least if I could contact the European distributor I could order some Dyna-Bands and we could get the body conditioning class going. Well – life is never easy! The distributor in Europe didn't stock the band. He was more interested in the Hygenic Corporation's other products which were all related to the medical field – eg surgery equipment for hospitals and dentists. However, he told me of a planned visit by the vice-president of the Hygenic Corporation to London in the near future. I was luckier here – the vice-president agreed to meet me when he came to London but I had a whole month to wait – a month to get started on my campaign to market the Dyna-Band in the UK.

I decided to place a small order with the Americans for 80 Dyna-Bands so that I could test the reaction in my area. My fitness instructor introduced them into her existing classes and the response was so positive that she decided to set up a new 'Dyna-Band class'.

We immediately contacted the local papers feeling that a new style of exercise class deserved some press coverage. One journalist even joined in with the class himself and found the Dyna-Band to be really effective. He also thoroughly enjoyed himself! Even so, getting him to commit himself on paper in an article proved difficult. He said that he couldn't do anything unless I got exclusive UK distribution rights from the Hygenic Corporation. He probably thought that I was just a crazy housewife who had latched on to yet another exercise gimmick that wasn't going to last.

Convincing people was hard going at first. I found that people tended to be sceptical, particularly if they'd had experience of other rubber bands in the past. My tactic was to get them to hold the Dyna-Band – to stretch it and use it, to feel it working their muscles. Most people were easy to convince once they'd experienced the effects of the Dyna-Band working. The new class set up by my fitness instructor was going fantastically well and all the women were seeing improvements in their figures after only three weeks. By now I was utterly convinced that the Dyna-Band was going to feature for a long time in our exercising lives so I didn't miss an opportunity to promote it. Also – at long last – I had found something that worked for me. My figure was noticeably improving – and what's more – with very little time and effort compared to other exercise programmes I'd tried.

During my meeting with the vice-president of the Hygenic Corporation I obviously managed to convince him that my enthusiasm for the Dyna-Band would be an invaluable marketing asset. I was granted exclusive distribution rights in the UK and Channel Islands – needless to say I was delighted! Now to approach the reluctant journalist – surely he would now agree to publish an article about the local Dyna–Band class? I was wrong – he was still not convinced and I virtually had to threaten him with strangulation by a Dyna-Band if he didn't publish the article! My determination paid off as he printed the article the following week, probably because he was frightened of any further confrontations with me! I felt it necessary to push like this because I knew that the Dyna-Band worked and I wanted others like me to benefit from its fantastic effects.

It all proved to be worthwhile in the end as the Daily Mail saw the article in my local paper and followed it up with a full-page spread on the Dyna-Band. This article generated a lot of response; major department stores, such as Harrods and Selfridges, became stockists and I began to import the Dyna-Band by the thousand.

At this stage I needed lots of help and support as I began to panic about the amount of work I had taken on. Was I really up to it – how could I manage a husband, children and home and build up the reputation of the Dyna-Band? I needn't have worried as my family was marvellous.

My eldest son, Simon, had already accompanied me to one of my meetings with the American vice-president and he continued to offer his support. He collected my VAT registration certificate – confirmation that I really was in business. He has continued to accompany me on other occasions which are important stepping stones in building up the success of the Dyna-Band.

My youngest daughter, Jane, kept saying 'You can do it Mummy' when she could see me looking a little down with the pressure of marketing a new product that some people were still very sceptical about. 'Go on Mummy, you can do it' always seemed to be said at the right time – when I really didn't think it was worth continuing.

My youngest son, Paul, started to collect my Dyna-Band orders which were delivered by air freight, and my mother just stayed quietly in the background providing cups of tea and meals when they were needed. If it weren't for her the whole household would have ground to a halt! I had Dyna-Bands waiting to be cut and packaged in the lounge, the kitchen, the dining room – everywhere in fact! Throughout this chaos the family were all wonderfully supportive except for the one person I haven't yet mentioned. My husband, Christopher, thought the whole thing was just a disruption to the normally orderly routine of the household. He didn't believe in the Dyna-Band – in fact he was annoyed with it for making some of his meals late! He just wanted his wife to return to domesticity and to her most important job of looking after him – I'm sure you recognise the type – you may have one like him yourself! It was because Christopher was so unsupportive that I became even more determined to make the Dyna-Band successful. After all, if he ran a successful business why couldn't I? Nowadays he couldn't be more helpful and I rely on him for his help and guidance. He can see now that I was right all along about the Dyna-Band but I wouldn't go as far as to risk saying 'I told you so!'

MEETING ANDRÉE

One of my biggest breakthroughs came when my eldest daughter, Zara, who by this time believed in the Dyna-Band as much as I did myself, decided to go on an exercise teacher training course so that she would feel capable of teaching Dyna-Band classes of her own. She enrolled on a course that the Sports Council recommended to her which was run by Shape – a training company directed by Andrée Deane. Halfway through the course Zara showed some Dyna-Bands to Andrée who was immediately impressed and borrowed some Dyna-Bands to give a demonstration class on her next course. It took Andrée just a couple of days to become convinced that the Dyna-Band was the best form of resistance band on the market. She built a session into her course timetable where she demonstrated exercises using the Dyna-Band so that her students could appreciate this new form of resistance exercise. These exercise teacher training students then started to tell their exercise classes about the Dyna-Band – at last word was beginning to spread and my efforts were paying off.

THE BOOK

At the beginning of 1990 I was approached by Ebury Press who wanted to publish an exercise book using this new revolutionary piece of exercise equipment. I needed to find a writer and a fitness consultant to work with as, although I was convinced of the benefits of using the Dyna-Band, and had devised some of my own exercises, I was in no way a fitness expert. Professional advice was necessary to make sure that the exercises were safe and medically approved.

Andrée Deane immediately sprang to mind for several reasons. Firstly she was already converted to the benefits of using the Dyna-Band and was using it regularly on her training courses; secondly, I had discovered from several people in the fitness profession that she was a highly qualified, respected and well-known lecturer and exercise teacher who was running one of the most successful exercise teacher training courses in the country. Andrée also regularly wrote articles about exercise.

Andrée devised a programme of exercises that could be done at home, took minimum time, fuss and effort and yet still gave quick results. Between us we thought that 10 minutes a day every day was reasonable, or 20 minutes three times a week.

The problem was to get a group of people together who were willing to try out the exercises over several weeks so that we could check on their progress and give the book some case-histories. I decided to advertise! I asked for volunteers who were willing to spend 10 minutes a day exercising for 10 weeks altogether. They had to agree to 'before' pictures, 4-week pictures and then final pictures at 10 weeks. In return I promised them that their figures would improve. And as you can see from the photographs of our case-histories – I certainly fulfilled my promise! They are genuine photos that have not been altered or 'touched up' in any way and they show the results of the Dyna-Band General Challenge.

I know that a lot of people will look upon this as just another exercise gimmick, but they will be totally wrong. Resistance exercise using rubber bands has been around for a long time but nobody yet has seemed to get it right. With the Dyna-Band it is right. It is not just another gimmick that has taken us by storm. The Dyna-Band has been used in British hospitals under the name of 'Thera Band' for the past 7 years so some of you may have already exercised with it. And what better recommendation could it have? Being used by medical practitioners and physiotherapists gives the Dyna-Band top marks as far as safety goes.

HOW THE DYNA-BAND HAS AFFECTED MY FIGURE

I speak from personal experience when I say that the Dyna-Band does work. I started to exercise with the Dyna-Band in January for 20 minutes three times a week. I felt that the 20 minutes suited my busy lifestyle more than 10 minutes every day. By mid-February, which was only three weeks later, friends were coming up to me and saying – 'Well – it's certainly worked for you.' By the end of February I had lost inches from my waist, my stomach was firm and my trousers and skirts fitted beautifully. I couldn't believe it – an exercise programme that actually worked! And it wasn't just an overnight wonder. I still do the Dyna-Band exercises three times a week and I have now progressed to the Ultimate Challenge. The exercises don't take up too much of my time and, most important of all, they work – so how could I get bored with the exercises when my figure is constantly improving?

I was also getting very favourable reactions from my husband Christopher. At the beginning of March, after only six weeks of exercising with the Dyna-Band, Christopher, in a playful mood, patted my bottom and said, 'Now your bottom's so nice and firm I could almost mistake you for Jane!' As our youngest daughter, Jane, is only thirteen years old I was naturally very pleased about this – who wouldn't be! Anyway, he then continued with more compliments. '. . . by the way, sex is great lately. Is that anything to do with the Dyna-Band?' I didn't know but I was certainly going to try and find out! Could the exercise routines have improved my body in an area that couldn't be seen in a mirror?

HOW THE DYNA-BAND CAN IMPROVE YOUR SEX LIFE

I telephoned a close friend who was also doing the Dyna-Band Challenge and asked her, very tactfully, if she'd noticed any improvements in her pelvic floor muscles. Immediately she said yes – that her sex life had improved and her husband had been the first to comment on the improvement. She also went on to say that the fluid retention she had been so used to experiencing before a period had improved over the last few months – since she had been using the Dyna-Band in fact. Naturally she had been delighted about these changes but hadn't related them to the Dyna-Band.

I wondered who else I could speak to on such an intimate subject. I decided to ask my eldest daughter, Zara, who has two very small children. She told me that her husband had decided that the Dyna-Band must improve 'the underneath muscles that you can't see'. At the time I hadn't really understood what she meant so I didn't take much notice. But obviously her husband had also noticed an improvement in the tone of her pelvic floor muscles. Zara had also found that she was not so bloated before a period.

I consulted Andrée on this coincidence (or was it?) of three of us with husbands who had noticed improvements in sex. She said yes - that it was definitely possible. On the tummy exercises where you lift your legs off the floor and contract the lower part of your stomach your pelvic floor muscles can also be contracted. You just have to squeeze in, pretending that you are stopping in mid-flow whilst urinating. Also on some of the buttock exercises you are instructed to squeeze your bottom and your pelvic floor muscles at the same time.

I'd done all of those pelvic floor exercises that they give you in hospital after your baby is born – they hadn't really worked then so how come they should work now? Apparently the increased resistance provided by the Dyna-Band makes you work your pelvic floor muscles even harder as you concentrate the exercise on one part of the body – like your stomach or bottom. Also, once the exercises start working for you and you feel stronger, fitter and healthier, you will improve your body awareness. Your posture will improve and you will become aware of where your pelvic floor muscles are (something women often find difficult). You will therefore be able to squeeze them more effectively.

Fluid retention before a period can be minimised with any form of exercise as waste products are eliminated more efficiently in a healthy, well-exercised body. The Dyna-Band seems to be particularly effective in preventing that horrible bloating before a period and is much safer and healthier than resorting to diuretics.

As weak pelvic floor muscles are so common amongst women, particularly those who have had several children, we were very anxious to get some more information about how the Dyna-Band was helping to improve this area of the body. We decided to send out a questionnaire to all the Dyna-Band class members as we had several classes running by now. As well as questions about figure improvement we asked some more personal questions about improvements in their sex lives. In every case the women who had had children had noticed real improvements in the quality of sex with their partners and in 90% of these cases the partner had remarked upon it.

This was marvellous – my husband hadn't been imagining things! The Dyna-Band was obviously providing very real improvements to women's pelvic floor muscles if they followed the exercises regularly. And this was a totally unexpected and added bonus. We had seen fantastic improvements in the shape of these women which would have been enough for them – but to also improve on the quality of their sex lives was wonderful.

I said earlier that some people out there will think that this is just another exercise gimmick. If you feel sceptical – do yourself a favour. Have a go at the exercises in this book and feel your muscles working. Spend just 10 minutes a day on the Dyna-Band General Challenge for a few weeks and then decide whether this is another gimmick that will fade away. I think that you will become, like me, a firm believer in the Dyna-Band.

CHAPTER THREE

CASE HISTORIES

'Everyone keeps saying — what diet are you on?'

'Incredible — really amazing — my husband noticed a difference after only four weeks.'

'Two years ago my doctor said I needed a bladder repair operation — he says it's not necessary now!'

'In all the years I've been exercising this is the thing that works for me.'

'My boyfriend says I've got more of a figure now.'

'Ten minutes is easy to find.'

Here are just some of the quotes from the ecstatic volunteers who took part in our Dyna-Band Challenge experiment. You are about to see some amazing improvements to their figures in just ten hours of exercising, in fact in some cases after only four hours.

Hilary advertised in local newspapers asking for volunteers to take part in a ten-week exercise programme using the Dyna-Band. As an incentive she guaranteed that we could improve their figures. The response was disappointing at first and you can well imagine why. There are so many gimmicks promising figure improvement advertised in newspapers that people have become wary. Usually they consist of diets which are uninteresting, unappetising and sometimes even dangerous. Nobody had heard of the Dyna-Band so they probably thought that it was yet another gimmick designed to make vast amounts of money for the seller.

Eventually Hilary got a large enough group together (unfortunately they were all women so we have no male representative) and explained what they would be expected to do in exchange for a fantastic new figure. This then gave them the chance to back out if they wanted to! We asked the group to agree to these six conditions.

- They had to exercise using the Dyna-Band for either ten minutes a day or twenty minutes three times a week. It didn't matter what time of day they exercised although most of them did stick to a regular time each day.

- They were asked not to take up any other new form of exercise at the same time as this could affect the results of the 'experiment'.

- They needed to do the complete programme of exercises for all parts of the body so that we could see an overall improvement rather than just concentrating on their worst area!

- The experiment would last for ten weeks – although hopefully they would see such an improvement in their figures that they would want to carry on with the exercises after this period.

- They were not expected to diet at all but to just carry on eating normally (which hopefully meant a reasonably healthy diet!).

- Photographs would be taken before the project started, four weeks after exercising and finally at ten weeks.

The photographs were the biggest 'turn off'. Would you put on a leotard and face a camera looking your absolute fattest? The ladies we eventually used as our case-histories did, which must have taken them a lot of nerve. For some of them it was a painful process – seeing the awful truth in black and white.

Eventually we selected six women who represented a cross-section of ages, shapes and sizes to show you that you can improve on your figure with the Dyna-Band Challenge whatever your age and shape – whether you are very large or only need to tone up in a few places.

Before you look at any of these photographs just remember that none of them has been tampered with in any way, they show genuine figure improvements. They also represent only four and ten weeks exercising with the Dyna-Band – in other words we haven't cheated by asking the women to work for more than one hour a week and for more than ten weeks.

JAN

Jan was in a very depressed state just before she started the Dyna-Band Challenge. She had caught sight of herself in a mirror at the family's Christmas celebrations and was disgusted at what she saw. She was size 16 and had plenty of spare tyres. Jan said, 'Christmas should have been the best time of year for me but it wasn't – I just wanted to crawl into a corner and hide!' Jan had tried to improve her figure lots of times before but she felt that none of the exercise or diet books she had tried had really worked. She has four children and had 'never been able to get rid of the flab from having kids'. She could never wear a swimming costume and always made excuses when her children asked her to go swimming with them. She also didn't want to go to aerobics classes because she felt self-conscious and ashamed of her body. Jan began the Dyna-Band Challenge and her husband noticed a difference after only four weeks. She goes into raptures when she talks about the effects the Dyna-Band has had on her figure! 'Incredible – really amazing!'

After ten weeks of working out for ten minutes a day with the Dyna-Band she has gone from a size 16 to a size 12! She didn't diet at all but says that she's always been 'reasonably careful' about what she eats. Jan says, 'It's down to the individual – if you want something badly enough you have to give it a go. I saw that the Dyna-Band was working

Before

After 4 weeks

10 weeks

for me so I made sure that I never missed a session and that I did all the exercises properly.' She also feels great after every Dyna-Band workout and says that she has become addicted to it!

Jan has not just toned up in specific areas but all over her body and is probably our best example of the effect the Dyna-Band can have on your figure. Her husband thinks that he is married to a 'new woman'. The most fantastic improvement that Jan has experienced though is one that can't be seen in a mirror. Two years ago her doctor told her that she would need a bladder repair operation sometime in the near future. She just recently had another examination by her doctor who told her that the operation was no longer necessary. The exercises with the Dyna-Band had strengthened her pelvic floor muscles and got rid of her incontinence problem. Jan used to 'trickle' a bit when she coughed, sneezed or jumped – but not any more. She could never do a mid-stream specimen of urine for the doctor as her pelvic floor muscles were so weak that she didn't have enough control to stop the urine in mid-flow. Just recently she has given such a specimen – and perfectly!

Jan's husband is disabled and confined to a wheelchair. He has a muscle wasting disease that is hereditary as other members of his family also suffer with the same condition. Jan has encouraged all of them to use the Dyna-Band in some gentle exercises so that their muscles are stimulated to contract and to remain as strong as possible. I think this story is fantastic as it shows how versatile the Dyna-Band is. Sitting in his wheelchair he is able to isolate parts of his body with the Dyna-Band and exercise them without endangering the badly affected areas. Hopefully, his Dyna-Band exercises will mean that he can remain independent and self-sufficient for as long as possible.

MO

Mo saw Hilary's advertisement for 'guinea pigs' for the Dyna-Band project but didn't want to go along on her own so she persuaded her daughter, Lorna, to go with her. Mo had been going to keep-fit classes for many years so she had always been figure conscious.

At first Mo started with the green band but she moved very quickly onto the purple one. She does her Dyna-Band exercises for 20 minutes three times a week on a Monday, Wednesday and Friday so she has made it into a regular routine.

She says that '20 minutes is easy to find'. She often puts music or the television on whilst she's exercising as it gives her something to concentrate on.

Before   10 weeks

Mo noticed improvements in after only four weeks. She says that the Dyna-Band Challenge has 'lifted my bottom and tightened up my waist'. She knows this because her skirts are now much looser. Mo hasn't dieted at all and, the last time I spoke to her, admitted to having eaten a box of chocolates that very day! 'In all the years I've been exercising this thing works for me. It doesn't tire you out and yet you still feel good afterwards.'

Mo has also improved the strength of her pelvic floor muscles. When she used to go to keep-fit classes a couple of years ago she had to wear a tampon to stop any embarrassing leaking when she jumped up and down. She also tended to leak if she coughed or sneezed. Since the Dyna-Band Challenge this problem has completely disappeared. Mo regularly jogs without needing a tampon as her pelvic floor muscles are now a lot stronger. Until I asked Mo about any improvements to her pelvic floor muscles she hadn't really thought about it – 'It's the sort of thing you take for granted,' she said. Having realised that there was a big improvement she decided to ask her husband whether he'd noticed any difference in their sex life recently and he agreed that there definitely had been. He had noticed an improvement a couple of weeks before but hadn't mentioned the fact to Mo – now she is even keener to continue with her Dyna-Band exercises!

CAROLINE

We are very proud of Caroline because her figure has improved so much after ten weeks of using Dyna-Band that she has gained enough confidence to appear as a model in the book (she performs the lower leg exercises). We would have liked Caroline to wear the same leotard for her ten-week photographs as she did for her 'before' ones but it was not possible – her original leotard was far too big! To show off her achievement Caroline decided to wear a skimpy leotard. 'I'd never have dared to wear anything like this before!' she said at the photo session.

Caroline is 20 years old and wanted to see more definition in her shape, particularly her waist and tummy. She answered Hilary's advertisement for volunteers because she had tried aerobic classes and they hadn't improved her figure so she thought she'd try something different. Caroline did the Dyna-Band Challenge three times a week for 20 minutes, usually in the evenings as she works in an office during the day. After about five or six weeks the girls at work started commenting on her change in shape. Her waist was starting to go in, rather than following a straight line from her hips, her thighs had toned up and her bottom was a lot firmer. On Caroline's ten-week photos you can see that her posture has improved and her bust has also lifted. 'I feel as if I'm getting more of a figure.'

Before   Before   After 10 weeks   After 10 weeks

Her boyfriend is delighted – 'It's an all over effect,' he says. Throughout the ten weeks Caroline just carried on eating normally so she found that her motivation stayed high – she only had to exercise for an hour a week and eat more or less what she wanted. 'I haven't lost a whole lot of weight – I just trimmed up in some areas.'

LORNA

Lorna wanted to improve her figure but only if she could do it without any effort! (Wouldn't we all!) Mo dragged her along to the first Dyna-Band class and Lorna enjoyed it so much that she decided to continue with the ten-week project. Lorna has been dancing and horse riding most of her life but had just recently stopped both of these activities and, to make matters worse, started taking the pill. Her figure began to expand and Lorna felt that she ought to do something about it. Mo says that Lorna 'puts no real effort into the exercises when she uses the Dyna-Band – she does it half-heartedly'. Also Lorna has not dieted at all – and she has got a large appetite according to her mother!

Even though Lorna has made no real effort you can see that after only four weeks she has made some improvements to her figure. Her bottom has lifted and her hips have slimmed down a little. She feels more comfortable in her clothes and, after seeing the improvement in black and white, says she might make a bit more effort. Lorna's case just goes to show that the Dyna-Band Challenge can still improve your figure with no real effort on your part. But just think what it can do for you if you give the exercises your whole-hearted attention!

Before

4 weeks

CHRISTINA

Christina was a size 18 before she started the Dyna-Band Challenge – now she is a size 14! Understandably she is very pleased with the Dyna-Band. Until then Christina had found it difficult to improve her figure. She had been on several diets but her weight always crept back up again as soon as she stopped dieting. She didn't really want to be on a permanent diet all her life as 'it's no fun having tonic water when your friends are enjoying themselves. You can't go out to a restaurant very often – it's really miserable.'

Christina started going to a gym but felt intimidated by the bodybuilders there so she soon gave it up. She had also been to aerobic classes but didn't like 'jumping around'.

Christina went along to the Dyna-Band class and enjoyed herself so much that she agreed to take part in the 10-week project and went home with a green band. She does the Dyna-Band exercises for 10–15 minutes a day (she adds in a few exercises from the specific section as well as the Dyna-Band General Challenge) and fits in her workout between getting home from work and going out in the evening.

You can clearly see the effect that the Dyna-Band exercises have had on Christina's figure. After ten weeks her hips have slimmed down and her trousers and skirts are a lot looser around the waist.

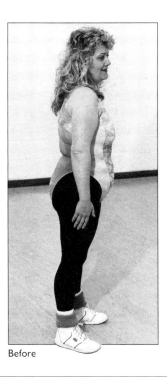

Before

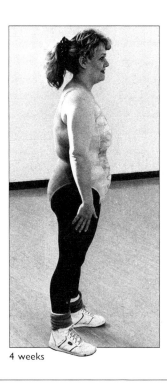

4 weeks

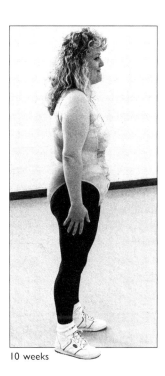

10 weeks

'Everyone keeps saying – What diet are you on?' Everyone she works with and all of her family and friends have noticed a difference in Christina's figure. Of course she realises that she has still got more improvements to make but this is a good start after only ten hours of exercising!

Christina has not been dieting as she has had enough of it. Instead she says, 'I'd prefer to exercise with the Dyna-Band and eat sensibly, rather than diet all the time.'

NICOLA

Since exercising with the Dyna-Band Nicola can now get into her size 12 black ski pants – something she hasn't been able to do for years!

Nicola has not always been able to complete a full hour of exercising with the Dyna-Band every week but she has done her best. She feels that her figure has become much firmer, especially her hips and bottom, and her clothes feel much more comfortable. Her friends and family have noticed a massive improvement in her figure and her sister says that she 'looks great'. Nicola finds it difficult to get down to the exercises in the evening after work and really has to push herself. Once she has made the effort though she feels much better and makes a resolution not to miss any sessions in future!

Before

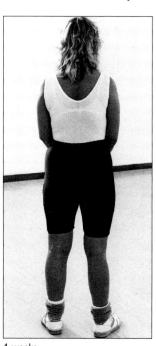
4 weeks

10 weeks

CAN YOU EXPECT THE SAME IMPROVEMENTS?

C an you see now how easy it is to gain a fabulous figure in only ten hours? All of our case histories said that the Dyna-Band Challenge was easily manageable and involved no big effort or commitment.

They all liked the fact that you don't have to get changed into exercise clothing every time you work out – loose clothing is fine, and that you don't break out in a sweat and have to clean yourself up afterwards. Often, when you go to an aerobics class or go out for a run you waste a lot of time getting changed. It can turn your exercise sessions into a whole evening's drama – the sort where you make excuses like 'It's raining tonight, I don't think I'll go' or 'There's a good play on television, I'll exercise tomorrow'. These excuses will not be used for the Dyna-Band Challenge as you can slip your exercises into an odd few minutes any time.

So can you expect the same improvements as our case histories? The Dyna-Band Challenge will tighten and tone your muscles so that you will look firmer and shapelier. You will lose inches off your body but not necessarily weight. To lose excess weight you either need to go on a calorie-controlled diet or do an aerobic form of exercise in addition to your Dyna-Band Challenge, eg jogging, brisk walking, swimming or cycling. Try not to become too obsessed about your weight as this is not necessarily the vital factor in looking slim and healthy. Of course if you know that you are well overweight you must become concerned because of the risks to your health. But if only a few extra pounds are involved, concentrate on toning your body so that it looks lighter even though your scales still read the same! None of our case histories dieted or took part in any other exercise and yet still they achieved results. If you want to put an extra effort into the programme and extend your daily Dyna-Band routine and possibly diet as well – just think of the results you could achieve!

If you do decide to diet at the same time as starting the Dyna-Band Challenge make sure that it is a well-balanced diet where the calorie intake is at least one thousand per day – a diet that you can safely follow for quite a while without your health being affected. Don't go for these crash diets or diets that are based on the same foods every day. Firstly they can be dangerous and secondly the weight loss is never permanent. Be sensible as you need some energy to cope with your new Dyna-Band exercises. So please don't record your progress with the Dyna-Band by weighing yourself. If you want to measure how much you are improving try a tape measure and observe the changes in your vital statistics because, believe me, they will change for the better – and I can guarantee this so long as you follow the challenge carefully, and above all – don't cheat.

CHAPTER FOUR

THE WARM UP

I t is vitally important that you follow these warm up exercises before your day's Dyna-Band Challenge. I know that it will be tempting to miss them out if you are short of time but you will not get the best out of your body if you go straight into the Dyna-Band Challenge. These exercises will:

- Help prevent muscle and joint injuries.
- Increase the benefits of the Dyna-Band exercises as warm muscles and joints will work more efficiently.
- Help you to get more out of the toning and conditioning exercises – therefore you will achieve better results.
- Psychologically prepare you for the time you are about to spend on yourself.

You will need enough room to extend your arms, and a mat or thick carpeting for the floor stretches.

To begin with, perform these exercises smoothly and slowly to allow your joints and muscles time to adapt.

POSTURAL CHECK

Ideally you should check your posture standing sideways to a full-length mirror. Stand with your feet slightly apart, bottom tucked in and your stomach pulled in tightly. (This movement will have the effect of tilting your pelvis.) Shoulders need to be pulled back but not tense – make sure they are down and relaxed. Your head should be lifted with your chin parallel to the floor. Breathe in a normal and relaxed way throughout the exercises.

Incorrect posture

Correct posture

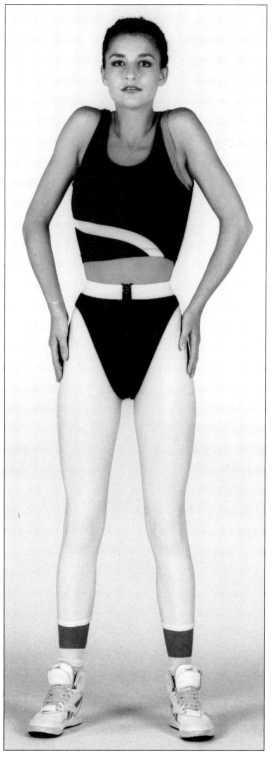

SHOULDER LIFTS

- Check your posture and stand with feet hip distance apart and knees slightly bent.
- Leaving your arms down and relaxed by your side, gently lift both shoulders up towards your ears and then lower.
- Repeat the lifts 15 times.

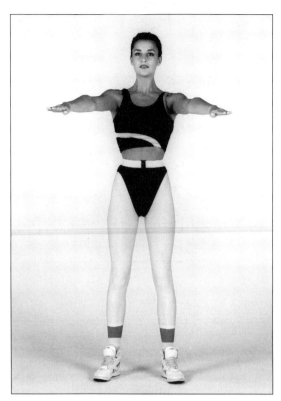

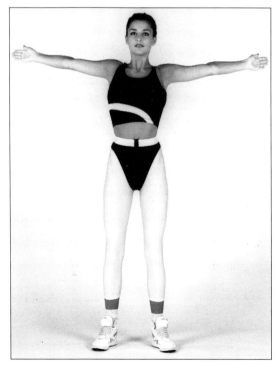

ARM CIRCLES

- In the same position extend both arms and circle them round smoothly.
- Repeat the circles 10 times.
- Make the circles larger by extending your arms further.
- Repeat the larger circles 10 times.

HIP CIRCLES

- Continue in the same position with your knees bent and slowly circle your hips round. Restrict the movement to your hips only by keeping your knees bent and your legs still.
- Repeat the hip circles 5 times round to the right and 5 times round to the left.

SIDE BENDS

- Stand in the 'postural check' position.
- Place your hands on your hips and bend to one side from your waist. Keep your legs still, only moving at your waist.
- Do 5 bends to the right followed by 5 bends to the left.

SIDE STEPS

- Take a large step to your right and then back to your left.
- Bend your knees as you step. (The more you bend your knees the warmer your leg muscles will become.)
- Repeat the side steps 20 times altogether.

SIDE STEPS WITH ARM SWINGS

- Take the same steps as in the previous exercise.
- Swing your arms from side to side with the steps.

- Make the swinging movements bigger as you warm up.
- Take 20 steps with arm swings altogether.

SKI-DIPS

- Stand with your arms above your head.
- As you bend your knees swing your arms down as if you are holding ski sticks and are pushing the snow away.
- Bring your arms back above your head as you straighten your knees.
- Do 15 ski-dips altogether.

MARCHES

- March on the spot with your arms swinging. You can make the march into a gentle jog if you wish.
- Perform 30 marches or jogs. You should be feeling warm by now. If you are not, perform the last three exercises again as you must be warm before you do any of the following stretching exercises.

WARM UP STRETCHES
Upper Body

CHEST

- Stand in the 'postural check' position.
- Clasp your hands together behind your back and squeeze your shoulder blades towards each other.
- Hold this stretch position for a slow count of six.

Note: it is important that all stretches are *held* and not 'pulsed' or 'bounced' into.

WARM UP STRETCHES

WAIST

- Stand in the same position as for the previous exercise.
- Place one hand on your hip and the other behind your head.
- Bend to the same side as your hand on hip.
- Hold the stretch position for a slow count of six.
- Change arm positions and repeat the stretch on the other side.

WARM UP STRETCHES

UPPER ARM

- Stand in the same position as for the previous exercise.
- Place one hand on the back of your opposite shoulder.
- Use your other hand to gently assist by pressing the arm further over your shoulder.
- Hold the stretch position for a slow count of six and then repeat on the other arm.

WARM UP STRETCHES

LUNGE

- Stand with your feet wide apart and toes pointing diagonally outwards.
- Stay facing forward and bend one knee. Remember your knee should stay in line with your ankle.
- If you cannot feel a stretch in your inner thigh take your legs further apart and lean your body forward more.
- Hold the stretch position for a slow count of six.
- Repeat on the other leg.

You will need your mat for the rest of the warm-up stretches.

WARM UP STRETCHES

BACK OF THIGH (HAMSTRING)

- Lie on your back with your knees bent and your feet flat on the floor.
- Hug one knee in to your chest and then extend the leg as far as you comfortably can. Note – you do not have to straighten your leg – not many people are flexible enough to do this.
- Hold the stretch position for a slow count of six.
- Repeat on the other leg.

CALF

- Lie in the same position as for the previous exercise.
- Hug one knee in to your chest and flex your foot. You should feel a stretch in your calf muscle.
- Hold the stretch position for a slow count of six.
- Repeat on the other foot.

These stretch positions should feel comfortable. You should feel no pain during any of them but just a mild tension as the muscle is being lengthened.

Do not bounce in any of these stretch positions or you may damage your muscles. Be patient and hold the stretches for the suggested length of time in a static position.

You will feel invigorated and ready to begin your Dyna-Band Challenge!

CHAPTER FIVE

THE GENERAL CHALLENGE

Here are the exercises that can work wonders for you in only ten minutes a day, providing you follow them as advised. Those of you who are fairly new to exercise may need to build up to the suggested number of repetitions gradually to avoid post-exercise soreness. And remember – these exercises should not give you any pain or discomfort but rather give your muscles a healthy feeling of mild tension.

The General Challenge is based on six ten-minute sessions per week. You can either perform the exercises every day for six days as suggested or, if it suits your schedule better, you can put two days together and workout for twenty minutes only three times each week. If you choose the second option I suggest that you leave a rest day between each exercise session to allow your muscles to recover.

Many of you will wish to concentrate on specific areas of your body. To make the exercises easy to identify we have 'coded' them by using the same model for each body part.

Corinne – chest and upper back **Andrée** – waist and stomach **Linda** – thighs and buttocks **Valda** – arms **Caroline** – lower leg

Remember though that you will not reap the full benefits of the Dyna-Band Challenge, which is a complete body workout, if you skip some of the exercises.

When you get used to the exercises, which shouldn't take long as they are all very simple, you can just refer to the table at the end of the chapter and perform your day's Challenge with minimum time and fuss. You may find it time consuming at first to tie the band in the correct position and to get used to the amount of tension you require to work at a comfortable level. This will mean that the Challenge could take rather more than ten minutes each day at first. Don't worry though as you will soon become familiar with the

SAFETY REMINDER
Check with your doctor if:
- **You have high blood pressure or a history of heart disease.**
- **You are suffering from any joint injuries, disabilities or pain.**
- **You are more than 35lb overweight or have not exercised for a long time.**
- **You are receiving medication on a long-term basis.**

exercise positions and will naturally move from one to the other with ease. I can now perform the General Challenge in about eight minutes because I am so used to it.

TYING AND GRIPPING THE DYNA-BAND

W hen an exercise requires you to tie a knot in the Dyna-Band there is no need to pull the knot tightly. The knot will tighten up anyway as you work. You will find a tightly pulled knot very difficult to undo and risk damaging your Dyna-Band by straining the rubber as you attempt to pull it apart or by digging your fingernails into it. Use a loosely tied double knot as shown in the picture.

Always remove large rings as they may also damage your Dyna-Band.

And one word of warning to male users of the Dyna-Band! It you wear shorts for your Dyna-Band workout protect the hairs on your legs with long socks – the rubber does tend to stick to hairs and pull them out which, as you can imagine, can be quite painful! For exercises where you need to grip the ends of the Dyna-Band you may find that you have to wrap the ends around your hands in order to get the right tension and to provide a steady

Follow these photographs which show how to tie and hold the Dyna-Band.

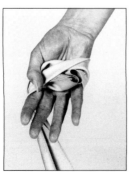

hold whilst working. You may have to experiment with comfortable positions for you but here are a couple of suggestions for ways of wrapping the ends of the Dyna-Band around your hands.

Training Shoes All of the models are wearing training shoes because they provide a firmer base for the Dyna-Band to attach to in exercises that require you to hook the band over your instep. You can easily perform the exercises without shoes though, and certainly for the cool-down stretches you do not need training shoes.

DAYS 1, 3 AND 5

CHEST, ARMS AND ABDOMINALS

Those of us who have had children, and possibly breast fed them, may find that our bust-line is a little lower than we would like it to be! Not only can a sagging bust spoil the line of a close-fitting t-shirt, it can also be uncomfortable and damaging whilst exercising. Of course a good fitting bra should always be worn whilst exercising to prevent any over stretching of supportive tissue but often damage has already been done in the past. The breasts themselves have no muscle tissue and rely on the strength of the chest, or pectoral, muscles to support them. The chest exercises shown here using the Dyna-Band are particularly effective because of the resistance involved and the versatility of the band, providing a large range of exercises to choose from.

And for those of you who wish to increase the size of your bust (and don't wish to invest in silicone implants!) try these exercises as the increased strength in the chest muscles will lift your bust upwards, giving you a more youthful shape and the illusion of increased size.

All of the standing exercises require you to check your posture, preferably sideways in a mirror. Your feet need to be slightly more than hip distance apart, knees relaxed, your bottom tucked in and your stomach pulled in. Shoulders need to be down and relaxed and the chin horizontal to the floor. A padded mat or piece of carpet will be necessary for the floor exercises.

DAYS 1, 3 AND 5   **CHEST, ARMS AND ABDOMINALS**

CHEST PRESS

- Place the Dyna-Band around the upper back and under the armpits.
- Hold on to the ends of the band, adjusting the length by wrapping around your hands to maintain tension.
- Keeping the elbows bent and the hands at head height, press the elbows into the centre of the body and then return to the starting position.

If you look in the mirror whilst doing this exercise you will see your chest being lifted as your elbows squeeze inwards. The movement should be slow and controlled.

Suggested repetitions – 10, rest and repeat if possible.

CHEST, ARMS AND ABDOMINALS   DAYS 1, 3 AND 5

EXTENDED CHEST PRESS

- The Dyna-Band stays in the same position as in the previous exercise.
- With the arms extended move your hands towards each other so that they meet at arm's length in front of your chest.

Again the movement is slow and controlled.

Suggested repetitions – 10, rest and repeat if possible.

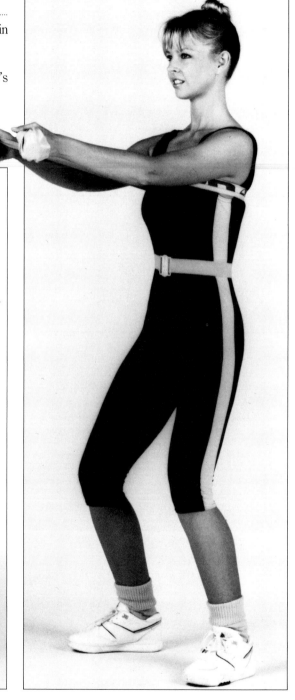

DAYS 1, 3 AND 5

CHEST, ARMS AND ABDOMINALS

SCISSORS

- The Dyna-Band remains stretched across the upper back and under the armpits.
- Extend your arms in front of you as in the extended chest press on the previous page and, keeping the band tight, scissor, starting at waist level and taking four scissor movements to reach head height.
- Return to waist level with another four scissors making sure that you squeeze the arms in towards the chest as you perform the exercise.

The eight scissors in total (four scissors up and four scissors down) make one repetition.

Suggested repetitions – 5, rest and repeat if possible.

CHEST, ARMS AND ABDOMINALS   DAYS 1, 3 AND 5

PULL DOWNS

This exercise will tone up the muscles along the sides of your back and into the waist (latissimus dorsi). This is the area where fat can bulge over a tight-fitting bra or bikini, just below your arm pits on your back.

- Hold the ends of the Dyna-Band in each hand behind your head, maintaining a fairly strong tension. Adjust length by loosely wrapping band around hands.
- Lower your arms, keeping your elbows slightly bent, to waist level.
- Raise again in a controlled manner to return to the starting position.

Suggested repetitions – 15, rest and repeat if possible.

DAYS 1, 3 AND 5　　　　　　　**CHEST, ARMS AND ABDOMINALS**

SEATED ROW

It is important, after working the chest muscles, to follow with exercises for the upper back to maintain and improve the upper body posture. Make a special effort to do this exercise if you tend to be round shouldered.

- Sitting in an upright position hook the Dyna-Band around the soles of your feet holding each end in either hand at about knee level.
- Pull the ends of the band towards you, keeping your elbows close in to the sides of your body. Keep your back in an upright position throughout.
- Return to the starting position with control.

Suggested repetitions – 15, rest and repeat if possible.

YOU CAN NOW STAY IN THIS POSITION READY TO DO THE ABDOMINAL EXERCISES.

The Abdominals and Waist

Some of you will probably be eager to dip straight into this section of the Dyna-Band Challenge as the stomach and waist are classic problem areas. It's perfectly okay to home in on this section, and to increase the suggested number of repetitions if you want to, but remember that the success of the Dyna-Band Challenge is in the combination of exercises for all body parts – so don't neglect the other exercises for the chest and arms. The abdominal area is often very weak, particularly in women who have had several children. Because of this weakness, posture is often poor and the muscles of the low back are placed under considerable strain. The overall result can be a pot belly and arched lower back. Unfortunately, not only does this posture look ugly and unflattering, it can also cause medical problems, eventually causing parts of the vertebrae in your lower spine to rub together – the result of which is the dreaded backache! You don't even have to be overweight to have a pot belly either – it can occur just from years of poor posture and incorrect exercises. I have taught many students over the years who are naturally thin, with slim arms and legs, but who have a pot belly due to weak abdominal muscles and poor posture. Often they have made the problem much worse by going to exercise classes taught by unqualified teachers or copied unsafe exercises from books. Of course, if you are overweight as well as having weak stomach muscles the problem is exaggerated.

So – why should these Dyna-Band stomach exercises be any more successful than the hundreds of others you've already tried?

- They are an expertly balanced combination of exercises working the four abdominal muscles in rotation. Therefore it is important that you keep to the suggested order for this section.

- The resistance provided by the Dyna-Band will force your muscles to contract strongly. You can really feel those muscles working deeply and powerfully.

- If you pull in the lower part of your stomach and push your back down into the floor whilst doing these exercises you will feel a tightening in your pelvic floor muscles. In other words – your sex life can improve! (See the case histories in chapter 2).

- In some of the positions the Dyna-Band acts as a postural aid and support enabling you to perform the exercises safely and correctly.

- These exercises are safe and easy to perform.

NOTE – Some of the exercises require you to loop the Dyna-Band around a heavy fixed object such as a table leg or heavy chair. I use my dining room table leg – you may have a heavy chair or desk, a stair banister, or even a pedestal wash basin or bidet that you can loop the Dyna-Band around! Whatever object you use it must be immoveable for the exercise to be safe (I don't want you to have furniture toppling down on your head!) and effective as an abdominal exercise.

SAFETY REMINDER

- On *NO* account perform these exercises if you are pregnant or think that you might be pregnant.

- If you regularly suffer from backache, substitute these exercises with the abdominal exercises from the specialist section in chapter 5.

- If you experience pain or discomfort in your neck during these exercises try to relax your neck and shoulders; keep the movements slow and controlled and cut down on the number of repetitions if necessary, building up gradually to the suggested number. If your neck continues to cause pain or discomfort, substitute these exercises with the specialist abdominal exercises from chapter 5.

CHEST, ARMS AND ABDOMINALS

LOWER TUMMY TIGHTENER

- Lie on your back, pull your stomach in and press your low back firmly into the floor.
- Take each end of the Dyna-Band in either hand and hook the band over the soles of your feet.
- Bring your knees into your chest.
- Push the soles of your feet into the air stretching the Dyna-Band. (You don't need to straighten your legs completely.)
- Relax the knees back into the chest.
- As you push the band away from your body breathe out.

Suggested repetitions – 10, rest and repeat if possible. Whilst doing this exercise squeeze your pelvic floor muscles in as you push your legs up. (In case you don't know where your pelvic floor muscles are, imagine you are stopping yourself urinating whilst midstream!)

CHEST, ARMS AND ABDOMINALS

WAIST TWIST

- Take each end of the Dyna-Band in either hand and place it across your back and under your armpits.
- Lie on your back with your knees bent and your feet flat on the floor. Press your low back firmly into the floor.
- Keeping one elbow on the floor, lift the other arm off the floor, holding firmly onto the Dyna-Band aiming the elbow to meet the opposite knee.
- Relax slowly back down to the floor and then repeat with the *same* arm.

Suggested repetitions – 10 on one side, 10 on other side and then repeat.

This will do wonders for your waist if you can keep the non-working elbow on the floor causing a twist as you cross.

CHEST, ARMS AND ABDOMINALS   DAYS 1, 3 AND 5

STOMACH CURL

- Loop the Dyna-Band around a heavy fixed object and take one end of the band in each hand.
- Bend your knees in the air keeping them directly above your hips. Cross your ankles.
- Lift your head, shoulders and arms off the floor bringing both elbows in towards the thighs. Breathe out as you lift up.
- Relax your head and shoulders back down to the floor.

Suggested repetitions – 10, rest and repeat if possible.

WAIST WHITTLER

- Remain in the same position, with the Dyna-Band looped around a fixed object.
- Bend your knees and place your feet flat on the floor.
- Keeping one elbow fixed on the floor reach the other hand across to the opposite knee pulling one shoulder gently off the floor.
- Relax back down to the starting position.

Suggested repetitions – 10 on each side.

CHEST, ARMS AND ABDOMINALS

STOMACH CRUNCH

- Keep the Dyna-Band looped around a heavy fixed object.
- Lie on your back holding the ends of the Dyna-Band in each hand and bend your knees placing your feet flat on the floor.
- Press the small of your back firmly into the floor.
- Lift your head and shoulders off the floor, bringing the band with you, and *at the same time* bring your knees in towards your chest. Aim to meet your elbows to your knees.
- Breathe out as you 'crunch' in.
- Relax back down to the floor.

Suggested repetitions – 10.

This is a demanding exercise and it may take a little while for you to get used to it – but be patient because you will be thrilled with the results it gives!

Exercises for the Upper Arms

Y ou may not notice that the tops of your arms are getting flabby during the winter months as we have very little opportunity to display them. A sunny spell in the spring may persuade you into sleeveless dresses and t-shirts and it's only then that you realise emergency measures are needed before summer arrives!

The fronts of our upper arms (biceps) don't tend to be as much of a problem as the backs (triceps). The back of the arm tends to be a very flabby area in women because it is a little-used muscle compared to the front of the arm which is used regularly in everyday household chores such as lifting, carrying and shopping. Exercises without added resistance tend to be very unsuccessful for the arms. With the Dyna-Band, however, they are fantastic as your muscles will work against the resistance without you hardly realising it. The exercises then become really effective.

There is hardly anything as ageing as flabby arms so if this is your particular problem you may decide to do more than the recommended number of repetitions. Also remember that you can turn to the specialist exercise chapter for additional exercises for this part of the body.

Valda is the model for these exercises as she feels that she is at the age where she needs to start worrying about her upper arms. As you get older the backs of your arms do tend to lose their tone more quickly so Valda was very pleased to have a go at these – she is using the pink band which is suitable for the older age group.

Kevin is shown in some of the arm exercises in the Ultimate Challenge as he has been working out with the Dyna-Band for several weeks now and is a wonderful advertisement for the success of the band because he feels that the arm exercises are just as effective for him as his daily workout in the gym. So the Dyna-Band really is an exercise product for the whole family; men can use the purple or grey band and strengthen their muscles with simple exercises that are neither particularly feminine nor masculine. Women can tone up their muscles to gain better definition and shape, and children can follow the exercises that are specially recommended for them. Get the whole family working out together!

DAYS 1, 3 AND 5   **CHEST, ARMS AND ABDOMINALS**

FOREARM CURL

This exercise works the front of your upper arm.
- Secure one end of the Dyna-Band by standing on it with your right foot.
- Hold the other end of the Dyna-Band in your right hand winding it loosely around your hand if necessary so that there is plenty of tension.
- Stand with your knees slightly bent, your bottom tucked in and your tummy pulled tight.
- Starting position is with your hand at waist height.
- With the palm of your hand facing upwards pull the end of the Dyna-Band towards your shoulder.
- Relax the Dyna-Band back to waist height but still keeping the band 'tight'.

Suggested repetitions – 10 on each arm.

UNDERARM KICK BACK

This exercise will tighten up the backs of your arms and make you proud to wear evening dresses and summer clothes if you are female, and singlets if you are male!
- Remain in the same position as for the exercise above.
- Keeping the elbow close to the body extend your arm behind you. You don't need to completely straighten your elbow.
- Relax back to the starting position.

Suggested repetitions – 10 on each arm.

HIPS, THIGHS AND BUTTOCKS

I f you feel that the shape of your legs closely resembles a pair of jodhpurs and that your thighs appear to be wearing saddlebags – this section is definitely for you! Firm and well-toned thighs can also reduce the 'dimpling' effect that cellulite produces – a common problem, particularly amongst women. If you go back to our case-histories in chapter 2 you will notice that results on the hip, thigh and buttock areas are outstanding. For some women inches were dramatically lost and in all cases a firmer shape was achieved. Results were often noticeable after as little as three or four weeks of performing these exercises, and for relatively little effort. This is because the Dyna-Band enables you to isolate the thigh and buttock area very effectively and the added resistance means that fewer repetitions are needed than when performing the same exercise without the band. Linda, the model who is performing these exercises, has always had a problem with her thighs and buttocks as they are out of proportion to the rest of her body. She has been doing these exercises three times a week for several weeks now and is delighted with the effect.

For exercises where the Dyna-Band needs to be tied, use a loosely tied double knot and take care not to use your fingernails when untying it or you may cause damage to the latex rubber and shorten the life of your band. Also, try to keep the natural width of the band before tying, as this will prevent the band from rolling up and becoming uncomfortable and as a result less effective. I have organised these exercises so that you will not have to tie and untie the Dyna-Band too much so it will be time saving if you follow the suggested order of exercises.

Remember only to perform what is comfortable and to stop if you feel any pain or extreme fatigue. Gradually build up to the suggested number of repetitions if you are a beginner.

DAYS 2, 4 AND 6   **HIPS, THIGHS AND BUTTOCKS**

SIDE LEG RAISES – BENT KNEE

This exercise works wonders for the outer thigh area.

- Tie the Dyna-Band securely around your thighs just above your knees.
- Lie on one side with your knees bent and line your heels up with your bottom.
- Keeping your toe and kneecap facing forward (this is very important or you won't focus on the correct muscle) slowly raise and lower the upper leg in a controlled manner. The knee must stay in line with the foot throughout the movement.

Suggested repetitions – 15 and then repeat on the other leg.

HIPS, THIGHS AND BUTTOCKS   DAYS 2, 4 AND 6

GLUTEAL PRESS

This is a very demanding exercise but is great for the outer thighs and buttocks. Take care though – if you feel tired or uncomfortable don't attempt the suggested number of repetitions.

- Keep the Dyna-Band tied in exactly the same position as for the previous exercise.

- Lie on one side, knees bent, heels in line with bottom as in side leg raise on previous page.
- Press the knee of the top leg towards the floor and then, with the sole of the foot facing the ceiling, press the leg upwards.

Suggested repetitions – 10 and repeat on other leg.

INNER THIGH RAISES

Often used this position is still the most effective for working the inner thigh area. Note though that this position only allows for a small movement in the working leg and will therefore be performed at a much quicker pace than the two previous exercises.

- Tie the Dyna-Band quite tightly around your ankles. Lie on one side.
- Bring your top leg to rest on the mat in front of you and extend your lower leg.
- Hook the Dyna-Band over the instep of your lower, extended leg.
- Lift and lower the extended leg making sure that you keep the foot and knee of this leg facing forward. The Dyna-Band needs to be kept 'tight' throughout this movement.

Suggested repetitions – 15 and then repeat on the other leg.

HIPS, THIGHS AND BUTTOCKS

BUTTOCK SQUEEZES

- Keep the Dyna-Band in the same position as in the previous exercise (tied around your ankles) and carefully roll over onto your stomach.
- Rest your forehead on your hands.
- Raise one leg as high as you can.
- Squeeze in your buttock at the same time.

- Release the leg and the squeeze gradually. To make this exercise really work you must not be tempted to cheat by raising your hips off the mat. Keep your hips pressed firmly into the mat throughout.

Suggested repetitions – 15, rest and repeat on the other leg.

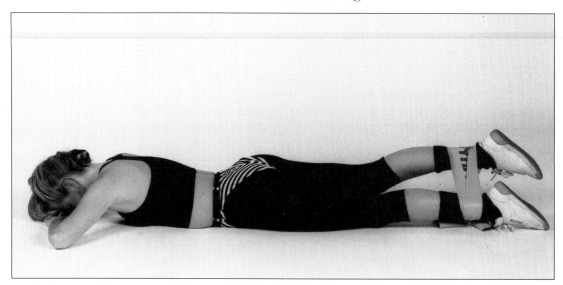

BACK OF THIGH (HAMSTRING) CURL IN

This exercise will work the backs of your thighs and buttocks.

- Remain in the same position as for the previous exercise with the Dyna-Band tied around your ankles but hook the band over one instep.
- Rest your forehead on your hands.
- Slowly curl one leg in to about 90 degrees. (You are NOT aiming to curl in as far as your bottom.)
- Resist by pressing the opposite leg down into the floor.
- Slowly lower the curled leg.

Suggested repetitions – 15 and repeat on the other leg.

HIPS, THIGHS AND BUTTOCKS   DAYS **2, 4** AND **6**

BUTTOCK LIFTS

- Transfer the Dyna-Band to your thighs from the previous exercise. (You will have to re-tie the band to give you maximum length.)
- Keep natural width of band.
- Pin part of the band to the floor with one knee.
- Raise the other leg, with knee bent, as high as you comfortably can making sure that your hips face the floor, your head is down and that your back is straight.
- Lower the knee only to hip level when you release.

Suggested repetitions – 15 and repeat on the other leg.

DAYS **2, 4** AND **6**   **HIPS, THIGHS AND BUTTOCKS**

TAUT THIGH PUSH

You should feel this exercise working the fronts of your thighs which is very important as we rely on this group of muscles (the quadriceps) in everyday activities such as walking, bending, straightening and climbing up stairs.

- Hook the Dyna-Band around one foot. Sit in semi-reclining position (leaning back on your elbows) and hold the ends of the band in each hand.
- Bend the knee of your other leg and place that foot flat on the floor.
- Bend your knee of the leg that has the Dyna-Band attached but keep the band tight. (You may have to wrap some of the Dyna-Band loosely around your hands to keep this tension.)
- Push your foot away from your body but keep your hands in close to your waist so that the Dyna-Band is stretched fully.
- Relax back to the starting position.

Suggested repetitions – 15 on each leg.

Tom (age 11) is shown doing a variation of this exercise.

HIPS, THIGHS AND BUTTOCKS

CALF AND SHIN STRENGTHENER

This exercise will be good for you if you have weak ankles and need extra muscular support in this area. It will also strengthen your shins which is important if you have ruined them with high-impact aerobics.

- Remain in the same position as the previous exercise with the Dyna-Band hooked around one foot or you can sit up if you feel more comfortable.
- Keeping the tension on the band slowly point and flex your toe working as hard as possible against the resistance the Dyna-Band provides.

Suggested repetitions – 20 on each foot.

SUMMARY OF EXERCISES

DAYS 1, 3 AND 5
CHEST, ARMS AND ABDOMINALS

EXERCISE	REPETITIONS	EXTRA
CHEST PRESS	10, rest, 10	5
EXTENDED CHEST PRESS	10, rest, 10	5
SCISSORS	5, rest, 5	2
PULL DOWNS	15, rest, 15	5
SEATED ROW	15, rest, 15	5
LOWER TUMMY TIGHTENER	10, rest, 10	5
WAIST TWIST	10 each side, rest, 10	5
STOMACH CURL	10, rest, 10	5
WAIST WHITTLER	10 each side	5
STOMACH CRUNCH	10	2
FOREARM CURL	10 each arm	5
UNDERARM KICK BACK	10 each arm	5

DAYS 2, 4 AND 6
HIPS, THIGHS AND BUTTOCKS

SIDE LEG RAISE	15 each leg	5
GLUTEAL PRESS	10 each leg	2
INNER THIGH RAISE	15 each leg	5
BUTTOCK SQUEEZE	15 each leg	5
BACK THIGH CURL IN	15 each leg	5
BUTTOCK LIFTS	15 each leg	5
TAUT THIGH PUSH	15 each leg	5
CALF AND SHIN STRENGTHENER	20 each foot	5

When you are able to comfortably manage all of the suggested repetitions, make sure that you can also do the number in the 'extra' column before you either progress on to a stronger Dyna-Band or move on to the Dyna-Band Ultimate Challenge.

To remind you, here are the different colours of Dyna-Band in order of increasing strength:
PINK Very beginner level, older age groups, pre- and post-natal.
GREEN Beginner level, new to exercise or unfit and out of condition.
PURPLE General to intermediate level, exercising regularly.
GREY Advanced, experienced exerciser.

CHAPTER SIX

THE ULTIMATE CHALLENGE

I have called this the 'Ultimate Challenge' because it is a daily workout that you will, hopefully, ultimately build up to and one that will become your goal. And when you finally do get to this stage of the book you will most definitely have achieved a new and more beautiful body. Having said this, do not feel under any pressure to move on to this more advanced workout. Our case-histories used only the General Challenge to achieve their fantastic results – and you *DO* only need 10 minutes a day with the Dyna-Band to tone your muscles and change your shape.

Some of you though will just get 'hooked' on the Dyna-Band way of exercising. You will love feeling in control of your body and will be proud of your self-discipline in fitting your exercises into a chaotic lifestyle. Some of you may become addicted to that feeling of euphoria which occurs after exercising when a chemical substance is released giving you an 'exercise high!' You may be finding everyday chores and tasks easier. Everything becomes less stressful. The saying 'healthy body – healthy mind' is certainly true. It can be stressful to be called upstairs to the children for the umpteenth time whilst trying to get them to go to sleep – but less so if your leg muscles are strong and fit and less likely to tire! It can be tiring having to tidy up after a boisterous and messy family but less so if your arm and leg muscles are well conditioned and can cope with extra work. And of course – not only are you beginning to find life less tiring and chores less tedious – your body is also looking good!

For these reasons you may decide to take on a more challenging workout by moving on to the Dyna-Band Ultimate Challenge. If, on the other hand, you are quite content to continue with the General Challenge that's fine, but try not to let your Dyna-Band exercising lapse as you will need to keep it up to maintain and improve your new shape.

Who is the Dyna-Band Ultimate Challenge For?
The exercises have been designed for either:
- Those of you who have successfully worked through the Dyna-Band General Challenge several times and are beginning to feel that you are ready for a more demanding and stimulating workout, or
- Experienced exercisers who have regularly followed a programme of exercise and feel that the General Challenge will not maintain their level of fitness.

How do you know when to progress on to the Dyna-Band Ultimate Challenge?
- When you have progressed through the four different colours and strengths of Dyna-

Band – pink, green, purple and grey (see the chapter on page 14 about selecting the right Dyna-Band) and feel that the exercises are 'comfortably' manageable. In other words – you no longer feel tension in your muscles after about 8 or 10 repetitions.

- When you have become familiar with the exercise positions in the General Challenge and are able to tie the Dyna-Band with ease and work comfortably with it.
- When you can allow yourself a bit more time each day to spend on yourself and your Dyna-Band exercise programme.
- When you have achieved results and have become 'hooked' on the Dyna-Band method of exercising.
- When you feel that you are both physically and mentally ready for a further challenge.

What can you expect to achieve from this advanced Dyna-Band workout?
The programme is a carefully balanced combination of conditioning exercises that will give your body a more clearly defined shape if you follow it regularly.

- You will feel in control of your body as it becomes physically stronger and fitter.
- Your body awareness and posture will improve – aches and pains may disappear.
- Your sense of achievement will increase your confidence and self-awareness.

If, by now, you have decided that it is time for you to move on to the Dyna-Band Ultimate Challenge – great, then let's go for it!

The Dyna-Band Ultimate Challenge is based around 15 minutes exercise each day and is in the same format as the General Challenge. You work the chest, abdominals and arms on days 1, 3 and 5 and the thighs and buttocks on days 2, 4 and 6. Alternatively you can work out for 30 minutes every other day by working through all of the exercises in one session three times a week, depending on which suits your lifestyle best. When you start this new challenge you don't have to drop right down to the pink band. This depends on the colour you were using at the end of the General Challenge. If you had worked up to the grey band then I suggest you drop down to either green or purple. If you were working with the purple band before you definitely need to drop down to the green to start with. If you had been using two bands together for the General Challenge you will have to drop one of them for a while until you have got used to the exercises again. It will be very much a case of 'trial and error' – just remember that your muscles should start to feel the workload after about 8 to 10 repetitions of the exercise. Any sooner and the band is too strong for you and any easier means that it is not strong enough.

Once you have worked out which Dyna-Band to use you are ready to go.

CHEST, ARMS AND ABDOMINALS

DON'T FORGET YOUR **POSTURE CHECK** FOR ALL OF THE
STANDING EXERCISES –

- feet slightly more than hip distance apart
- bottom tucked in and stomach tight
- knees relaxed
- shoulders back and down
- chin parallel to the floor

CHEST PRESS

- Place the Dyna-Band around your upper back and under your armpits as shown.
- Hold on to the ends of the band, adjusting the length by wrapping around your hands to maintain tension.
- Keeping your elbows bent and your hands at head height, press your elbows into the centre of your body and then return to the starting position.

Exercise chest muscles with slow and controlled movements.

Suggested repetitions – 20, rest and repeat.

DAYS 1, 3 AND 5   CHEST, ARMS AND ABDOMINALS

EXTENDED CHEST PRESS

- The Dyna-Band stays in the same position as in the previous exercise.
- With your arms extended move your hands towards each other so that they meet at arm's length in front of your chest.

Again the movement should be slow and controlled and you should feel your chest muscles working even harder.

Suggested repetitions
20, rest and repeat.

CHEST, ARMS AND ABDOMINALS   DAYS 1, 3 AND 5

PULL DOWNS

- Hold the ends of the Dyna-Band behind your head maintaining a fairly strong tension. Wrap loosely around hands to adjust length.
- Lower your arms, keeping your elbows slightly bent, to waist level.
- Raise your arms again in a controlled manner to return to the starting position, behind your head. *Suggested repetitions* – 25, rest and repeat.

DAYS 1, 3 AND 5   **CHEST, ARMS AND ABDOMINALS**

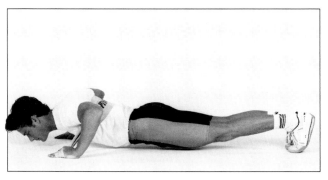

PRESS UPS

There are two positions for this exercise depending on how strong your chest and arm muscles are! Choose the appropriate one from the illustrations – either on your knees which is the easier alternative, or on your toes in a full press up as Kevin is showing.

- Stretch the Dyna-Band across your upper back and under your armpits.
- Either kneeling or on your toes in your selected position pin either end of the Dyna-Band to the floor with your hands which should be wider apart than your shoulders.
- Try to maintain the natural width of the band.
- Lower your body, bending at your elbows, until your nose is just off the floor, keeping your back level. (Do not stick your bottom up in the air!)
- Straighten your elbows and lift your body back to the starting position.

This is a very strenuous exercise and you may have to build up gradually to the suggested number of repetitions. You will feel your chest (pectorals) and upper arm (triceps) muscles working.

Suggested repetitions – 10, rest and repeat.

Abdominal and Waist Exercises

LOWER TUMMY TIGHTENER

- Lie on your back, pull your stomach in and press your low back firmly into the floor.
- Take each end of the Dyna-Band in either hand and hook the band over the soles of your feet.
- Bring your knees into your chest.
- Push the soles of your feet into the air stretching the Dyna-Band. (You don't need to straighten your legs completely.)
- Relax your knees back into your chest.
- As you push the band away from your body breathe out.

DON'T forget to squeeze in your pelvic floor muscles (as if you're trying to stop urinating midstream) as you push the Dyna-Band away from you.

Suggested repetitions – 20, rest and repeat.

CHEST, ARMS AND ABDOMINALS

CRUNCH CURL

- Tie the Dyna-Band around both legs just above your knees.
- Lie on your back and pull your knees into your chest.
- Reach around the outside of your legs and take hold of the Dyna-Band with both hands at the back of your knees.
- Pull your knees towards your chest against the Dyna-Band.
- At the same time lift your head and shoulders off the floor.
- Either leave your hands in the same position or press them forward to increase the resistance.
- Lower slowly.
- Breathe out as you curl in.

Suggested repetitions – 15, rest and repeat.

The rest of the waist and stomach exercises require a heavy or fixed object, such as a heavy chair, sofa, table, stair banister etc, to loop the Dyna-Band around. Alternatively you can ask a partner to fix the Dyna-Band in place for you.

CHEST, ARMS AND ABDOMINALS   DAYS 1, 3 AND 5

BICYCLE

- Loop the Dyna-Band around a heavy object and lie on the floor holding either end of the band above your head.
- Bring one knee in to meet the opposite elbow, lifting your shoulder off the floor to meet the knee and stretching the Dyna-Band.
- The other leg extends outwards at about a 45 degree angle.
- Change legs and arms in a cycling movement.

Suggested repetitions – 20 bicycles, rest and repeat.

NOTE – Make sure that you keep your extended leg quite high. You may damage your back if your leg is extended close to the floor.

DAYS 1, 3 AND 5   **CHEST, ARMS AND ABDOMINALS**

STOMACH CURL

- Stay in the same position as for the previous exercise.
- Bend your knees and cross your ankles in the air.
- Lift your head, shoulders and arms off the floor bringing both elbows in towards the thighs. Breathe out as you lift up.
- Relax your head and shoulders back down to the floor.

Suggested repetitions – 20, rest and repeat.

CHEST, ARMS AND ABDOMINALS   DAYS 1, 3 AND 5

WAIST WHITTLER

- Remain in the same position – with the Dyna-Band looped around a fixed object.
- Bend your knees and place your feet flat on the floor.
- Keeping one elbow fixed on the floor reach the other hand across to the opposite knee pulling one shoulder gently off the floor.
- Relax gently back down to the starting position.

Suggested repetitions – 20 on each side.

DAYS **1, 3** AND **5**   **CHEST, ARMS AND ABDOMINALS**

STOMACH CRUNCH

- Remain in the same position.
- Lie on your back holding the ends of the Dyna-Band in each hand and bend your knees placing your feet flat on the floor.
- Lift your head and shoulders off the floor, bringing the band with you, and – *at the same*

time – bring your knees in towards your chest. Aim to meet your elbows to your knees, without forcing.
- Breathe out as you crunch in.
- Relax back down to the floor.

Suggested repetitions – 10, rest and repeat.

CHEST, ARMS AND ABDOMINALS   DAYS 1, 3 AND 5

Arm Exercises

DIPS (TRICEPS)

- Sit down and place the Dyna-Band across your stomach. Pin either end of the Dyna-Band down with your hands.
- Adjust the length so that the band is tense across your stomach. Maintain the natural width of the band.
- Your hands must face your bottom and be directly under your shoulders.
- Your feet should be flat on the floor and hip distance apart.
- Lift your body off the floor by straightening your elbows.
- Keep your back straight as you lift.
- On the return don't release back down to the floor but continue to lift from an already lifted position if you can.

Suggested repetitions – 15, rest and repeat.

Valda is performing the easier version here – with both feet on the floor. Kevin has gone for an advanced position with one leg extended and held off the floor. Build up to this advanced one if you want to.

DAYS 1, 3 AND 5   **CHEST, ARMS AND ABDOMINALS**

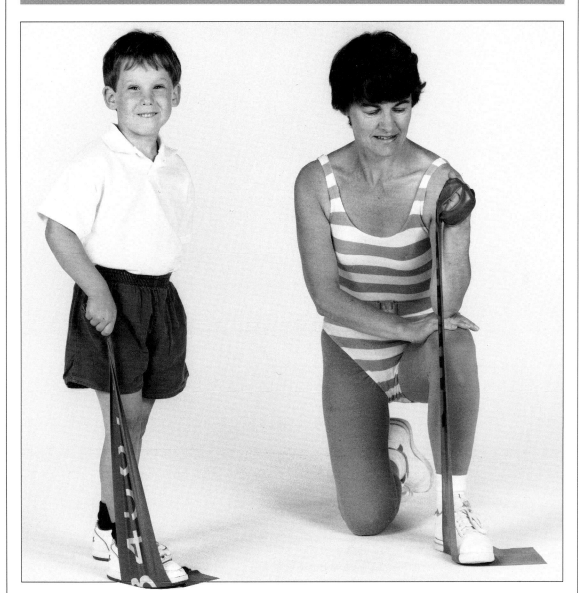

FOREARM CURL (BICEPS)

- Kneel on one knee. Place the Dyna-Band under your foot.
- Hold the end of the Dyna-Band and curl your hand up to your shoulder stretching the band.
- Keep your elbow on the inside of your knee.
- Slowly return.

Suggested repetitions – 20 on each arm.
You can make this harder by shortening the band by loosely wrapping around hand.
Gregory is performing his own version of this exercise by pulling his child's Dyna-Band up as far as he can!

CHEST, ARMS AND ABDOMINALS   DAYS 1, 3 AND 5

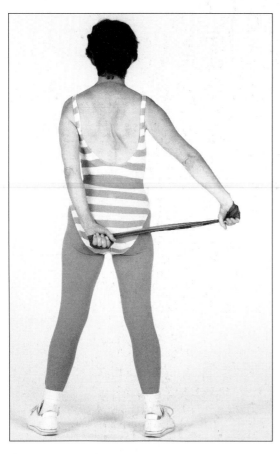 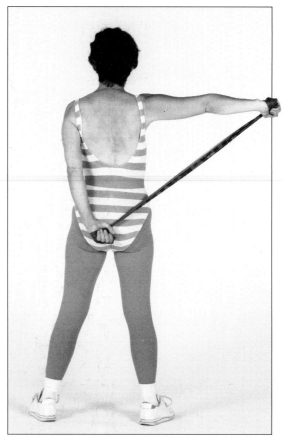

SHOULDER LIFTS

- In a standing position, check your posture.
- Grip one end of the Dyna-Band behind your back and rest it against your bottom.
- Grip the other end of the Dyna-Band with your opposite hand.
- Relax this opposite hand alongside your body.
- Raise your arm to shoulder level.
- Slowly lower back down to your side.

Suggested repetitions – 20 on each arm.

DAYS 1, 3 AND 5

CHEST, ARMS AND ABDOMINALS

ARM PULL

- Keep the same standing position as for the previous exercise.
- Wrap the Dyna-Band loosely around both of your hands which should be shoulder width apart.
- Face the palms of your hands upwards.
- Extend your arms in front of your body.
- Pull your arms apart pinching your shoulder blades together.
- Slowly return your arms to the starting position.

This exercise will work your upper back and shoulders. Again, Gregory is performing his own version of the exercise!

Suggested repetitions – 10, rest and repeat.

HIPS, THIGHS AND BUTTOCKS

Remember that you do not have to complete the suggested number of repetitions – build up to them gradually and take rests whenever you need them. When you get to the stage where the repetitions suggested are comfortable there is nothing to stop you increasing them, although your daily challenge will then take rather more than 15 minutes.

GLUTEAL PRESS

- Tie the Dyna-Band around your thighs, just above your knees.
- Lie on one side, knees bent, and your hips in line with your bottom.
- Press the knee of the top leg towards the floor and then, with the sole of your foot facing the ceiling, press your leg upwards.

You will feel this exercise working your outside thigh and into your buttocks.

Suggested repetitions – 20 on each leg.

DAYS **2, 4** AND **6**   **HIPS, THIGHS AND BUTTOCKS**

SIDE LEG RAISES – STRAIGHT LEG

- Transfer the Dyna-Band to your ankles and lie on your side. (You may not have to tighten the band – it depends how strong your outer thighs are. The slacker the Dyna-Band the easier the exercise.)

- Straighten your legs out and slowly lift the top leg as far as you can.
- Keep your hips and knees facing forward.
- Lower the leg under control.

Suggested repetitions – 20 on each leg.

HIPS, THIGHS AND BUTTOCKS   DAYS 2, 4 AND 6

INNER THIGH RAISES

Note that this movement will be performed at a quicker speed than the exercise before as it involves a more limited range.

- Tie the Dyna-Band quite tightly around your ankles. Lie on one side.
- Bring your top leg to rest on the mat in front of you and extend your lower leg.

- Hook the Dyna-Band over the instep of your lower, extended leg.
- Lift and lower the extended leg. Make sure you keep the foot and knee of this leg facing forward.

The Dyna-Band needs to be kept taut throughout this movement.

Suggested repetitions – 20 on each leg.

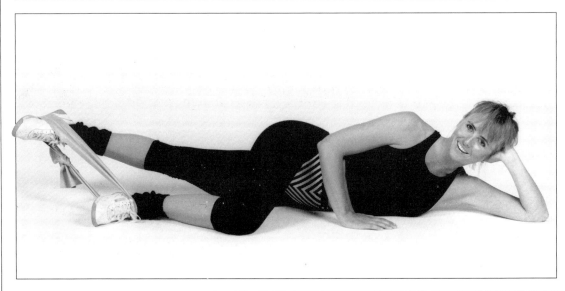

DAYS **2, 4** AND **6**   ## HIPS, THIGHS AND BUTTOCKS

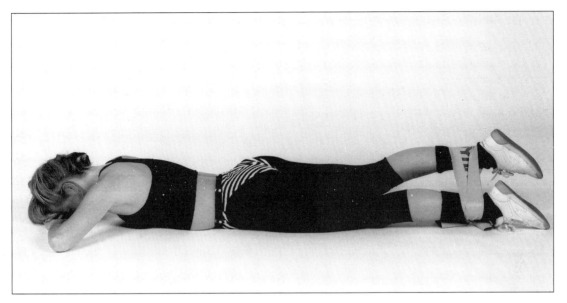

BUTTOCK SQUEEZES

- Keep the Dyna-Band in the same position as in the previous exercise.
- Rest your forehead on your hands.
- Raise one leg as high as you can and squeeze in your buttock at the same time.

- Release the leg and the squeeze gradually. Lower the leg.

Keep your hips pressed firmly into the mat throughout this exercise.

Suggested repetitions – 30 on each leg.

HIPS, THIGHS AND BUTTOCKS   DAYS 2, 4 AND 6

HAMSTRING CURL IN

- Lie on your stomach in the same position as for the previous exercise with the Dyna-Band still tied around your ankles, but hook the band over one instep.
- Rest your forehead on your hands.
- Curl one leg in to about 90 degrees (you are *not* aiming to curl in as far as your bottom).
- Resist by pressing the opposite leg down into the floor.
- Slowly lower the curled leg.

Suggested repetitions – 15 on each leg and then repeat.

OUTER THIGH PULL

- Remain lying in the same position with the Dyna-Band tied around your ankles.
- Pull one leg out to the side as far as you can.
- Keep your hips and toes in contact with the floor.
- Relax the leg back to the starting position.

Suggested repetitions – 10 on each leg and then repeat. This is a great exercise for the outside of your thighs but it is quite strenuous! Build up to the reps gradually if it tires you.

DAYS **2, 4** AND **6**   **HIPS, THIGHS AND BUTTOCKS**

LEG PRESS

- Tie the Dyna-Band around your thighs, just above your knees. Try to maintain the natural width of the band.
- Get into the elbows and knees position.
- Slide the Dyna-Band down one leg and onto the instep of one foot.

- Extend this leg straight back – NO higher than your buttocks.
- Return the leg slowly.

Your stomach needs to be pulled in and your back kept flat throughout this exercise.

Suggested repetitions – 20 on each leg.

HIPS, THIGHS AND BUTTOCKS   DAYS 2, 4 AND 6

BUTTOCK LIFTS

- Transfer the Dyna-Band to your thighs (just above your knees) from the previous exercise. You may not need to untie the band.
- Pin part of the Dyna-Band to the floor with one knee.
- Raise the other leg, with your knee bent, as high as you comfortably can making sure that your hips face the floor and that your back stays flat.
- Lower the knee to hip level only when you release.

Suggested repetitions – 15 on each leg and then repeat.

HIPS, THIGHS AND BUTTOCKS

THIGH EXTENSION

- Tie the Dyna-Band around your ankles.
- Sit on the floor and lean back on your elbows.
- Bend your knees so your feet are flat on the floor pinning the Dyna-Band to the floor with one foot.
- Extend one leg.
- Lower but try not to touch the floor between the movements.

Suggested repetitions – 15 on each leg and then repeat. This exercise will tone up the fronts of your thighs.

DAYS 2, 4 AND 6   HIPS, THIGHS AND BUTTOCKS

CALF AND SHIN STRENGTHENER

- Sit upright and hook the Dyna-Band around the instep of one foot.
- Keeping the tension on the Dyna-Band slowly point and flex your toe working hard against the resistance provided by the band.

Suggested repetitions – 20 on each foot and then repeat.

SUMMARY OF EXERCISES

DAYS 1, 3 AND 5	
CHEST, ARMS AND ABDOMINALS	
EXERCISE	REPETITIONS
CHEST PRESS	20, rest, 20
EXTENDED CHEST PRESS	20, rest, 20
PULL DOWNS	25, rest, 25
PRESS UPS	10, rest, 10
LOWER TUMMY TIGHTENER	20, rest, 20
CRUNCH CURL	15, rest, 15
BICYCLE	20, rest, 20
STOMACH CURL	20, rest, 20
WAIST WHITTLER	20 each side
STOMACH CRUNCH	10, rest, 10
DIPS	15, rest, 15
FOREARM CURL	20 each arm
SHOULDER LIFTS	20 each arm
ARM PULL	10, rest, 10

DAYS 2, 4 AND 6	
HIPS, THIGHS AND BUTTOCKS	
EXERCISE	SUGGESTED REPETITIONS
SIDE LEG RAISES (STRAIGHT LEG)	20 each leg
GLUTEAL PRESS	20 each leg
INNER THIGH RAISES	20 each leg
BUTTOCK SQUEEZES	30 each leg
HAMSTRING CURL IN	15 each leg and repeat
OUTER THIGH PULL	10 each leg and repeat
LEG PRESS	20 each leg
BUTTOCK LIFTS	15 each leg and repeat
THIGH EXTENSION	15 each leg and repeat
CALF AND SHIN STRENGTHENER	20 each foot and repeat

CHAPTER SEVEN

COOL DOWN STRETCHES

Throughout the exercise classes I have taught over the years I have often found that the stretching section is the part of the class people often consider to be of least importance. It's the part where people tend to 'slope' off with excuses about 'going somewhere in a rush' or 'I've got to get back for the babysitter'. People often feel that all the 'real' work is over – that the exercises where muscles are worked by repeatedly contracting them is the only part worth doing. They often feel, quite wrongly of course, that stretching is only for relaxation and provides no exercise-related benefits.

You may be tempted to do the same thing and skip the following stretches that should be done at the end of your daily Dyna-Band Challenge. There are several reasons why this would be unwise. These stretches will return muscles to their normal length after they have been repeatedly shortened in the Dyna-Band Challenge. This means that:

- Your muscles are less likely to become tight, knotted and bulky. (Have you ever noticed how runners who don't stretch after training end up with bulky calves and bulging leg muscles?)
- Muscles are less likely to become stiff and sore after exercising. Extreme muscle soreness could stop you exercising for the next few days which would interrupt your Dyna-Band Challenge programme.
- Stretching will help to improve your posture.
- You should feel refreshed and alive again after the stretching exercises rather than tired and exhausted!

Match the appropriate stretches with your day's exercises. For example, days 1, 3 and 5 concentrate on chest, abdominal and arm exercises – for these days you need to look at the stretches for those areas. Days 2, 4 and 6 concentrate on calf, shin, thigh and buttock exercises to which you need to match the correct stretches. If you have chosen to do your Dyna-Band Challenge every other day for 20 minutes, performing all of the exercises in one session, you will need to stretch out all areas of the body.

I'm sure you've noticed that some of us are more flexible than others. How far you can stretch largely depends on the shape of your joints and how the bones meet together. (There is no such thing as being 'double-jointed' by the way! The expression just means hyper flexible.) How flexible your joints are also depends on how regularly you stretch – you should find that your flexibility improves a great deal if you perform these stretches daily.

Before you begin these stretching exercises it is important to bear in mind that:

- Stretching is very individual and therefore you must only stretch as far as is comfortable. No pain should be felt at all, only a mild tension in the muscle being lengthened. Hilary is very flexible in her hip area and can get into all of these positions comfortably. You may not be able to stretch as far as her at first but that does not matter – the stretch will still be effective for you.

- Some of the stretches have a general and an ultimate label. Start with the general exercises if you haven't stretched for a while and know that you are not very flexible. After a while you may want to experiment to see which is the most suitable level for you. You could find that in some areas of your body you are flexible and can do the ultimate stretch and yet in other areas you may have to stick with the general level.

- You must make the time to spend a few well-deserved minutes relaxing and stretching after your daily Dyna-Band Challenge. Play some soothing music if you are able and, if it is the end of the day, dim the lights. Ease slowly and carefully into the stretch positions and hold each one for about 8 to 10 seconds before you release.

CHEST, ABDOMINAL AND ARM STRETCHES

REMEMBER ALL STRETCHES SHOULD BE HELD FOR ABOUT 8 TO 10 SECONDS. ON NO ACCOUNT MUST YOU 'BOUNCE' IN ANY OF THE POSITIONS AS YOU COULD DAMAGE YOUR MUSCLES OR JOINTS.

UPPER ARM (GENERAL)

- Sit upright on an exercise mat or carpeting.
- Either cross your legs or bend your knees, whichever is the more comfortable.
- Bring one arm across your chest resting your hand on the back of the opposite shoulder.
- Use your other hand to gently push the arm across the chest. (Press on the upper part of the arm and not the elbow.)
- Repeat the stretch with your other arm.

You will feel the stretch in your shoulder and the back of your upper arm (triceps).

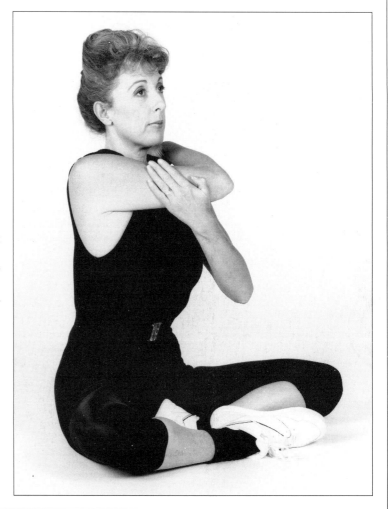

UPPER ARM (ULTIMATE)

- Sit upright with your legs crossed or knees bent.
- Take one arm over your shoulder and let it travel as far possible down your back.
- Bring your other arm behind your waist to join hands. (You may only be able to brush your fingers together.)
- Change your arms around to repeat the stretch.

You will feel the stretch in your shoulder and the back of your upper arm (tricep).

CHEST, ARMS AND ABDOMINALS DAYS 1, 3 AND 5

CHEST (GENERAL AND ULTIMATE)

- In the same position as the previous stretches.
- Clasp your hands together behind your back.
- Squeeze your shoulder blades together.

By doing this exercise properly, you will feel the stretch across the front of your chest (pectorals).

DAYS 1, 3 AND 5　　　　　　　　**CHEST, ARMS AND ABDOMINALS**

UPPER BACK AND SHOULDERS (GENERAL AND ULTIMATE)

- Sit in the same position as before.
- Clasp your hands together in front of you.
- Push your arms away from you at about chin level.

- Round your shoulders as you push your arms away.

You will feel this stretch across your upper back (trapezius).

CHEST, ARMS AND ABDOMINALS   DAYS 1, 3 AND 5

SIDE (GENERAL AND ULTIMATE)

- Sit upright with legs crossed in front of you.
- Rest one hand on your waist or thigh.
- Reach the other arm up and over your head as far as you comfortably can. Don't lift your bottom off the floor.
- Change arms to stretch on the other side.

You will feel this stretch up the side of your body and into your waist.

DAYS 1, 3 AND 5   CHEST, ARMS AND ABDOMINALS

WAIST AND ABDOMINALS (GENERAL)

- Lie on your back on a mat.
- Bend your knees and let them flop down to the left.
- Bring your arms gently across your chest and let them rest over to the right side of your body.
- Swop the arm and leg position to stretch the other side of the waist.

CHEST, ARMS AND ABDOMINALS   DAYS 1, 3 AND 5

ABDOMINALS (ULTIMATE)

- Lie on your stomach on a mat.
- Resting on your forearms gently push your upper body off the floor.

- Keep your hips on the floor throughout. DON'T DO THIS STRETCH IF YOU HAVE A LOW BACK PROBLEM.

ALL OVER (GENERAL AND ULTIMATE)

- Lying on your back, stretch your arms and your legs away from each other.
- You should feel the stretch throughout your body. This is probably similar to the stretch you do before you get out of bed in the morning! It always feels good!

DAYS 2, 4 AND 6

BUTTOCK, THIGH AND LOWER LEG STRETCHES

REMEMBER THAT ALL OF THESE STRETCHES MUST BE HELD FOR ABOUT 8 TO 10 SECONDS. DO NOT BE TEMPTED TO 'BOUNCE' IN ANY OF THE POSITIONS.

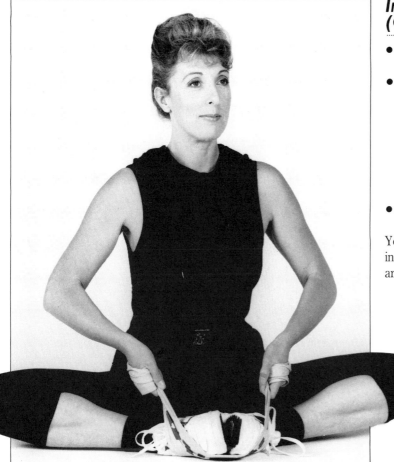

INNER THIGH (GENERAL)

- Sit upright on a mat with the soles of your feet together.
- If you find it difficult to sit with your back straight in this position wrap the Dyna-Band around the soles of your feet and around your hands. Use the Dyna-Band to pull yourself up straight as Hilary has done.
- Press your knees towards the floor.

You will feel a stretch along the insides of your thighs (the groin area) and possibly in your back.

BUTTOCK, THIGH AND LOWER LEG   DAYS 2, 4 AND 6

INNER THIGH (ULTIMATE)

- Sit upright and extend your legs outwards.
- Lift up straight so that you are not in a slouched position. (If you cannot straighten up the stretch position may be too difficult for you or you may simply need to bring your legs closer together.)
- Lean forward to increase the stretch.

You will feel the stretch in the groin area.

BUTTOCK, THIGH AND LOWER LEG

OUTER THIGH (GENERAL)

- Lie on your side, your body in a straight line.
- Cross your top leg over the lower leg and let it drop down onto the floor in front of you.
- Roll over and repeat the stretch on the other leg.

You should feel the stretch on the outside of your thigh.

BUTTOCKS AND OUTER THIGH (GENERAL AND ULTIMATE)

- Lie on your back and bring your knees into your chest.
- Put the heel of one foot onto your opposite knee.
- Straighten the leg that is acting as a support for your heel.
- You can pull the straight leg closer to your body with your hand if you wish (as Hilary is doing in the picture).

BUTTOCK, THIGH AND LOWER LEG   DAYS **2, 4** AND **6**

BACK OF THIGH – HAMSTRINGS (GENERAL)

- Lie on your back and bend both knees, placing both feet flat on the floor.
- Hug one knee into chest then extend lower part of leg towards the ceiling.

NOTE – your leg does not have to straighten at your knee – you only need to go as far as is comfortable. Keep your knee close to your chest.

DAYS 2, 4 AND 6   BUTTOCK, THIGH AND LOWER LEG

BACK OF THIGH – HAMSTRINGS (ULTIMATE)

- Sit upright with your legs straight out in front of you.
- If you find it difficult to sit up straight, wrap the Dyna-Band around the soles of your feet and pull yourself upright.
- Gradually lean forward if you wish to increase the stretch.

CALF (GENERAL AND ULTIMATE)

- Sit in the same position as for the previous exercise.
- Flex your feet so that your toes point up to the ceiling.
- Hold for 8 to 10 seconds and then repeat the stretch again.

FRONT THIGH – QUADS (GENERAL AND ULTIMATE)

- Lie on your stomach or on your side (whichever position you find most comfortable).
- Take hold of one foot and gently pull towards your bottom (if you are lying on your side this will be the top leg).
- Change legs and repeat on the other side.

IF YOU HAVE A KNEE INJURY DON'T PULL ON YOUR FOOT.
When you have completed all of your stretches stand up slowly, rolling up through your spine, and give yourself a 'shake out' to loosen up your joints and wake you up a bit!

CHAPTER EIGHT

SPECIFIC EXERCISES FOR PROBLEM AREAS

Y ou may have an area of your body which you particularly want to tone up because it has always been a problem for you. For example you may have a 'pear shaped' body with heavy thighs and buttocks but a small waist and upper body. Your abdominals and waist may be weak after pregnancy and childbirth or other abdominal operations. Another problem can be flabby, out of condition, upper arms. If you are nodding and saying 'yes' to all of these things then the General Challenge will give you an 'all over body' workout which will help you in all of these areas. If, however, you do have one or two particular problems dip into this section and look for the appropriate exercises. You really need to do these exercises in addition to your daily Dyna-Band Challenge to gain your fabulous new figure. The advantage is that you don't have to do them at the same time as your daily workout but you can slot them in wherever you have a few spare minutes. If you do this remember that you may not be fully warmed up and that you must take care to go slowly and carefully.

I have not suggested numbers of repetitions for any of these specific exercises. I think you should be beginning to appreciate your own strengths and weaknesses and also your own limitations. You will also be getting more used to using the Dyna-Band and should feel happy and comfortable with it. Work until your muscles feel pleasantly tired but not exhausted or painful. It is better to do several repeats of an exercise, rest and repeat again rather than continue until you are dropping. Your exercise technique will suffer and you may put your body in danger. If you are realistic in your goals you will finish feeling relaxed and keen to return to the exercises another day. If you exhaust yourself the exercises are more likely to be a 'one minute' wonder, never to be returned to again!

REMEMBER

You should consult with your doctor if:
- **You have a history of heart problems**
- **High blood pressure**
- **You have a medical condition that requires medication**
- **You are unfit or overweight.**

SHOULDERS

D o you find that your shoulders tire easily when your arms are raised in the air and held for a while? Do you find it a strain to carry heavy bags of shopping? Do your shoulders ache after strenuous lifting and carrying exercises? If the answer is 'yes' to any of these you probably need to strengthen your upper back and shoulder area.

Some men want to build up the muscles in their shoulder area. This can be achieved by using the grey Dyna-Band for these exercises.

FORWARD ARM RAISE

- Place one foot slightly ahead of the other.
- Relax both knees.
- Stand on the end of the Dyna-Band with the forward foot.

- Loosely wrap the other end around the hand on the same side.
- Raise your arm in front to shoulder level.
- Slowly lower. Repeat on other side.

SHOULDERS

SINGLE ARM RAISE

- Stand on the Dyna-Band with one foot.
- Loosely wrap the Dyna-Band around your hand on the same side.
- Check your posture.
- Raise your arm out to shoulder level.
- Keep your elbow slightly bent.
- Slowly lower.
- Change sides to work the other shoulder.

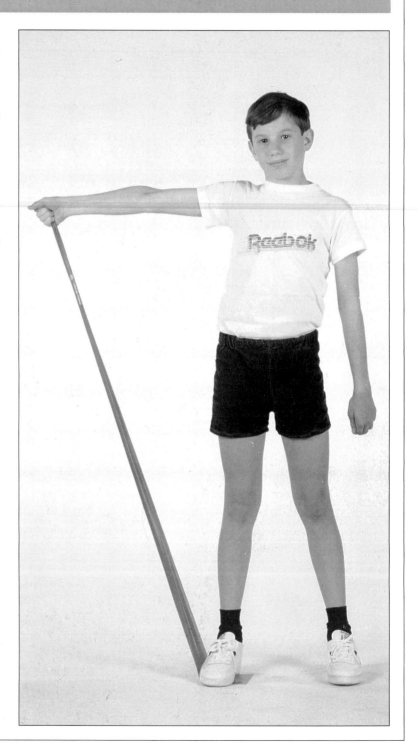

SHOULDERS

DOUBLE ARM RAISE

- Lie on your mat with legs bent, feet flat on the floor.
- Hook the Dyna-Band around the soles of your feet.
- Hold the ends of the Dyna-Band in each hand.
- Raise both elbows up to shoulder level.
- Slowly lower.

This exercise will work your shoulders and upper back. Kevin is working the same area of the body by pulling the Dyna-Band out to the side.

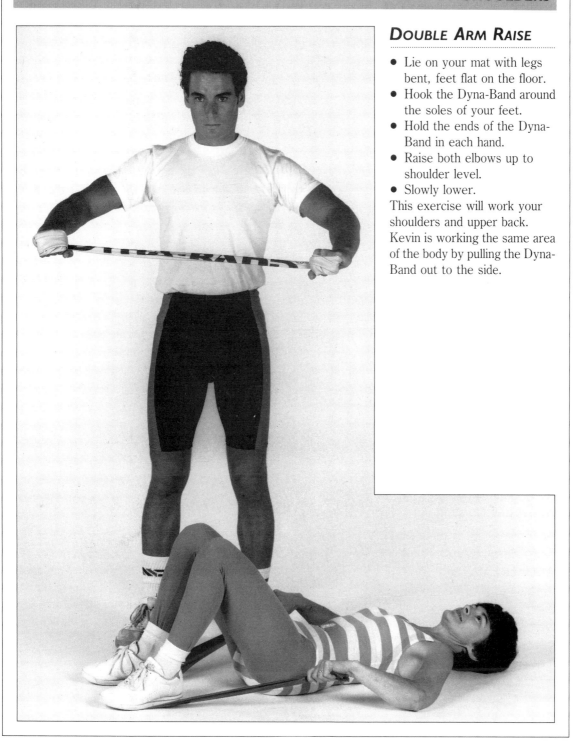

UPPER ARMS

E mergency action is often necessary for the upper arms when we get into spring and short sleeves come into sight! There is nothing as ageing or as unflattering as flabby upper arms – and don't think that to get rid of the flab you can only do boring, traditional exercises like press-ups. There are masses of exercises that you can do for the arms with the Dyna-Band and here are only a small selection.

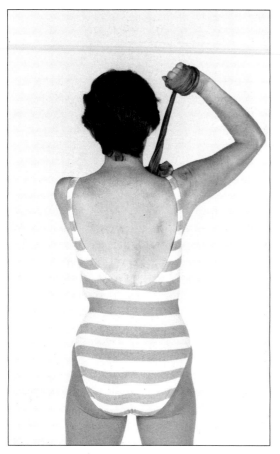 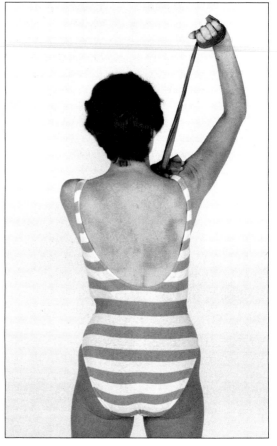

TRICEP PRESS

- Hold the end of the Dyna-Band with one hand and place it on your opposite shoulder.
- Loosely wrap the other end of the Dyna-Band around your opposite hand and push upwards to the ceiling.
- Keep your arm directly above your shoulder.

- Slowly release to the start position.
- Change sides to work back of other arm.
- On the next page Kevin is performing a harder version of the tricep press in a standing position. Try it if you feel you can cope with it!

UPPER ARMS

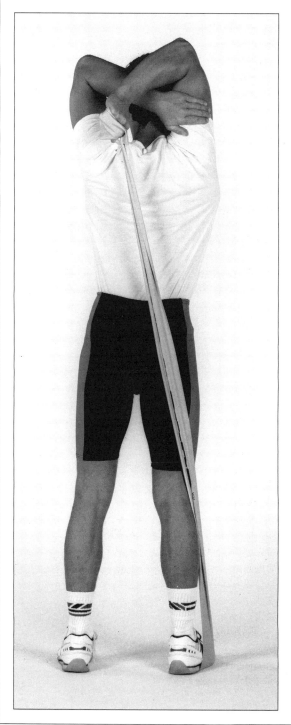

UPPER ARMS

BOW AND ARROW

- Wrap one end of the Dyna-Band around each hand. Keep one arm extended out at shoulder level.
- Raise other arm in line with opposite shoulder.

- Pull your arm across your chest.
- Slowly return to the start position.

Tom is performing the same exercise to strengthen his arms and shoulders for playing tennis.

UPPER ARMS

DOUBLE ARM CURL

- Stand with one leg in front of the other (a split stance).
- Bend the front leg.
- Hook the Dyna-Band around your thigh, just above your knee. Try to maintain the natural width of the band.
- Hold both ends of the Dyna-Band with your hands.
- Curl your hands up towards your shoulders.
- Slowly return.

UPPER ARMS

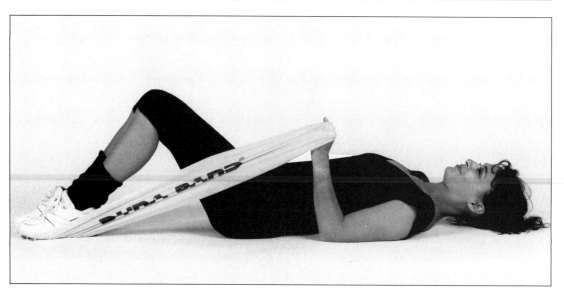

LYING ARM CURL

- Lie on your back with your stomach held in and your back pressed into the floor.
- Bend your knees and place your feet flat on the floor.
- Stand on the end of the Dyna-Band with one foot.
- Hold the other end of the Dyna-Band in one hand (you will probably need to wrap it around your hand quite a bit).
- Curl your hand up to your shoulder.
- Keep your elbow close in to your body.
- Relax back to the start position.
- Repeat the exercise with your other arm.

CHEST AND UPPER BACK

If I were given money for every student on my exercise teacher training course who was round shouldered I would be very rich indeed! You only have to look around you in the street and you will see dozens of people stooping over in that classic round-shouldered posture. You are very likely to have this problem if you work at a desk all day long, drive for a living, are a hairdresser, dentist or involved in any profession that makes you lean over in some way.

Often though the problem starts much earlier in your teenage years. Girls may become conscious and sensitive about their rapidly developing bust and will round their shoulders in an attempt to hide their chest. Teenage boys often grow so rapidly that they cannot cope with their lankiness and increased height and so stoop to appear shorter.

Sometimes round shoulders occur as a result of laziness – it just becomes too much effort to pull yourself up straight. There are, of course, some cases where round shoulders are caused by a medical condition – exercise will still be beneficial in most of these cases but you would have to consult your doctor first.

The problems caused by round shoulders are not just aesthetic – eventually pain and discomfort will occur. The muscles of your upper back will be over-stretched in contrast to the muscles of your chest which will become shortened. Your upper back will become too weak to support the weight of your head and shoulders and you will feel tired and uncomfortable by the end of the day. When muscles are not strong enough to support the skeleton, problems related to this instability can occur. As a result your upper spine may become threatened and a prolapsed disc can be the end result.

As you can see it is very important to work on your upper back to correct any posture deficiencies if you don't want to spend a lot of your time with a chiropractor or osteopath. It is also important to work on your chest muscles, not just to support your breasts if you are female, but also to encourage a balance of strength between the upper back and the opposite muscles in the chest and to encourage good posture.

CHEST AND UPPER BACK

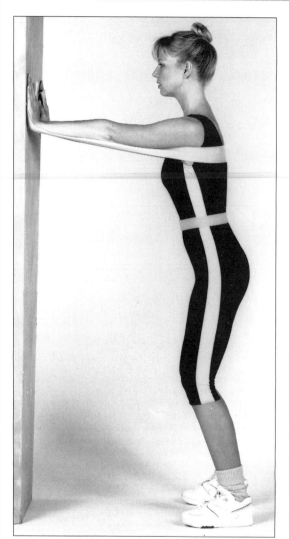
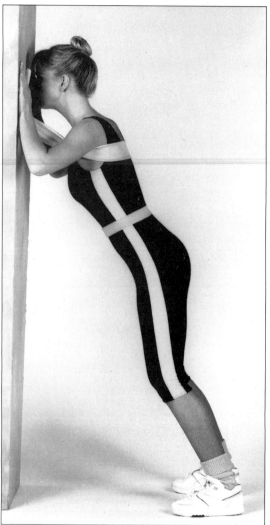

WALL PRESS

This exercise is an easier version of the box and full press-ups in the Dyna-Band Ultimate Challenge.

- Stand about 18 inches away from a wall.
- Wrap the Dyna-Band across your upper back and under your armpits. Maintain the natural width of the band.
- Pin the ends of the Dyna-Band against the wall keeping it taut.

- Your hands should be further apart than your shoulders and flat against the wall.
- Lean forward so that your nose is almost touching the wall bending your elbows.
- Push away from the wall by straightening your elbows to return to the start position.
- Keep your back straight and your stomach pulled in throughout the movement.

STANDING ROW

- Using a split stance (one foot in front of the other, front knee bent) stand on one end of the Dyna-Band.
- Hold the other end of the Dyna-Band in the same hand.
- Raise your elbow no higher than shoulder level.

Remember to keep your hand close in to your body.
- Lower slowly.
- Repeat with the other arm.

This exercise will work the muscles that pull your shoulders back.

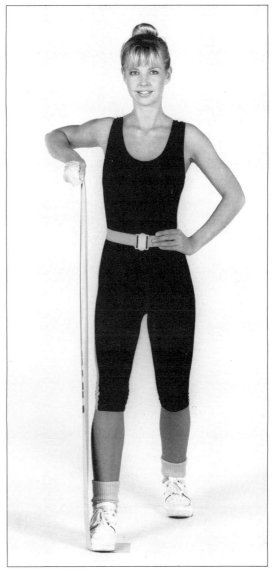

CHEST AND UPPER BACK

BENT OVER ROW *(Also for the upper back)*

- Stand on one end of the Dyna-Band and wrap the other end loosely around your hand on the same side.
- Bend your knees and lean forward with a straight back and your stomach muscles pulled in.

- Pull the Dyna-Band upwards keeping your elbows close to your body until your hand is near your chest.
- Slowly return to the starting position.
- Change sides to work the other side of your back.

CHEST AND UPPER BACK

ARM PULL DOWN

- Loosely wrap the Dyna-Band around your hands until the length is about shoulder width apart.
- Raise your arms over your head.
- Pull your arms down and out to the side to about shoulder level.
- Slowly raise your arms over your head.
- Repeat as many times as you can to strengthen your upper back and shoulders.

ABDOMINALS AND WAIST

These first two exercises are designed to whittle away your waist. You will need a door knob or handle to tie the Dyna-Band onto or possibly a stair banister – anything that is fixed, secure and about waist height.

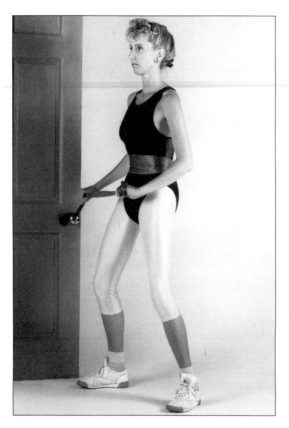 

SIDE BEND

- Tie the Dyna-Band securely onto your door handle.
- Stand with feet apart, knees slightly bent, stomach pulled in and sideways on to the door.
- Take hold of the Dyna-Band with both hands, wrapping it round to a suitable length.
- Lean away from the door bending from your waist directly to the side.
- Return to an upright position.
- Turn around and bend using the other side of your waist.

Throughout this exercise you must keep your knees bent and lean directly to the side, not tipping your shoulders forward or back.

ABDOMINALS AND WAIST

SIDE TWISTS

- Stand in the same position as for the previous exercise.
- Holding the Dyna-Band securely twist away from the door to look over your shoulder.
- Return to the start position. Keep your knees bent and your hips facing the front throughout this exercise so that you get a good twist in your waist.

ABDOMINALS AND WAIST

SIDE TWIST (SEATED)

Also for the waist, this exercise does not require the door.

- Sit on the floor with your legs slightly bent.
- Hook the Dyna-Band around the instep of one foot.
- Hold firmly onto both ends of the Dyna-Band. Wrap loosely around hands.
- Sitting upright with your back straight and your stomach held in turn and twist to look over your shoulder away from the foot which has the Dyna-Band around it.
- At the same time draw your elbow out behind.
- Change the Dyna-Band to the opposite foot and twist in the opposite direction to work the other side of your waist.

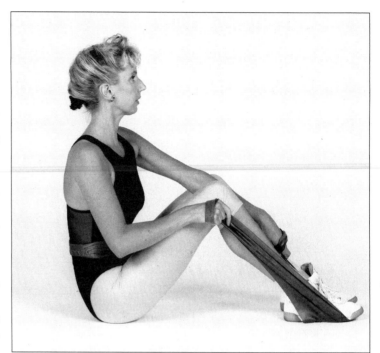

ABDOMINALS AND WAIST

The following abdominal exercises are great for those people with stomach muscles that are very weak and who find some of the exercises in the General Challenge uncomfortable or difficult.

These exercises use the Dyna-Band as a postural aid and support and enable you to perform the exercises correctly and therefore get the best out of them.

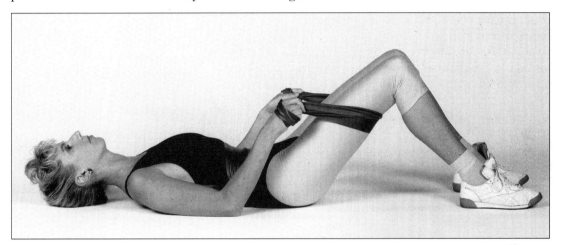

CURL UP

- Lie on a mat with your knees bent and your feet flat on the floor.
- Hook the Dyna-Band around your thighs just above your knees. Keep natural width.
- Loosely wrap the ends of the Dyna-Band around your hands and, using the band to help you, slowly lift your head and shoulders off the floor.
- Press your back into the floor as you lift up.
- Breathe out as you lift up.
- Slowly return to the floor.

ABDOMINALS AND WAIST

MORE ADVANCED CURL UP

- Lie in the same position as for the exercise before.
- Raise your legs off the floor at right angles to your body and keep your knees slightly bent. Cross ankles.
- Use the Dyna-Band to help you as you lift your head towards your knees.
- Breathe out as you lift up and press your lower back into the floor.
- Lower slowly to the floor.

THIGHS AND BUTTOCKS

I suspect that a lot of you will want to work hard on your thighs and buttocks in addition to your daily challenge. It seems to be a common problem area and very few people are satisfied with their legs and hips. Remember though that if you are naturally big hipped with a classic 'pear' shape these exercises will not make you into a slim-hipped, long-legged beauty! Your body type is mainly determined by genetics. In other words, if your family has a tendency to large thighs and bottoms you may have inherited it. However, there is no need whatsoever for flabby thighs and bottoms even if they are large. These exercises will tighten up the muscles in this area if done regularly.

Inner Thigh

SITTING INNER THIGH PULL

- Tie the Dyna-Band around both ankles.
- Sit up with legs out in front.
- Support your upper body on your elbows.
- Keeping your foot flexed pull one leg up and across your bottom leg.
- Slowly return.

You can make this exercise easier by moving the Dyna-Band up to your thighs.

Outer Thighs

STANDING LEG LIFT

This is another exercise which can be done free standing or alternatively with the Dyna-Band tied around a heavy fixed object like a table leg or stair banister.

- Tie the Dyna-Band around both ankles or around one ankle and the table leg.

- Free standing or sideways on to the table lift your leg directly out to the side.
- Return slowly to the starting position.
- Repeat using the other leg.

Emily is performing the same exercise sitting on the chair but on the opposite leg to Linda.

THIGHS AND BUTTOCKS

ROVER'S REVENGE

- Tie the Dyna-Band around your thighs just above your knees. Maintain natural width of band.
- Get into the 'all fours' position on your knees and elbows.
- Raise one leg directly to the side no higher than your hips.
- Slowly lower.
- Change legs.

This exercise is often incorrectly performed. To make it safe and effective your back must remain flat and your hips facing the floor. It is a great temptation to twist as the leg is raised but you could damage your back if you do this. Only your leg moves and nothing else.

THIGHS AND BUTTOCKS

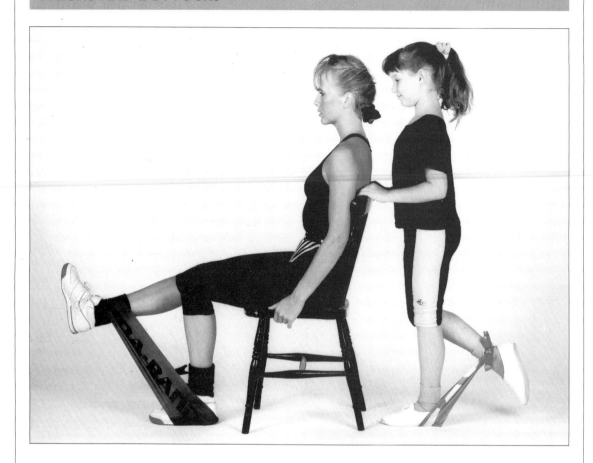

Front and Back of Thighs and Buttocks

SITTING LEG EXTENSION

- Sit on chair.
- Tie the Dyna-Band around your ankles.
- Bend your knees so your feet are flat on the floor.
- Extend one leg, keeping your knees parallel.
- Slowly lower.
- Repeat on the other leg.

You can perform the same exercise lying flat if this position is more comfortable than sitting in a chair.

STANDING LEG CURL

- Tie the Dyna-Band in a loop around your ankles.
- Hook the Dyna-Band around one instep.
- Lean your hands on a chair or the wall for support.
- Stand with your feet together and curl up the leg inside the Dyna-Band behind you.
- Return the foot slowly to the floor.
- Change feet to work the other leg.

THIGHS AND BUTTOCKS

STANDING BUTTOCK SQUEEZE

- Stand in the same position as the previous exercise.
- Place the Dyna-Band around your ankle and not your instep this time.
- Lift your leg behind you keeping the knee slightly bent.

- As you lift squeeze your buttock in.
- Release slowly to the floor.
- Change legs to work the other buttock.

Emily is working the front of her thigh by extending her leg in front from her comfortable sitting position.

THIGHS AND BUTTOCKS

BUTTOCK PUSHES

- Tie the Dyna-Band around your ankles. The knot needs to be at the end of the band, giving you plenty of length.
- Rest on your elbows and knees in an 'all fours' position.
- Hook the Dyna-Band over one instep.
- Bend your knee and press the sole of your foot up towards the ceiling no higher than your hips.
- Return slowly.

Keep your back flat and your stomach pulled in throughout this exercise.

LOWER LEGS

You may want to do extra work on your shins and calves because your ankles are weak. Perhaps you need to build up your lower legs – spindly shins and calves are very unattractive. Or maybe your calves are flabby and need tightening up.

SHIN STRENGTHENER

- Tie the Dyna-Band around the instep of both feet.
- Sit up straight and extend one leg keeping the other slightly bent.
- Loop one arm under the bent leg for balance.
- Pull the toe of your bent leg towards your shins.
- Hold for a count of 4. Release.

- Repeat on the other leg.
- You can make this into a calf exercise by pointing your toe of the straight leg instead of flexing. Hold point for a count of 4 and then release (picture shows).

SHIN ROLLS

- Tie your feet together around your insteps with the Dyna-Band.
- Lie on your back and hug your knees into your chest.
- Point your toes away from each other.
- Hold for a count of 4.
- Relax the feet and repeat.

This is a really effective exercise for those people with sore shins from doing too much aerobic exercise or jogging on hard roads and pavements.

Chapter Nine

EXERCISES FOR THE YOUNG AND OLD

Pictures of my children exercising with the Dyna-Band are scattered throughout the book because I thought it would be good to show you that children can easily work alongside an adult who is performing the Dyna-Band Challenge. How often have the mothers among us prepared for our exercise session – got down onto the carpet all set to go – only to find that within minutes your child is crawling all over you, anxious to join in the game? After all – what else could you be doing lying down on the floor other than pretending to be an animal? With the Dyna-Band Challenge you may be able to bribe your children with one of the colourful children's bands. This will not only occupy him or her but improve their muscular strength and endurance as well.

The Dyna-Band is safe for children of pre-school age as long as it is treated sensibly. The rubber will never snap and cause facial or bodily harm as it is too soft and flexible but one or two safety precautions have to be taken when very young children play with the Dyna-Band.

- The Dyna-Band must never be placed around the head, neck or face.
- Don't allow your child to play with their Dyna-Band without adult supervision.
- Don't let your child stand too near another person when playing with the Dyna-Band.
- Do not allow your child to put the Dyna-Band into his or her mouth.

Unfortunately I cannot advise you to let your child perform all of the exercises in the book with you. This is because, unlike adults, children's bones are not fully calcified and therefore hardened until late into their teens. Their joints are vulnerable and any excess pressure or strain placed upon them may cause injury.

Several of the Dyna-Band General Challenge exercises can be made suitable by dropping the number of repetitions – although a child will tend to stop automatically when he's had enough anyway. Some of the specialist exercises, and certainly the Ultimate Challenge, involve positions where the Dyna-Band's resistive strength will put too much strain on bones and joints.

Here is a guide to help you decide how much of the Dyna-Band Challenge your child can participate in.

Pre-School Children

For this age group the Dyna-Band is very much a toy rather than a piece of exercise equipment. If you ask a small child where his muscles are he will probably indicate his arms and show you his biceps. It's a good idea to let small children strengthen their arms so that they can start to carry heavier objects. Also, the arm exercises are easier to co-ordinate than some of the leg exercises and tend to involve more straight-forward positions. Let your child play with the Dyna-Band by stretching it in his hands, pulling it across his chest pretending to be Superman! My son, Gregory, who is just 5 years old, had tremendous fun pulling the Dyna-Band with his hands like a chest expander, standing on one end and pulling it upwards and outwards and generally just experimenting.

Exercises where the Dyna-Band is tied will be unsuitable for this age group – unless you want to stop working out every few seconds to untie the band again! Don't worry about the Dyna-Band Grip – just let him hold the band where it feels comfortable for him.

The sitting exercises in the General Challenge are safe and comfortable for very small children. The seated row can be good fun as it will seem like rowing a boat. This exercise can also be performed using another child as a partner.

Young children's upper bodies are often quite weak so it is very important that they do only as much as they comfortably can. Keep your child motivated by giving him or her plenty of encouragement as, if he is interested in the Dyna-Band, there's more chance of you completing your Dyna-Band Challenge without interruption!

Five to Fourteen Year Olds

When children are growing and developing it is important that they have some body awareness, are able to carry themselves erectly and to sit properly rather than to slouch. Bad habits begun in childhood are often ingrained for life and this refers to diet as well as posture. Overweight children tend to grow into overweight adults but exercise and a healthy diet can help to prevent this problem.

I began my exercise career teaching physical education in a secondary school and my eyes were opened to poor eating habits and, in many cases, a disturbing lack of exercise. Surveys showed that in the mid-1970s only a very small percentage of children between the ages of eleven and sixteen did more than a few minutes of exercise each day – and often that few minutes merely involved a short and leisurely walk to school. The same statistics for the 1980s were even more of a concern. I found it appalling to think that most teenagers were already leading the type of sedentary lifestyle that leads to our western society diseases – namely heart disease and cancer. Clearly exercise needs to be made enjoyable enough to motivate these sometimes rather lazy youngsters.

If you have a child in this age group, try to tempt him or her with the Dyna-Band. The General Challenge can be adapted to suit this age group in the following ways:

- Forget about the suggested number of repetitions with each exercise. Just let your child do as many as he or she feels comfortable with.
- Do not let them attempt the Ultimate Challenge or the special exercises as some of these positions may be difficult and uncomfortable for them.
- Exercises with a supporting aid are good for children, eg where a chair is involved to either sit or lean on.
- Exercises on all fours (on elbows and knees) should be replaced with lying completely flat on their tummy so that the spine has plenty of support.
- The abdominal exercises which use a chair or a table leg need to be omitted because they require strong stomach muscles. Children may have to force themselves up therefore putting a strain on other body parts.
- Exercises that require co-ordination should be encouraged so that motor skills are developed, eg the cycling exercise in the General Challenge that does not use a chair or table leg.

My daughter, Emily, is well co-ordinated because of her dance experience, but my eleven-year-old son, Tom, struggled at first with the techniques of some of the more complicated exercises.

Let your child work to his or her own level. Unlike adults children don't tend to push themselves to their limit – probably because they are not yet at the stage where they are thinking about a new skirt or pair of trousers they want to get into by next month!

FIFTEEN YEAR OLDS AND OVER

This age group can quite safely perform the General Challenge unless they have any injuries, disabilities or contra-indicative medical conditions. The level of work must be progressed very gradually, starting with a low number of repetitions and building them up session by session. Teenagers may be more inclined to take up the Dyna-Band Challenge as a form of exercise, particularly if they are not 'sporty' and don't like participating in team sports and games. In this activity they will be able to achieve their rewards by observing the progress they are making which can be a more positive experience for them than being driven unwillingly into hockey, netball or soccer.

I have given a few brief ideas about the possibilities for children using the Dyna-Band. There are many more – in fact the Dyna-Band is flexible enough to devise a separate programme of exercises for children only – but that is the subject for another book!

Dyna-Band and The Older Age Group

The pink Dyna-Band has been specially made with this age group in mind. These days it is very difficult to define 'elderly' and very easy to offend when using the term. Those people who have maintained an active lifestyle will be more physically able and capable than their old school chums who have led a sedentary lifestyle. In my aerobics classes and teacher training courses I regularly have men and women in their fifties and sixties but I wouldn't term them 'elderly'. Valda, for example, is our model for the arm exercises and is in her mid-fifties – she has certainly managed to delay the ageing process as she is slim, fit and healthy and it is all due to her active lifestyle.

Unfortunately though, however well we may have looked after ourselves and however fortunate we may have been in remaining free from sickness, few of us will have avoided some disability by the time we reach the latter part of our lives. But how will this disability affect us in relation to exercise?

It is usual to advise consultation with your doctor before you begin any new programme of exercise, and this is sound advice in the case of exercise for the older age group. Commonsense is also valuable though, as you will have come to understand your body over the years, in some cases better than your doctor.

Whilst many of the older age group will have normal, but unfit, bodies, there will be some who have incurred disabilities such as arthritis, paralysed limbs or possibly a strained heart. Whether chair bound or otherwise incapacitated, a Dyna-Band pro-gramme of exercises can still be structured into your daily life. Even if this exercise is restricted to the arms and shoulders, blood flow will be increased, the heart will become stronger and circulation will improve – and all this can be done without even putting on a tracksuit or a leotard!

Heart disease is a particular concern for the older age group, especially when considered in relation to exercise. Our bodies will adapt comfortably and well to various physical demands, provided those demands are not markedly greater than our normal activity. Our bodies adapt to exercise slowly and progressively in a 'step ladder' method and doctors use this principle with their patients during rehabilitation after illness.

Heart failure occurs when, due to disease or damage, the heart can no longer cope with its task and cannot push the blood around fast enough to keep the tissues adequately supplied with the oxygen they need for their work. If this is so, then surely exercise, by increasing the demands upon the heart, will make the situation worse?

If exercise is vigorous then further cardiac strain is likely to occur and should be avoided. On the other hand, if we progress slowly and carefully we can gradually improve the efficiency of our lungs, circulation and muscles in the transportation and the usage of oxygen. A benefit of this is a decrease of stress whilst the heart is at rest so the exercise has had a 'tuning up' effect on the heart. In other words we need exercise to lessen the strain on the heart and consequently avoid heart failure.

Hypertension, or raised blood pressure, is one of the commonest medical conditions today, affecting mainly the middle aged and the elderly. Raised blood pressure can eventually lead to a heart attack or a stroke but regular moderate exercise will decrease blood pressure and the Dyna-Band Challenge is ideal as a form of moderate exercise. Take care though to progress carefully through the exercises if you suffer from high blood pressure and follow your doctor's advice. Increase your repetitions and the strength of your Dyna-Band very gradually. You must also work to a steady momentum and avoid holding or straining on any exercise positions. Isometric exercises (where muscles are held in contraction for several seconds) will cause a high increase in blood pressure and should be avoided. Also try to breathe evenly throughout the exercises, don't force breathing to an unnatural pattern and, above all, don't hold your breath.

Another common disability in the older age group is arthritis – the inflammation of a joint. Osteoarthritis develops with advancing years due to repeated wear and tear of the joints. We all experience this to some degree as we get older. In those who have done a lot of manual work or contact sport (eg football) osteoarthritis can come at an earlier age.

Exercise can be beneficial in mobilising affected joints – as a basic rule acutely inflamed or painful joints should be rested as exercise will not only prolong the inflammation but also increase the risk of permanent joint damage. As soon as the inflammation dies down exercise is the best treatment the joint can have. Physiotherapists often use the pink Dyna-Band to help ease the problems associated with arthritis –

stiffness and soreness. The Dyna-Band General Challenge exercises can all be done by arthritis sufferers when their joints are not inflamed but the repetitions must be built up very gradually. Try starting with just five repetitions and adding one more every other day. The light resistance provided by the pink Dyna-Band will give fast gains in strength but not put the joints under any stress or strain.

As always though, prevention is better than cure and one of the best antidotes to arthritis in later life is regular exercise over a full range of movement. This maintains strength, stops excessive wear on one particular angle of the joint, and can improve the condition of cartilage and ligaments provided that the exercise is not sudden or jarring.

The message is, then, to progress slowly and carefully through the Dyna-Band Challenge if you are one of the 'older' age group. If your body is unfit a gradual progression is the safest and, although results may take a little longer than our case histories you will definitely improve your posture, shape and strength after a relatively short period of time – shorter than in most other exercise programmes. You may even rid yourself of niggling pains that are caused by poor posture. If you suffer from one of the above disabilities, or others that I have not mentioned, your care must be even greater – but do not be put off as in all cases exercise, and most particularly Dyna-Band exercise, is the best medicine you could have.

The Dyna-Band has a huge potential for the older age group to exercise with – doctors in hospitals have recognised this for a long time. We have only skimmed over the surface of the subject here but I hope, if you are in the 'older' age group (whatever it is) you will be inspired to exercise with the Dyna-Band.

THE DYNA-BAND CHALLENGE VIDEO

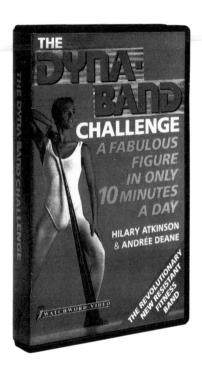

Based on the book, the video programme gives clear demonstrations of the exercises, with step-by-step instructions.

Only $19.95

Available from all good video retailers and bookshops, or by mail order at $19.95 from:

Crown World Marketing Ltd.
Telephone U.S.A. 813-951-0767